The Voice
Celestial

Other books by Ernest Holmes

The Science of Mind
Creative Mind and Success
How to Use the Science of Mind
This Thing Called Life
This Thing Called You
Words That Heal Today

Science of Mind Publishing Edition

THE VOICE
CELESTIAL

Thou Art That

An epic poem

Ernest S. Holmes
&
Fenwicke L. Holmes

Questions all thoughtful men have asked,
Answered from the Wisdom of the Ages

Science of **Mind** Publishing
Los Angeles

Originally published by Dodd, Mead & Co., New York
Copyright © 1960, by Ernest S. and Fenwicke L. Holmes
Foreword copyright © 2004, by Dr. Christian Sorensen

Science of Mind Publishing
2600 West Magnolia Blvd.
Burbank, CA 91505

Design by Randall Friesen

Contents

See "Notes" on page 361.

Second Book

Foreword

I first became enamored with *The Voice Celestial*, the epic poem by Dr. Ernest Holmes and his older brother Fenwicke Holmes, when I was growing up. I would hear my father reading the book aloud around the house. By the early 1980s my family was performing adaptations of this seminal work in various churches and at conferences around the United States. As I performed in many of the scenes, I felt as though I were the Farer searching for answers to solve the riddle of human life; my mother would be the Scribe tying the scenes together with her observation of the conversations between the Wayfarer and the Presence. My father was the "Voice Celestial," reading his lines from offstage with his booming theatrical voice resounding across the speakers from some ethereal realm with the revelations to life's piercing questions.

The Farer represents every person in his search for greater understanding of life and he asks the tough questions that every searching soul aches to have answered. Fortunately, the Farer develops an inner ear and becomes aware of the guidance that is available to all of us as he struggles with his emerging awareness. This great book is about the individual journey of awakening to the Universal Life, for which the potential lies within all of us. One of the amazing facts about Science of Mind that Dr.

Holmes brought forth is that it predates, by decades, humanistic and transpersonal psychology as well as right brain and left brain theories.

I enjoyed a lunch recently at a restaurant on the California coast overlooking the blue Pacific with Rev. James Pottenger. This brilliant Religious Science minister lived with Ernest Holmes at his home in Los Angeles for over two years during the time Ernest and his brother Fenwicke were writing *The Voice Celestial*. Rev. Pottenger reported how Ernest would use him as a sounding board as he shared some of the beautiful phrases from the book. Rev. Pottenger was also a member of Dr. Holmes' Tuesday morning class, by invitation only, at the Institute where he would read this evolving epic poem to his selected students for feedback. Rev. Pottenger reported how Ernest was concerned that *The Voice Celestial* would make his textbook, *The Science of Mind*, obsolete, because it reveals to the reader that we evolve from the cause and effect of Science of Mind to the acceptance of preexisting wholeness discovered in "Idealistic Monism" or Universal Mind.

It has been said that Fenwicke was the scholar and Ernest the mystic while working together to bring forth Ernest's final literary piece in a poetic form. After preparing for a lifetime to complete this work, one witness felt that both brothers were automatically writing their epic poem together. It appeared that they were actually tapping into the revelation of Universal Mind. This book takes us through the individual subjective to the Universal Transcendence. The Farer moves from personal cause and effect to an inside acceptance of the Presence, which is what Ernest often called "Practicing the Presence." This monumental book moves the reader from the realm of mind to one of spiritual wholeness.

With its beautiful phrasing, this epic poem may challenge the reader's current belief system but will open the reader to the spiritual truth of his being. It moves one from potential into actualization. Yet this is accomplished not by parroting back these potent spiritual truths but by applying them to one's present life. One must move beyond linear understanding to vertical acceptance of our preexisting wholeness.

Join the Farer as we take this journey together, actualizing the gift our spiritual inheritance has given us. This gift, emerging as we advance into a greater acceptance of the true Self which Ernest Holmes lived throughout his life, is what Ernest called Universal Mind.

Dr. Christian Sorensen
Encinitas, California

The Voice Celestial

The Farer or Wayfarer, you or me or anybody who tries to solve the
   riddle of human life

The Presence or The Voice Celestial, becoming audible to all who
   develop the inner ear

The Scribe or Observer, who reports the conversations between
   the Farer and the Presence or Voice

The Masters of the Ages, who appear to the Farer while he is in higher
   states of consciousness

Had I the genius, I would pluck each star,
Proclaimed by these great souls, and with them form
A new and brilliant galaxy, and set them
So in place that they would shine as one.
Too long, men analyze, dissect
And into parts divide philosophies and faiths.

Reverie of the farer

1

He came at sunset to his home at last,
Unchained at night from slavery to the day.
"Ah, night," he breathed, "angelic specter, thou
Who dost possess a million eyes—or fears,
I shall relax and in a sweet content
Review the day. For good outweighs
The ill; and when tomorrow comes (it comes,
No doubt), I shall arise and spin the wheel
Of fortune once again."

But then he faltered, for the word Tomorrow
Was overcast by doubt. Are there "Tomorrows"?
How swift the change in all things manifest,
Illusive, beckoning and, like a wraith
Dissolving into air, washed out by light.

Today—tomorrow—what are they? And what
Was yesterday? Where are they now—these days
Of which I speak as real? Are they but dreams?
Perhaps "the Now" is all that does exist.

I wonder if when I am dead that I
Shall know that I am dead—
Why am I here and who and what am I?
I heard, I think, (or does it rise in me?)
That man is soul and lives the mortal span
To save his soul by deeds and thoughts and prayer
To clothe himself in immortality.

What joke is here! What laughter for the gods,
If gods there be! I, too, shall laugh
At those who fictionalize a living soul,
A wraith, a specter of the mind, and then
Go out into the wastes to find and bring
It back again. And I,
Had I a soul and knew I had a soul,
Would gladly work to save the soul I had
And all the other souls of overburdened men.

But who is there to prove and justify
A faith toward which I lean without a hope?

Creeds, dogmas, candlesticks and sandalwood,
Gold, ivory, and marble-chiseled walls—
All these are still of earth! While I have need
Of the unearthly, if such there be! I
Must find the REAL behind the things that *seem.*
But *where,* oh, where to look and what to do!

I know that poets, seers and those they call
The avatars—embodiments of gods—
Declare they know by other means
That there exists another world beyond.
They say it was revealed to them or to
Another who stood behind another whom they knew.
The mystery, they say, has been unsealed
Unto a "chosen few."

BUT I WOULD LIKE TO KNOW WHAT I MYSELF CAN KNOW.
I crave to know the meaning of great words;
I ask that LIFE may be defined, and what
Is LOVE. Perchance I, too, can grasp a key
That opens up the door and for myself
Unveil the Mysteries. Or I may hear
A Voice beyond earth's hearing, or see
A PRESENCE which shall REVEAL TO ME!

I know in part, at least, the sayings of
Old faiths, religions great and small—and creeds,
And creeds and creeds! I shudder here
Within my lonely room. Complex and dread,
How often they affirm damnation each to each!
From them no answer comes to me unless
A Something stirs within me, and I hear
A Voice from out the Void, if such there be.

The Scribe

His mind was spinning like a whirling wheel
That comes to rest by chance yet never moves
Beyond its orbit to a higher plane.
He seemed himself to be upon the wheel,
Bound there by dread necessity and fate.

He knew the wheel had spun and once again
Had come to rest upon the same old shibboleth,
A form to hide the emptiness that lies
In ancient, mystic abracadabra.
"Though folly pass from age to age and through
Ten thousand years of tonsured heads, it still
Is folly at the end. 'Tis so with Truth
But how am I to know, though true or false?"

He laughed at this, a bitter laugh. "How now,
O Timeless Sphinx," he said, "thou face inscrutable,
Cold, calculating, cruel question mark
Who dost bestride the ages like a god,
Will Delphic speech break from thy sandstone lips
To shatter all the silence of the ages?

The Farer

Perhaps I am myself the Sphinx, the dumb
Unblinking stone that broods but does not think.
O God, if God there be, O Soul of souls,
I cannot bear the hollowness and pain
That fills my heart with loneliness and grief;
How can I bear the emptiness of ignorance?
I WANT TO KNOW AND KNOW I KNOW.

Alas, alas, should I concede the Heaven,
That some have taught, with angel-choirs and wings,
I must accept their Hell as well
With cries from purgatory, and bats' wings!
Far better this, dumb as I am, to build

4

My heaven or hell out of myself!
I have the stuff for one; perhaps, the other.

Oh, mystery on mystery so piled
That I would welcome death could it display
The figured tapestry beneath the shroud.

'Tis said that Jesus knew and that the cord
Which binds the body to the soul remained
Unbroken and that he rose and walked...
I was not there. O how then shall I KNOW
If this sweet tale be true? 'Tis sweet enough,
I swear. I was not there!

We sail a storm-racked sea and in the depths
The hulls of ships, the skeletons of men;
They will not rise and skim the sea again!
All things run to this sea at last. The rose
Is dying as it blooms; its perfumed breath
Is its own self, dividing in the air:
Its petals fall and in the end, the sea
Will claim the ashes in its depths.
Is this my fate? Is there no hope, no voice
To break the stillness of this deathly pall?

I had my hopes of it one night. I felt
A strange cold breeze that broke the stifling heat
And something passed me in the air and whispered...
Where was it? Let me see, can I recall?
Oh, yes, I see it now! The light was dim
And people strange to me were gathered there
In faith that they might speak and be bespoke
By entities discarnate, souls of men
Who broke the barrier that divides
The living and the dead. (This is their word,
Not mine. I know so little and must see
And touch and hear, before *I* can believe.)
"We have not died," it said. "You change your garb

Because your wrap is worn, your garment
Clay, but life is life and cannot die."
I do not know...I wonder...shall I say?
I know that those who claim to know—because
"Their Faith" proclaims no other source than theirs—
Affirm that things like this can never be;
Their "Faith, delivered to the saints," forbids...
Their saints have shut the out-hinged door of Heaven...
From faiths like this, sweet truth, deliver us.

And yet he had no rancor for he hoped
Behind the panoplies of every "Faith"
Some Truth was hid, some Presence felt;
"If some survive," he thought, "then all survive.
And since all life is change, then all will change."

He wondered why some took delight in fear
Or seemed complacent when they talked of Hell;
And, on their soul, declared there was no way
By which the soul *unshriven* could escape
Eternal doom, nor even pass into
Oblivion beyond Elysian fields.

The Farer stirred and shuddered on his bed:
He wondered why such thoughts should come to him.
"For I know none who knows," he said,
"Or if he knew, I would not know he knows."
He laughed with mirthless humor. "How well I know
I do not know. Can I aspire to find a way?
But woe, most awful woe, besets me if
I fail to try—a living death! but where
Shall I begin?"

"I shall begin with *life*," he said, "Of this
I am assured: I am alive. And what is it
To *live*, save that I *think*? And I can think
Back from "effect to cause."
The very greatness of the thought o'erwhelmed him—

6

"How swiftly reason points the mind
To unknown cause," he said, "but does it verify?"

The Scribe

He could not sleep,
Excited by the bigness of his quest
And more excited by the thought that he
Must hold within himself the answer,
For through his mind must march the serried ranks
Of masters, hierophants, and sages
And all their sayings, all their works, and all
Their lengthened shadows in those who follow after
Who chant their articles of faith. And he
Must pass upon theologies, philosophies,
And all the songs inspired by faith; for men
Do build cathedral spires of hymns and songs;
For poetry is priestess to the soul
And tends the fires which, by Prometheus filched,
Were first to heat cold reason.

"All these must play their part upon my stage
But in the end *I* must decide, accept,
Reject, for I and only I can know
Within myself and for myself that which is true
For me. Not even God can faith compel,
Not even He reject."
He sought for Truth, he said, and not alone for God:

The Farer

If there be God, why, it is well, but I
Seek *Truth* and whether there be Mind or no
Within the Cosmic Scheme: and should it be,
Then shall I further quest a way to speak,
Perhaps to hear; and should It speak to me,
Then gladly to obey.
But Truth Itself can never lay commands;
For dogma is the mummy of the past,

Long since embalmed but not interred,
Wrapped round with gravecloths of intolerance.

The God of such belief is not the God I seek,
Nor can be real to me. I search for God,
Unfettered, free from cloying garb
Of priests whose bony hands and tonsured pates
Bespeak a niggard faith.

The Scribe

He laughed aloud for to his vision came
The images, the sculptured forms, the gilded
Domes, the naked paunches cast in bronze;
Hawk-headed Horus, son of Osiris;
And gargoyles, leering, frightful
To minions of the nether world;
For superstition ever molds a form
For ignorance to worship or to fear.

The Farer

Then what is judgment, justice, hell or heav'n
But that which man creates? Is this not true?—
The hell designed by those who seek to put
The fear of God in man, with flame and fork,
And Satan and his horde, is crude, and bears
The imprint of an atavistic age,
A throwback infantile. For so it seems to me.

It cannot be that Heaven stands aloof
From prayer, if so it be the soul's desire
Of him who prays. But as for me,
I cannot hold with those who claim to pray
The sinner out of hell and so transport,
Like some Aladdin's rug, the rascal soul,
Unscathed, from those hot flames so dearly loved
In theologic lore. Else would the flames
Unfed, and withered, die; a sorry thing

For those who hold to fear as best designed
To frighten souls to heaven.

The Scribe

    He fell into a state of wonderment
    And every cell of him was shaken
    Like aspen leaves that tremble in the night.
    Enthusiasm, that drunk'ness of the gods
    Which thrills the worshipper, thrilled him.
    He would himself launch out on such a quest,
    A Farer going forth to find the Truth.

The Farer

    My battle cry is Truth,
    My banner shall be faith. I think I can.
    But where shall I begin?
    I first of all must turn to mountain peaks
    Of personalities and what they saw
    Before men canonized and commonized
    And cracked the sacred crystal;
    To Vedic hymns that sang of the Creation;
    To Egypt, sacred keeper of the flame;
    To Hebrew prophets, to Moses and the Law;
    To Zendavesta, prayer-book of the Parsees,
    Transcribed by Zoroaster from the gods;
    Or wise Lao-tzu with his Tao old,
    Whose wisdom, lost to China, sealed her doom.

    I shall essay to sample all the ore
    Of ev'ry land and age but most of all
    Extract the gold of those rich mountain souls
    Who *lived* the message that they taught,
    Like Krishna, Buddha and the risen Christ.
    A tunnel I will run beneath the shaft
    That bears the gold of ev'ry age; and so
    From each will draw the wealth to build
    The temple spires that upward point to God!

I shall absorb from ev'ry source all that
I can of systems known to man; let them
Assume a single body with a Voice
That speaks to me as though it were
The Primal Voice, which first proclaimed,
"Let there be light."

The Scribe

'Twas then that laughter caught him unaware,
A kind of shame that he had dared to match
His wits with nature and with man—those men
Whose names were cut in stone, the seers
Of science, philosophy and faiths.
How did he dare to check his thought against
Such men as these...
But time ticked on and suddenly he thought—

The Farer

But this is NOW, not *then*—TODAY!
And I am heir to all they knew or claimed
To know, and I am scion of their Wisdom
Which may, through me, give birth
To knowledge and to clearer sight. For each
New soul is heir to all the past. And God
May make him prophet of the things to come.

The Scribe

He saw with comic inner eye the look
Of horror on faces of the past; of Jove
With readied thunderbolts; astrologers,
Blear-eyed with peering at the stars;
High priests of church and science, prepared
To nail him to the cross...And then
He laughed again with joy until it boomed
Across the ceiling and along the walls—
A cataract of sound that filled the air;
For on another highway he could see,
Advancing in the light, with banners high

And trumpets full-ablaze and clear, a new
Processional; and on each breast the one word, TRUTH.

To his amaze the vestments that they wore
Were those of priests and scientists and seers—
No other garb than such as others wore;
And with them marched initiates of rites
Of schools long gone, the mystic cults
Whose passion plays had introduced the Christ.
And there calm Plato marched with Socrates,
Aurelius, Plotinus, Paul and Jesus Christ,
And following close were many saints,
Saint Augustine, Saint Francis, and mystics
Small and great of yesteryear; and players
With their string'd lyres and instruments of brass,
With Mozart, Mendelssohn and sacred choirs;
And poets singing Songs of Deliverance
And hope and faith; and souls illumined, who through
The ages dark had kept alive the sacred flame.

The Farer
A goodly company, I claim; not Prodigals
Whose wasted hours are tarnished o'er
By fear to try. For they were Farers,
Not vagabonds like me. They pressed upon
The flying feet of wingéd goals and found
The happiness that lies in the pursuit.
And each drew some bright star from all
The galaxies of heaven.
Oh, would that I might be for that
Sweet caravan, the camel-driver who, in
The storm, lashed by the whirling sand
Might find oasis in a desert place.

Had I the genius, I would pluck each star,
Proclaimed by these great souls, and with them form
A new and brilliant galaxy, and set them
So in place that they would shine as one.

Too long, men analyze, dissect
And into parts divide philosophies and faiths.
Let me but posit this: the gold of truth,
If it be truly gold, will melt in one
Great crucible.
'Tis this, no less, that I shall now essay.

The Scribe

A trembling shook him but around his head
A nimbus formed so bright that to the eye—
Had there been eyes to see—it would appear
A brilliant microcosmic galaxy.
"Let me but posit this," he spoke again,
"All truths must fuse in one, for Truth *is* one,
And I shall find the Truth."

But then he laughed, it was his saving grace,
And that free laugh that rolled like thunder
All along the wall seemed suddenly
To leap through space and shake the trembling stars.
The tensions of his thought were stilled
For he at last had set the goal. He knew
What he would do.
And as he mused the Primal Light
Burned in the gloom and through the narrow gate
That opens to the soul, a Presence came.
He knew him not until the Presence spoke:

The Presence

Fear not, for I am He who sits behind the veil.

The Scribe

The Farer stirred and murmured tremblingly,

The Farer

I know you not, are you for death or life?

The Scribe
>The Farer felt a coolness like a breeze
>That rises with the morning light which springs
>From nowhere as though the day has breathed
>And as it breathes gives forth a glow to warn
>Of its approach. And first it shone like light
>Through alabaster lamps, so white it was;
>Then as the Farer stared, the Presence took
>On shape as though the air congealed to form.
>Half-filled with fear and half with hopefulness,
>The Farer gazed upon the apparition—
>While it appeared to clothe itself within
>A golden envelope, such aureole
>As artists paint around the heads of saints
>As though to magnify the soul and make
>It visible to men. It shone so bright
>The Farer could not look into the light.
>
>The Presence spoke to him as one who knew
>His thoughts as well as words, both old and new,
>Who, though he drew the truth from heights supernal,
>Employed but simple speech, kind and fraternal.

The Presence
>Thy voice has reached my ear, I hear thy cry,
>And though my brightness daze thy mortal eye,
>Yet here I am and I will give thee aid;
>Rest thou in peace and do not be afraid.

The Farer
>I cannot rest and I can find no peace,
>I am a pawn of fate, a mere caprice;
>There are so many lanes of wandering thought,
>So many moods of doubt and fear are caught
>Into the web of my uncertain mind,
>I cannot sleep and leave them all behind.
>Tomorrow holds such duties to be done,
>My mind leaps up before the rising sun

And pits its strength against the newborn day
Before I let the old one fade away.

The Presence

Yet even now a master waits your word,
A power-within which by your voice is stirred
To lift the weight of doubt, drive out the pain
Of throbbing drums that beat upon your brain—
The old regrets and stifled memories,
Suppressed emotions and uncertainties;
It bids confusion and all fear begone
That you may rest in peace until the dawn.

The Farer

Such is my deep desire; my soul in agony
Cries out for that which has eluded me.

The Presence

Be patient then, I come with this design
To wake thy Master-Self—the power is thine—
In you, the substance of a greater man,
In you, the purpose of a cosmic plan,
In you, the vision of a Central Flame,
The voice of Truth that calls you by your name.

The Farer

O God, if gods there be!

The Presence

Stand forth, O soul, flamed round with Cosmic Fire,
You shall achieve at length your heart's desire;
And while your body lies in sweet repose,
Your Never-Sleeping-Self expands and grows
Until your lesser self develops power
And you shall wake at last to that great hour
When Nature claims the triumph of Its plan
And shows through you *the Infinite in Man.*[1,2]

The Farer
>I am so small, so very small,
>I seem to be no one at all.

The Presence
>Out of the common stuff of earth
>God brings uncommon men to birth.
>The brazen gates shall ope...
>...Hold thou to hope...

Yet sometimes to us, as in sleep,
When all the earth is sunk in rest,
Out of the shadows still more deep,
There comes the vision of the blest.

The celestial presence

2

The Farer
"The brazen gates of doubt are riven to show
The wonder of the Whole!"...Would I could know
The meaning of the *part*...I who in pain
Have searched the wisdom of the world in vain!

The Presence
O foolish soul, O child of ignorance,
Who knows so much and knowing, does not know,
I come to thee as I to Moses came,
Unstopped his eyes and showed the Holy Land.
To know too much is not to know at all;
The vessel full, too full, to hold
The waters drawn from deeper wells
Cannot contain the draughts more newly drawn;
For how can Wisdom gain from Knowledge,
If knowledge be of that which is untrue?
A thousand falsehoods never make a fact.
Turn then from thy half-truths, thy mortal mind
And go with me. Nay, not to distant stars
The way of Truth is never out but in.

The Farer
You speak in riddles, for I know no way
By which to learn, unless I first do see,
And hear and taste and touch. Can Wisdom rise
From other source than these? With humble mind,
I beg of thee, be not annoyed.

The Presence
Why dost thou doubt? Have I not plainly said,
I come to you as I to others came?
For I would point a way to Truth for you.
It lies not out but in.

The Farer
Then will I yield myself, Celestial One,
For I do feel *Thou* art that light I seek.

I know not whence such thoughts should come to me,
Save it be true, as though, perhaps, my soul
Perceives both light and source of light as one.

The Presence
Nor flesh nor blood has said this thing to you,
This is indeed beyond the finite mind—

The Farer
You fill me with confusion and delight,
I do not know, but still have hope to know;
The more, that as I speak, some memory stirs,
As though in you the past returns to me
As present, and that I knew you long ago.
Did we, perhaps, go faring, each with each?
And is it true, that higher beings come
In man's great need, for I have need, such need!
O Angel of Celestial Light —I have
Great need. I HAVE GREAT NEED.

If beings come to earth from higher planes
And if it truly be that thou art such,
Thou art the first and only answer to
The prayers I prayed that such as you might come
With tidings from above, or from below.
Speak unto me that I shall surely find
And know some answer to my questioning.

The Presence
You may indeed, my friend, have hope to find
The sacred thread that leads you from the caves
Of dark despair.

The Farer
I pray thee, plainly speak, for I am dull,
Too gross to hear, too gross—too gross!

The Presence

> The neophyte, who by some inner urge
> Is set to find Infinity will first
> Of all be overwhelmed, like you, with loss
> Acute of all that once seemed real. The mind
> Is hung above a deep abyss between
> The solid world of sense material
> And that high sphere of inner thought in which,
> Though real, the soul feels not at home.

The Farer

> Thy words are true and over me a pall
> Does hang, a horror indescribable.

The Presence

> Then has your inner sight one moment glimpsed
> The Truth ineffable. Your soul must fare
> Upon a path so new, so strange that it
> Will seem unstable like walking on a sea.
> But have no fear; for I am close to you
> And I will walk with you.

The Farer

> Then shall my heart cry out with joy. I do
> Not care how long the road, how insecure
> If thou, O Presence, walk the way with me.

The Presence

> Then walk no more in utter gloom nor deep
> Regret. For men of earth
> Were not designed for gloom nor dread despair;
> Creator God did not ordain a sphere
> Of pain and sorrow; He who made the world
> Had also wisdom to make plain the course
> The stream of life would take, how to give form
> To beings put upon this earth, that they
> Might live in joy, in peace and happiness.
> And there is beauty—

The Farer
>The red upon the robin's breast!
>Long since I lost the robin and saw it,
>Alas, as but a bird! 'Twas so with all
>I saw—grey, dull, inanimate and dead.

The Presence
>Then look once more upon the mountains
>Which tow'r in beauty and in strength above
>The valley floor where running streams do feed
>And glorify the land whose vineyards fair
>Sustain the luscious grape from which is pressed
>The sacred symbol of the Life-of-All.
>Surely, the gardens of the gods are fair
>And all these things are placed upon the earth
>That living here might be a Paradise.

The Farer
>Why then is poverty upon the earth?
>Why do the dwellers of this blessed land,
>Like me, live on in wretchedness and pain?
>Make clear to me why men do fail to *act,*
>To enter and possess?
>The gardens of the earth do bloom indeed
>And wealth is his who dares or wills to claim
>The overflowing bounty—which lures me not,
>For I have hidden hunger which leaves me
>Truly famished. It gnaws upon my soul—
>If so it be, in truth, I have a soul
>Or reason for my being—It is for this
>I search. My hands are wet with my own blood
>In beating on the brazen doors of silence.
>There is no answer and I hear alone
>The far faint echo of my broken cry,
>"O what art Thou, O God, and what am I?"

The Presence

> Speak on, speak on. Release yourself of this
> Deep pain and all your memories of hurt.
> Once more I say, "He only can be filled
> Who first shall empty out—"

The Farer

> It is not grief. I weep not for a loss—
> And I am empty now, so empty!

The Presence

> If then 'tis happiness you seek—

The Farer

> Nay, not for happiness but bliss, for that
> Sweet bliss which seers have called Nirvana—
> To find eternal peace or nothingness!
> To all the sons of men does trouble come,
> And hurt and fear and awful doubts assail:
> We all are poor, we all are poor.

The Presence

> You have great need—

The Farer

> Aye, *need,* I have! So great a need that were
> The whole great bowl of heav'n turned upside down,
> It could not hold the vastness of my need,
> The need to know, the need to understand!
> The horror of my emptiness
> Is shadow cast on shadow in the dark.

The Presence

> But you shall see—

The Farer

> Ten thousand years have not revealed that which
> I seek. Across the human stage we stalk

As actors from the wings and back again
Into the wings. Nor do we understand
The part we played, nor what is man or why.

The Presence

I shall unfold—

The Farer

My life is short when measured by the lives
Of other men which end to end would stretch
Across the stage of time, yet what has come
From all *their* prayers? Have they not cried
As now I cry, their hearts as empty bled?
Their hands in bitter anguish raised
Toward what *they* hoped were gods.
No answer came from heaven nor from earth.
What is it came from *where* and *whither* goes?
Is there no ear to hear, no heart to pity,
No eye to see the tears? For men like me
Have raised their cry through endless time,
And not one whit have gained of Truth.

The Presence

Have you no hope, no comfort from some light
Within, some lamp that burns (though dark still reigns
Without)? For man can hope, though ignorant,
Until, his hope disproved, there is no room
For hope—

The Farer

The *hope to know* is greatest of all hopes—
It is disproved that man *can know*. At least,
His soaring thoughts, like eagle's wings, have beat
Against the bars of brass in vain.

The Presence

Have you yourself no hope at least?

The Farer
>My reason and emotions clash. My mind says, "No,"
>My heart affirms a hope. Although 'tis true
>That ears that vainly listen for a voice
>Do dull the hearing of the heart, and hope
>And faith are fled.
>
>Deal not I pray in subtlety. For I
>Am sick, my soul is sick, my mind is sick—

The Presence
>It is your heart—
>Be still awhile and let the heart speak out.
>And you shall find
>A jewel most precious in its brightness
>That shines not only in the realm above
>But rather scatters light upon the earth.
>This you yourself have felt at times, I think,
>'Til darkness gathered all around again
>And shadows fell, so that your jewel caught
>No ray. Your gem was held away from light
>By your own shadow. Despair does kill the gem.

The Farer
>I had a vision once, I seemed to see,
>Nay, more, I was caught up into a realm—
>Alas, it was a dream!

The Presence
>You have lamented well, but to what end?
>Your very eloquence does spite your heart.
>How often men become bemused by their
>Own speech, denying what they would believe,
>Believing what they falsely have affirmed.
>Do you, perchance, give room—when reasoning—
>For fault or blame in *logic* of your mind?
>Did you, perhaps, confuse yourself and stop
>The inner ear?

The Farer
>   I do not know, I do not know.

The Presence
>   Perhaps the gods could not make speech to you
>   Because you would not hear. Perhaps the god
>   Whom you addressed was not himself a god,
>   But just a specter sitting on a cloud
>   Projected from your doubting mind.
>   There are so many gods whom man has made
>   In his own likeness, who, when they reply
>   Do have the emptiness of their creator.
>   For lesser gods belong to lesser minds,
>   And lesser gods to lesser minds appear.
>   But all true gods to One True God belong.

The Farer
>   But *that* I have believed; if there be God
>   There is but one. How then could I conceive
>   A lesser God?

The Presence
>   You make a god of everything if you
>   Do give it power to rule your life:
>   And even good to evil turns—

The Farer
>   I do not understand. For how can good
>   Become to me an evil thing?
>   Let me but ponder this. Do I give power
>   To things or men or gods who then do rule
>   My life? Whom I endow with my
>   Own ignorance and then cry out for help?

The Presence
>   This is the law—look to the uncaused CAUSE,
>   For where causation is, there is your god.
>   Find Cause alone within; yea, find the One

True Cause within, whose center everywhere
Is found with naught to circumscribe.
The lesser gods must to this God comply
And if they be not subject unto Him,
They are no gods at all.

The Farer

In part I comprehend. I fear that I
Sought light from gods I did create and so
From them no light beyond my own could come.

The Presence

Most true. The gods whom men adore, too oft
Are not real gods at all, do not exist.
Had they been true, their answer would be swift;
For cause and Wisdom are not found alone
In upper realms beyond the cry of man
Nor do the gods in splendid solitude
Exist, since they themselves do but reflect
The splendor of the One, as does one wave
Reflect the glory of the Sun.
His essence is in all things hid—a piece
Of bread, a taste of wine, drawn from
The sacramental cup—or any cup
That man in faith uplifts.
He is the inner and the outer rim,
The center and circle infinite
Which circumscribes the whole.
From heaven comes no special gift,
To favored souls, but opens wide its gates
And from its windows pours a bounty great
Beyond the mind of man to comprehend.

The Farer

Such bounty failed to fall on me—

The Presence
> To each is *given all,* but he can take
> That only which he sees and does accept.

The Farer
> I am condemned by fate—

The Presence
> Your God does not condemn, and fate itself
> Is but a name for consequence. The weak
> And slothful seek to shift the blame
> To fate or God or any source without.

The Farer
> Then I am not condemned?

The Presence
> The Higher Power does not condemn nor does
> It pass some judgment dire upon the sons
> Of men; there is one law that as we sow
> We reap—no more no less; for God does send
> His sun to shine on good and evil men,
> And manna falls from heaven unto all.
> Put forth your hand and take the bread,
> Lean down and drink and quench your thirst.

The Farer
> Such words as these I cannot understand,
> I still am famished both for drink and bread;
> Dost think that *earthly* gifts are what I seek?
> I pray thee, trifle not; my heart is dead
> Within me: from tombs of age-old hopes
> I smell the stench—I cannot bear—Oh, I
> Could weep such tears—had I but tears to weep!
> How men have failed to touch the healing hem
> Of some great soul to cure their longing.
> And longing, they have died!
> Out of the empty void—nothing! Into

The yawning grave they fell, as I shall fall.
Or burned upon the pyre of dying hope,
I shall be wholly gone, my ashes swept
Along the waste to mix with desert sands
Where winds shall blow up transient forms to craze
Some farer such as I, who shall, like me,
Behold a false, ephemeral mirage;
And he and I and dust shall merge and blow
Insensate through all time.

The Presence
You do so damn yourself by bitterness!

The Farer
I taste the desert sand. My chalice is a skull.

The Presence
Beloved friend of mine, I long to soothe
Your grief. A heavenly light must break
Through that deep gloom by which you are embraced.
But first of all, take comfort, friend, in this,
That you yourself are source of all you fear,
And cause and circumstance lie deep within.

The Farer
I understand you not and why rejoice
If it be true that I am cause?
Would pain be less?

The Presence
What you create can be dissolved. If you
Are cause, you also are the remedy. Take heart
In this. For though the human sense is blind
And lives in its own darkness, there is a way—

The Farer
Show me that way—

The Scribe
    Then suddenly the air was stirred as by
    A fanning wing, and in it flamed the light
    So luminous it veiled the Presence from
    The Farer's eyes; although, bedazed, he knew
    Those lips had framed an answer to his need.
    Yet as he spoke, self-pity welled so high
    It choked his words and he was still.
    At which the Vision too began to fade
    Into the darkness of the room.
                        Alarmed,
    The Farer shook through all his limbs, yet half
    Relieved, for still his reason could not bear
    True witness to his sight, nor could he tell
    The nature of the apparition who
    Had come from Nowhere into Now, or man
    Or God, or what? Distraught, he wondered if
    Some evil visitant had come to claim
    His soul.
            And then he laughed in pure delight
    At his own fancy. "Who can claim my soul
    Until it first be proved I have a soul?"

    That same cool breeze which came to him before
    Which had announced and always would declare
    The advent of the Presence seemed to fan
    Again; the light began to glow as coals
    Appear in ashes blown upon, which flame
    To brilliance, so that the Farer saw him—
    Nor feared nor questioned whence he came nor why—
    But bowed his head to shade it from the light.

The Presence
    You have well said that men do oft convert
    Their faith or fear to *form* and give to it
    A pseudo-soul, bow down and worship it.
    It is for this I come, to bring the Truth
    That breaks the darkness down and sets you free.

Truth must be recognized and used and you
Are falsely led if you do think no souls
Have known nor used this truth till now, or ever can.

The Farer

I hope again! At least, I dare to hope.
If thou but lead, I follow though I die.
Far better die with hope than live with faith
In folly. I will believe not in myself but thee.

The Presence

Let it be known to you, my friend, that man
Doth live in twofold worlds, that which he sees
And the unseen, the world of form, and that
Which forms the form. The things of earth
Are patterned in a realm that lies above[3]
And all the things that men have wrought below
Are copied from the Unseen and the Real.
This real is essence from which all things proceed.

The Farer

Is Truth, then, something strewn upon the earth,
An emptiness that can be gathered up,
Held in a wishing-bowl of hope and faith,
And so from nothing, something comes?
To me, it still is echo, repeated
Along the canyon walls of emptiness.

The Presence

Not so, for Truth is from the just and wise,
A wisdom never held on earth by those
Who blindly do reject their heaven. For *Knowing*
Is a heav'nly thing. Beyond the reach of doubt,
Beyond the common faith or hope of finite mind,
The *soul* alone can know. The human mind
Would still deny though it should be set down
Within the walls of heav'n, because
It could not see. For it ignores the fact

That sight belongs to soul, and eyes themselves
Do never see what is the cause. It is
The *self* that sees and this same self may know
The truth without the eye or ear or sense.
He who would know must first be still
And listen for the Voice. He must become
The placid pool which will reflect
The beauty from above.

The Farer

                     Beset by doubt
My faith is but despair. I am afraid—

The Presence

    Give it but time, have faith in me and I
Will lead you into deeper faith. To this
Give heed, and I will guide you to belief.
Know this if you would enter and possess
The promised land and so partake
The banquet spread by Higher Powers: It is
The will of heav'n to give to all who ask.
Gods do withhold no good from those who seek.

Be like a child who looks to see the star
That first appears; and suddenly the whole
Bright galaxy has blossomed out of space;
And out of nothing, the visible appears.
It shall be so with you. The unseen stars
Of real, eternal things in shape
And substance will appear; and, as you look
The form of things divine will softly
Come to you amidst the shadows of the night.
As moonbeams trace the path across the sea
Or shine on forest pools unseen by man,
So shall the light ineffable touch you.
Behold the primal garden of the gods,
Wherein all things do bloom and fruit!
Reach out your hand, the fruit is yours to have

And to forever hold. Truth gives itself;
Rejecting naught, it should not be rejected.

The Farer

Almost thou persuadest me by thy sweet words,
And I do feel so closely drawn to thee!

The Presence

The ground on which you stand is holy ground,
You walk within the garden now. And you
Shall eat the fruit that satisfies
Your hungry heart. This is the first slow step
In your enlightenment. I will return
And in the days to come companion you...
I go, but going, leave with you these thoughts
On which to meditate, for inner growth
Is fed by what you think upon: speak thus:

> From Thee, O God, who dost impart
> To mortal man, immortal vision,
> I seek, with yearning in my heart,
> The Truth beyond the field of reason.

> The homesick soul cannot contain
> The longing once again to see
> The Face of Love and to remain
> Enraptured by Reality

> Too long the symbol has concealed
> What lies behind the things of sight,
> The mystery that, once revealed,
> Would fill the heart with pure delight.

> Too oft the weary watcher sees
> The half-formed vision fade from view,
> And hears the lisping of the leaves,
> " 'Tis not for you, 'tis not for you."
>   .   .   .   .   .

Yet sometimes to us, as in sleep,
When all the earth is sunk in rest,
Out of the shadows still more deep,
There comes the vision of the blest.

These wondrous moments—oh, how few!
They quickly come, as soon have fled;
Yet all the world is born anew
And life once more has blossomed red.

Again we breathe the air of heav'n,
And, in an ecstasy of soul,
The brazen gates of doubt are riv'n
To show the wonder of the Whole.

.   .   .   .   .

Each is a part of that great wonder,
And he himself is lock and key,
And none may break the gates asunder,
But only he, but only he!

Within, the angel of self-knowing,
Incarnate god, must wake and find
The torch of life, so faintly glowing
That it escapes the human mind.

Then hear again the voice supernal
That slipped long since from memory,
"If ye seek for life eternal,
Ye shall find it in the ME."

Your prayer is seed which strewn upon the soil
Of All-Creative Mind must grow for you
A harvest like the seed. If then your prayer
Affirms your doubt, declares your lack of faith
And loudly claims there is no love—
Why, then, your prayer will justify your faith
In nothing! From nothing, nothing comes.

Faith and hope

3

The Scribe

His hope lay dead against the Farer's heart—
Full lost the vanished dream! For so it seemed
In retrospect. The Presence came no more!
The bleakness of the afterglow was like
The coldness of a desert night; a dark
Unbroken stillness rolled across his soul
As is its wont when once the vision fades
From him who for a moment looks enthralled
Into infinity and sees the Whole
In light and love ineffable; and then
Is plunged into a deeper dark again.

How dread the night, how lost the soul appears
When faith is gone and hope rejects our tears!

The Farer

Thou art gone!
And through all the lonely reaches
Of my aching thoughts,
I seek out each shining memory of you.
How empty the world!

I grieve and yet I know somehow the years
Will pass. The pendulum of the universe
Will sweep its inexorable beat across
The tides of space—its galaxies grown old—
So old their suns will have turned
To unreflecting moons...
Then, O heavenly then,
In the dusk of a dying world
I will go seeking thee, calling thy name
Down the long echoing corridors of
Infinity until I find thee!
Or until I know thou hast forgotten
The beloved name I gave thee here
Or hast forgotten me.
No matter

If the empty corridors give back no voice
Save endless mockery of my calling;
No matter if the heartless reach of space
Remains a vast and lonely emptiness,
As empty as my heart—
                                            No matter if
No voice returns a joyous answer
To my call,
Still will I love thee,
I will love thee still!

The Scribe
Upon these words, the Presence reappeared.

The Presence
At last, you have unbarred the gate to me
Through which I could not pass. Your mind too full
Of doubt—

The Farer
I yearn for faith, but in my heart I know
Not even *hope*. Whence do they come and how?

The Presence
Against the lonely seasons of despair
And wintry wastes of utter unbelief,
The love of God prepares a reservoir
And fills it full, so full it overflows
And sweeps away despair. This is the pool
Of some deep *inner-knowing, soul-wisdom,*
God-substance, primal as the self.

The Farer
I do not know of what you speak
Whence cometh hope or to what end doth come?

The Presence

    Out of His wondrous wisdom, God designed
    A way to meet the yearnings of the mind—
    The way of hope, the first steps for the blind—
    To lead man's stumbling feet along the path
    That skirts the swamps of hopelessness and wrath,
    And through the floods of doubt; or up the slopes
    To high plateaus of faith and dearer hopes.
    Though He gave man the power to make his choice
    Of good or ill, He listens for the voice
    Of those who cry to Him amidst their trials deep,
    And sets out stars to guide the wandering sheep
    Or sends them shepherds and avatars to prove
    That none are lost who seek the Father's love.

The Farer

    I am as one who sleeps beyond the hour of dawn
    And cannot wake to glory of the morn.

The Presence

    How oft men fail to wake and be aware,
    And knowing naught of God, they would despair
    Save for the rays of hope that strike their eyes
    And bid them ope to view their Paradise.
    The night of darkest doubt and fear shall pass,
    And you shall wake where shadows on the grass
    Are but reminders that the night is done,
    With golden glory streaming from the sun.

The Farer

    Indeed, O Presence, what thou has seen from higher view,
    I have at times found true upon the lower sphere;
    For there were moments of my very own
    When hope newborn did lift me from the depths
    Of doubt and gave me wings to soar and soar;
    At such an hour I almost heard, or thought I heard,
    A voice that answered me—but then, but then...
                           I fell

Down to the depths again. And no response
Was made to my despairing cry. Oh me, I heard
Alone the echo of my cry...
I ask forgiveness for my grief and yet
Alas, I cannot weep, I have no tears.
The hidden stream of life again is dry
Like desert wastes so lone and bleak and bare!
Make plain to me, O Blessed One from Heav'n,
Can this be true? Is there a lamp whose light
Can never die, whose flowing oil is from within
And upward rises at the cry for help
That hope has uttered in its hour of need?

The Presence
The need of man is ever met. *It lies within!*
When God made man, He made him well,
He did not fumble with the clay;
And having made the lamp, prepared for it
A reservoir drawn from the infinite
Supply. Celestial oil forever flows!
Have, then, fresh hope and with your hope have faith,
For faith is inner *knowing,* assurance
Deep that you have filled your lamp and so the light
Must shine when once you light the wick...Or you
May think of faith in terms of seed—know this,
That seed and harvest are the same—seed does
Not weep in fear lest it shall bear no fruit
When harvest comes...The sower in the spring
Fares forth without a fear. And ev'ry path
Bears witness to its end. The goal is sure.

The Farer
But still there is no sun, I walk in fear
Beneath a cloud of sand, while darkness falls;
My burnished hope is vanquished by my doubt
And casts no glow reflected from above;
While peace and joy lie prostrate, even dead.

The Presence
>Yet in your mind have you no doubt of doubt?
>Have you no hope in hope or even faith
>In faith as though your groping hand might grasp
>Another hand? All is not dark. Look up.

The Farer
>Thou hast a strange uncanny sight, and thou
>Dost give me words to say what I myself
>Would not have skill to say; for even when
>My grief is deep and I am wrapped in robes
>Of darkest hue, I sometimes feel that just
>Behind the cloud of my unknowing, still
>A clearer vision might discern a star
>Of hope and follow through the dark.
>At such an hour the eastern sky shows dawn
>And out beyond the shores of time, I see
>Or seem to see eternal light, that for
>A moment shows to me the path across
>The dark abyss.

The Presence
>These fleeting moments have been given
>As beams of light from earth to heaven.
>Just as one ray, the sun reveals,
>One flash of vision oft unseals
>The tight-closed door that stands between
>Two worlds, one seen and one unseen;
>And men for just one moment see
>How time can pierce eternity,
>And can from Heaven filch the fire
>That satisfies the soul's desire.

The Farer
>Oh, that I might but have the vision given
>To see through nature into heaven!
>And stand assured, if so it be,
>If I see God, that He sees me.

If it be true that I have wrought
Through faith a view of Him I sought,
Does He know me or know me not?

The Presence
The Soul-of-All does in Himself know all.
There is One Power and He
Forever stands and like a mighty ocean holds
Within the changeless, self-existent sea
All living things, all substance and all form.
And human life, like mist, comes forth, takes shape
And for a time appears to live *apart*
And so in ignorance rejects the Source
From which it came; but all the time, like you,
The stream of life is yearning for the Cosmic Sea,
All unaware, save by a flash of faith
That even now it hastens to that Sea.

The Farer
What then, O presence luminous, what then?

The Presence
When once returned, the drop remains the drop,
The self remains a self, and co-exists
With all the selves and with the Whole; and so,
Eternally, each shares the essence and
Partakes in counterpart and in reaction
With the Whole.

The Farer
This still remains a mystery, remote;
I weary of the futile quest and toil of life.
Oh, tell me, Presence fairer than the morning,
How can I find a larger, deeper hope
That will mature in faith, the faith that knows
That even now the union is complete
Between the Whole and part? For I am lured
By memory of that small vision which I had

And which already fades. My yearning swells
To sorrow in my breast. I suffocate
With grief. I pray thee, answer me.

The Presence

Take comfort, friend, in this: Creator God
Himself does act by faith. For where no Will
Or Power exists beside His own, He does *decree*
And knows by faith that His creative word
Does bear within itself the fruit which will
Appear at length in action and in form.
It is by faith that God Himself creates.
And you—you can have faith!

The Farer

How then shall I acquire this faith; that I
May find within myself the living spring
That flows through Time into Eternal Life?

The Presence

Well have you spoken and inquired. And I
Shall answer and will show the way by which
Your seed of faith may grow and blossom and
Bear fruit. And first, I ask you this: Recall
How few there are who speak in terms
And language of the Higher Sphere. Do thou
Begin with speech, the speech of heaven,
And know that even now you have the power,
Through love and speech, to thus affect
In some small way that which has yet to come.
This gives you more than hope, it gives you pow'r
To KNOW and to believe, and this belief *is* faith.
And since by faith all things are made, your word
Creates what you believe; and knowing this
Your faith will larger grow, but larger still
Your union with that All-Sustaining Whole.
For Life decrees and all its laws are set
That nothing can resist the consummation

Of freedom born in union with the Whole,
Nor change one whit man's final evolution.
And hope and faith uniting into good
Shall speak the language of Eternal Word.
When joy and love and peace shall thus unite
In speech, they will drain down from Heav'n itself
That which the isolated intellect
Does not perceive, accept or understand;
But, held upon the outer rim alone,
Lacks that which is more deep and penetrating.

The Farer

O Presence, grant to me this larger good
That I may grasp and hold within my mind
The wonders of this vision you have told,
And bear to earth sweet messages from heaven,
The answer to its long sad years of waiting.
The endless ages have both come and gone
Amid a desert, long bereft of rain;
Nor branches from the tree of life give shade.
For men of earth do crave the life by God
Possessed, that doubt may not assail them.
O, once again I pray, Celestial One,
Impress upon my deep remembrance
The wonders of the things you have revealed,
So that the dead in faith shall rise in truth,
The destitute in hope shall sing again
And chains be struck from off the feet of pain.

O friend who reads the Mind of God, tell me
From whence yourself have come, what part you share
Within the Universal; your words are true,
And when you speak, my life again renews,
And all the stars that throng the Milky Way
Break forth in Vedic song as they did sing
When earth, newborn, broke through the cosmic cloud.
What is it that Thou art? Thy gracious face
Exalts my soul; thou art so very near

That with my hand I might reach out to touch
The light that clothes thy form in silver white
And casts a halo round about thy head.

The Presence
I do not stand, my friend, unmoved by your desire,
But even gods cannot be heard by ears
Untuned to higher speech, for those who hear,
Hear naught save sound as from a foreign tongue
Until the soul is tuned to inner speech.
Wait, work, believe, and when the hour has struck,
True Wisdom shall appear and you shall know
That which I am and whence both you and I
Have come and whither we are bound.
Stay not your search but seek the heavenly bread
That feeds the desert soul; and wine of life
That slakes the thirst but does not drown the sense.
For he who drinks need never empty out
The cup from which he drinks; it ever fills
From sources vaster far than space, more deep
Than are the wells of Time. This I assure.

The Farer
Your words are richer plumed than are the
Birds of Paradise, and are as truly winged
With flashing thoughts in heavenly flight.
Yet do I fear that they would blind and not
Reveal to mortal sight, and so would be
Rejected. Alas, how easy to reject!

The Presence
You speak inspired, for you have reached a point
Where you behold men as they are, and not
What they have claimed to be. From higher view
Man is an *angel* fallen out of grace;
But from below, a *beast* who vainly strives
To rise out of the mire. And those who see

The man as clay have worsted all the best
And bid him pass from dust to dust.

There is a field of higher consciousness,
As simple as the air man breathes. By it
He is surrounded everywhere; and, too,
It is within, breath of his breath. So God
In him and he in God exist as one.
The total power of All abides in each.
No attribute by God possessed
Is dispossessed in man. At every point
Within the Cosmic Whole exists the power
In *fullness,* of the All.

The Farer

In this I have no faith; I know too well
The evil in the dark caves of my mind
Where ghosts of memory, with bat-like wings,
Do flutter in the blackness of despair.
Truth is not there nor God nor any good.

The Presence

Yet have you not at times from tortured dreams
Awakened in the soft sweet light of day
And laughed when you recalled illusions stretched
Across the canopy of night?
So let it be with memories that cloud
The mind and heart. For he who looks into
The mirror of the past can only see
The ghosts of yesterday: unreal to him
Who looks into the mirror of today.
The evil shades that haunt your fearful mind
Do not confirm a vacuum in good
But rather prove an eye bewitched by doubt,
Until you cannot see the beauty close behind.
The green scum lying on the pool scowls at the sun
And hides the crystal depths; and thinks
To seize the beams of day and hold,

Nor mirror back again.
Yet all the while a deeper urge divine
Stirs in the pool, and rising, parts the filth
And forth appears the lily!
Fairest of flowers and rich in fragrance and in bloom,
It blows its perfumed breath across the waste;
And gathering all the sunbeams in its breast,
It glows in simple beauty and content.
Within its humble sphere.
No less is man!

The Farer

I have, O blessed One, no faith that I
Do bear such beauty in myself.
There is no soul within the bended walls
Of space with wit to comprehend
Arcana such as this; you speak in riddles,
And in mysteries so deep—

The Presence

A mystery is mystery alone
To him to whom it is a mystery.
The short-limbed dwarf with eye below
The level of the wall proclaims in strident tones,
"There are no blooms beyond, there is no fruit."
The smaller he, the louder is his voice.
Life is unreal to him who sleeps, and love
Cannot be known by him who does not love.
Too oft are you betrayed by inconclusive proof,
A path that ends in an abyss so deep!

The Farer

I do revere thy words and yearn to get
This Truth within my mind, too sore beset
By memories of seer on seer on seer
Who set all Babel babbling in my ear.
The wise and otherwise do oft invoke
The god whom other wise proclaim a joke.

Successive seers the other's god defame—
That god a devil now, but keeps its name!
And man himself most truly is enslaved
By that same creed through which he once was saved.
Until in wonderment, I greatly fear
That they have sold salvation far too dear.

The Presence
You have a bitter wit—

The Farer
Then is it bitter sweet, for it is sweet
With truth. How can the wise or otherwise
Find souls that have been lost? If they be lost,
Then are they truly lost, nor wit nor art
Of man can find in time or timeless space
That which is *naught* or give it any meaning.
What is salvation if the soul be gone?
From what to what can it be saved and who
Shall be the savior? I still will ask you
Though still I doubt; for deep within my heart
I yearn for light upon these mysteries.

The Presence
The world phenomenal is but the face
Or image of the Soul of Things: we trace
The forms we see, the visible, and make
Our judgments by appearances; we take
The insect and dissect its limbs to find
Its structure, but fail to search for mind.
A tree has soul: what tales the leaves can tell!
'Twas on a tree the final rout of hell
Was won by him who taught the truth that we
Must pierce the *form* to find reality.
"Not dead the maid—not dead is Lazarus.
Forgive their sins and let them come to us."
Know this, for nothing greater can be shown,
Your world reflects what in yourself is known;

No bound is set by fate, and its decrees
Can force no stalwart to his knees.
Horizons widen, soften, disappear
And fall away as you draw near.
As you expand, the circle, too, expands:
All fields lie fallow to your hands.
A wall is a mirage, a thing of naught,
Its only threat is in your thought.
For if the point-of-view be from the sky,
Both sides alike are open to the eye.
Appearances deceive, the Nothing seems
A Something in your frightened dreams.
Discard the haunting memories that seem
To fill your mind as in an evil dream.
No hand of God, no memory, no chance
Can do you ill nor force your circumstance.

The Farer

Is there not need of intercession, then?
Can one be saved unless a Savior come?

The Presence

All Saviors are illumined ones who do
Not pay a debt for sin[4], but point a way.
Salvation is to know but God alone.
He is the One and only light of Truth;
Too oft is light deflected and distort
By mirror-minds which dazzle and confuse.
It is from claims by those who do not see
That man is plunged into the great abyss.

The Farer

And what is this, I pray?

The Presence

This is the great abyss, that man is lost
In doubt, an emptiness beyond all speech;
Distraught by solitude he cannot bear,

Each carves an image to conform to that
Which he conceives[5] from what he hears; and this
He worships as the real, and thus creates
The phantom from which at length he seeks escape.

The Farer

You speak most truly as to me. But what,
Most gracious Presence, is the end? Is there
Some hope that something shall survive from this?

The Presence

Had men but bent their steps as they have bent
Their knees unto the lesser gods, they might
Have reached those lofty peaks whereon
The Higher Gods are found. Who shall unfold
His highest self shall closer come
To That Which Is both Real and Best.

The Farer

Whom you call "lesser," who are these?

The Presence

They are the vision of the highest good
That man perceives, the finger pointing on.
The movement of the Cosmic Mind is like
A stream whose ocean lies beyond and he
Who will unfold his best today
Will some day pour into the Cosmic Sea.
Put, first of all, resentment from thy heart.
Lo, giving and forgiving are one act,
For he who does forgive has entered in
The heart of the forgiven. Love's circle runs
About them both, and he who seeks forgiveness
Is also the forgiver.

The Farer

My heart confirms this mystery and I
Would sometimes like to hear the virtuous man

Who asks before the shrine in earnest prayer,
"Forgive me my transgressions, Gracious Lord,"
Pray also, this: "With equal grace, O God,
Forgive my virtues, too." Let virtue be
No outer gown with wide phylacteries,
But graciousness that lifts the hope and faith
Of those who stand with downcast face and heart.

The Presence

He who exalts the saddened heart, exalts
His God, and proves once more that worship is
The act of acting as his God would act;
And so the humble does possess
An equal greatness with the great.
Who loves the good creates the greater good,
Who loves the least has lost the most;
He is but dead who does not love at all.
The world is saved by love and not by thought,
For prayer itself is first of all self-giving.

The Farer

How hopeless is my fate! I have not reached
A plane of love impersonal as this.
I fiercely crave a love that gives me all;
Can I return that which has not been given?
How often have I flung my prayers upon
The empty void and hoped for love!

The Presence

Such prayers as yours might better not be prayed
If you have filled your speech with cries of doubt,
If you have said, "I am in pain, O Lord,
Deliver me. There is no hope and so
I come to Thee in deep despair. There is
No love for me on all the earth—"

The Farer

What better prayer than prayer to fill my need?

The Presence
    Your prayer is seed which strewn upon the soil
    Of All-Creative Mind must grow for you
    A harvest like the seed. If then your prayer
    Affirms your doubt, declares your lack of faith
    And loudly claims there is no love—
    Why, then, your prayer will justify your faith
    In nothing! From nothing, nothing comes.

The Farer
    Quite suddenly in grief, I realize that I
    Have worshipped unbelief, allowed belief to die.
    My faith was faith in doubt, my dreams were dreams of fear;
    Belief in unbelief has brought my failure here.
    What can I do to grow more faith and find
    Some way to soothe my anguishment of mind?

The Presence
    No better way can be than that you share
    What faith you have with those who need such care
    And have still less of hope and faith. Though dim
    Your torch, it still may light the lamp of him
    Who has a greater need and from your faint
    Belief, his soul may flare into a saint.
    The grace with which you act, the love displayed
    Will raise men's faith in love, and by such aid
    They will be healed. So seeing others healed,
    Your grain of faith becomes a harvest field
    And you shall reap what you yourself have sown,
    A greater faith which then becomes your own.

The Farer
    Your words are life, your love has lifted me
    To mountain peaks of hope and I can see
    Beyond the small horizon of today
    And what I cannot see, I now can feel.
    This is the wine of life to me, the blood
    Of consecrated love. And it is bread,

Which I shall eat that I may satisfy
My hungry soul. And I who dwelt in want
Shall throw my begging bowl away and cry
To every longing soul, "There is enough
And more for all; and gifts of hope and faith
I freely give to you. Take, eat and so
Be satisfied."

The Presence
                Well-spoken; who imparts
His little wisdom grows thereby still more.

The Farer
But more than all I yearn to lift my voice
In prayer to God; teach me what I should say
To help myself or others on the way.

The Presence
True prayer is not petition but perception
Oft clothed in affirmation and rejection:
With all your mind and all your faith intense
Reject the evidence of outer sense:
One "good" affirmed will drive ten evils out,
One man with God will put all hell to rout.
There is one only way, the final goal
Which meets the needs of body and of soul,
That man the cosmic source and center find
Within himself but deeper than his mind.
Then learn to pray the prayer of recognition
That finds the truth behind the superstition.
                                       For what is life
If man is unaware and does not feel
Within himself the love of God, nor see
The Inner Light which leads through darkness to
Eternal Light beyond the shores of time?
In quiet contemplation—

The Farer
>Cannot I feel and know that He is near
>The while I turn the wheel or grind the grain?
>If He be Father-God, is He not here?
>What then can I by such communion gain?

The Presence
>Life is not lived outside the man but in
>Himself, and growth requires expansion of
>His consciousness; for life is consciousness
>And in the soil of silence, knowledge grows;
>The wheel, the loom, sensations, feelings, all
>Are instruments by which the soul unfolds—
>Yet keep thine aim—forget not *these* are *seeds,*
>Lest worldly cares and your ten thousand needs
>Crowd out the sun and overgrow with weeds!
>Be still until you hear no more
>The whirling wheel:
>Wait breathless in the silence
>And you will pass beyond the reach
>Of sound and sight.
>Nor cleave to mind or soul
>Until you go behind the veil
>Of outward thought
>Into that holy place where you
>No longer feel
>That you are you: and God alone
>Is there and naught beside exists.
>Then let Him speak.

The Farer
>Is there no more, no other word to say?
>Is this enough to carry through the day?

The Presence
>Of every prayer this is the inner part,
>But learn to hold it closely to thy heart.
>Each moment of the day, you conquer fear

By simple affirmation, "God is here."
As swift as sunshine in the mist
That paints the sky with amethyst
So swift is faith to put to rout
The hosts of evil, fear and doubt;
And lo, before your gladdened eyes
The minarets of Paradise!

Turn thou thy mind to God and Good,
Affirm thy faith in Fatherhood.
Believe that heav'n is now and here
And ev'ry good you seek is near,
So near it fills you through and through
And thrills within the heart of you.
You are in heaven and no power
Can rob you of your glory hour.
The world that lately seemed to tell
A tale of evil and of Hell,
The world that broke your heart, no more
Shall knock upon your lonely door.
Claim thou but this:
                    I am in heaven
And all I ask is freely given.
When earth's discordant voices are so mute
You cannot hear the pipings of the flute,
Your soul will enter silences profound
And comprehend at last the soundless sound.
Here take your rest and let faith play its part
And let it heal your wounds and fill your heart.
For faith can serve the soul and heal all pain
And bring the mind to peace and joy again.
The life of man is measured by his soul,
And victory is his who plays the role
Of faith. Then let your soul with hope expand
He can win faith who first can understand.

The Farer
How can I grow in such capacities?

The Presence
>Rise up with prayer and calmly face the day
>With peaceful mien and greet in cheerful way
>Each one you meet, for he is part of you:
>Act unto him as you would have him do;
>And if he fails, let no offense be given,
>Affirm the healing words, "I am in Heaven."
>The common qualities when fully grown
>Like seed in early springtime freely sown,
>Will germinate and put forth root and leaves;
>Surviving storms, they bring at last the sheaves.
>
>Austere with self, indulgent with his friends,
>The steadfast mind is like the oak-tree, bends
>But does not break and, standing straight and strong,
>Commends the good, does not resist the wrong;
>Content to trust to laws of God and right,
>Seeks no revenge, no devious ways of night.
>Alike in solitude or in the clamoring crowd,
>He neither meekly bends nor cries aloud.
>In no extremes of meekness nor of wrath,
>He walks serene along the middle path,
>Save when a pilgrim falls beside the road
>He stoops to raise him up and bear his load,
>For he who shares his faith serves three,
>Himself, his neighbor and the Eternal Me.[6]

The Farer
>How great the power of faith! Is there another
>Or is this first and greatest of them all?

The Presence
>The greatest gift is love, for you can give,
>Not asking a return. Who gives himself
>In love has given more
>Than he who leaves at every door
>The food the hungry can devour
>Which fills the need but for the hour;

While love shall guide until the shelf
Is loaded by the man himself.⁶

The Farer

Will love indeed bring hope and faith?
If it be so, I shall henceforth pour out
My heart and soul with love so strong
That men shall know I—

The Presence

How swift and volatile you are! Beware
Lest you essay to mint your love and then
Exchange it for the coin of faith and hope.
Love does not barter, seeking for return.
For love that gives, contents itself to give.

The Farer

Then to what end is love if I gain not
Of faith and hope as honest in exchange?

The Presence

Love is a virtue which itself rewards.
For virtue is not something outward worn
But is a grace that will exalt the heart
And clothe the humble in the garb of kings.
Hold fast to love, for it alone expands
The total man and places in his hands
The power of all he is—the three-fold man—
And if he realize *himself* he can
Create the qualities he yearns to feel;
And what to him at first is but ideal
Becomes the fruited-harvest of the real.
Have faith in this, that man could not conceive
Some non-existent thing. You can achieve
The qualities of hope and faith when you
Hold fast your dream and keep it close in view
Until it grows into the dreamed-of goal
And you have built a body for the soul.⁷

The Scribe
>   A glowing glory filled the Farer's heart;
>   He improvised a song of adoration:

The Farer
>   O God, fulfill in me Thy dream
>   And mold me to Thy perfect plan
>   Make me the mirror of Thy thought,
>   Thyself incarnate as a man.
>
>   Here in this world ringed round with doubt,
>   With ever-changing form and face,
>   May I become that which Thou art,
>   And be Thy conscious dwelling-place.
>
>   Let me but body forth Thy dream,
>   Thy high design since Time began,
>   That man ascend to be a god
>   And God descend to be a man.

No death can come unto the soul *of man*
Though paths may wind through darkest gloom.
For God is Life and you are life, and life
And Life are One. More close to Him are you
Than shadow, deeper than the brain that thinks,
Than heart that beats, than self that loves and feels
Upon the earthly plane. Your self, immersed
Within the Cosmic Self can never know
An end. The soul of man endures.

Life and death

The Farer
    Thou Presence dear, through whom I fain would see
    Behind the veil of this mortality,
    Acquaint me now if there be meaning to
    The ceaseless search of man to bring to view
    That which the ages have not verified—
    Why man was born, why lived, and why he died.
    Is there some Monster Force who gave him breath
    To sing and dance, to swiftly lose in death,
    But soon forgot by gods who turn away
    To find some other joke, some other game to play?

    I bitter grow
    Because my very soul has pain to know.
    As surely as man lives, does he not die?
    As surely as he comes, does he not go?
    Nor leaves upon the trackless waste of time
    One forward step into the vast unknown,
    Beyond the blood-stained path his feet have trod
    In anguished questing through the endless years!
    Like insubstantial shadows, phantoms of
    The night, and in the dark, man vanishes
    To be no more, nor see, nor to be seen.
    From naught he comes, to naught does he return,
    And leaves no emptiness of space, save in
    The hearts that also die in pain of grief.
    For all the longings of the human race
    In utter loneliness do find no slightest hope
    To light the dark in which they vainly grope!
    O Presence, you who stand so near, I pray
    Is there no hope that I can find a way?

The Presence
    What is this all-consuming hope?

The Farer
                      That I
    May satisfy my mind of this, that death

Is not the end for me or mine. Is there,
Perhaps, some cave of thought, which once explored
Might lead man from the dark, one ray of light
By which life's mystery can be unsealed?
The fondest hopes, the dearest dreams mean naught
Unless man knows that he shall someday wake,
Somehow, somewhere, sometime to greater life
And find some healing from this plague, the dread
Disease, the fevered *need to know.*
I am undone!

The Presence
                    You are too soon dismayed,
Too tragic in your grief, who like the child
Exaggerates each moment of delay.
Fear not, the child doth grow into the boy:
The boy, though oft in melancholy held,
Disconsolate amidst ideas half-formed,
Becomes at length the full-grown man. Thy mind
Is young as yet. Thy soul awaits the hour
When mind matured shall see and know the truth,
That souls were never born nor can they die.

The Farer
Can man survive the change that we call death,
To find himself not less but more? Renewed,
Revitalized and self-aware?....Forgive
These tears, they are not grief, but I cannot
Contain myself, my heart beats high with hope
To hear thy words, that souls can never die.
For if man cannot die, then there is time
And place for him where he shall find himself
Renewed in vigor, where all that made him
What he at one time was shall make him more—
The infant grown into a boy, the boy to man,
The man to soul,[8] the soul to what? Is there
An end or does the spiral grow and evermore
Expand—and into what?

The Presence
'Tis not alone
In breadth and height, but depth the soul doth grow
Until it pass into the utter bliss
Of Being, where measurements dissolve in Him,
Transformed from thought to feeling and to love,
Where life and death and earth and heaven are one.

The Farer
I long to see this farther shore, beyond
The shadow of my doubts; and as the earth
Awaits the melting of the snow and as
The early springtime waits upon the harvest,
So do my hopes and all who dwell on earth
In greatest longing wait new life to spring
Like blades of corn from ancient harvesting.
Life still is dear to human hearts, though brief
And filled with pain, and tragic woe and grief.
Why is it that the gods above delight
In planting seeds that scarcely bloom 'til night
Draws on and, briefly flourishing, must die,
And dying, leave no answer but a cry?
One moment is my heart upheld by hope,
The next my hand with wildest fear doth grope.
How often would my mind dissolve the suture
That binds me to the past or to the future!
Unborn alike to outer self or in
And never know that I have ever been!

The Presence
Man, the master over forces,
Man himself selects the courses
He shall follow, he shall fly.
Man above the stars transcendent
Is with fate no more contendent,
He who now can rule the sky.
One more field alone to master,
Into which he presses faster,

Faster, faster soars on high!
Past the stars his course is sweeping,
Past the bars of death and weeping;
Life is life and cannot die.

The Scribe
The Farer gazed into infinity
With face so rapt it almost seemed that he
Had pierced the veil into eternity.
Then like the beast who fails to arch the wall
And gives one scream of anguish in its fall,
He cried, "Words, words, I do not know at all!"

The Presence
No death can come unto the *soul* of man
Though paths may wind through darkest gloom.
For God is Life and you are life, and life
And Life are One. More close to Him are you
Than shadow, deeper than the brain that thinks,
Than heart that beats, than self that loves and feels
Upon the earthly plane. Your self, immersed
Within the Cosmic Self can never know
An end. The soul of man endures.

The Farer
You draw a picture beautiful enough,
But even as you speak I hear a sound
That chills me to the bone, the stifled cries
Of those who mourn and bear their dead away.
Death gives the lie to life nor can the soul—
If there be soul—return to life again.
Beyond the measure of the stars in space,
Are those unnumbered hosts of coffined men
Across whose burial caves the stones were rolled
And ashes left with ashes, dust to dust,
While weeping kindred stood in mortal grief
And cried, "It is too late, O Christ, it is
Too late! Hadst thou but come, my brother then

Would not have died." Upon the earth alone
Can life be found. I weep because of death
And weep because of chaos and the night
That falls upon us all. Not one escapes!

The Presence

In just such scene as this was Jesus seen
And when they rolled away the stone, he gave
One shout to Lazarus, "Come forth!" and forth he came.
Deep in the soul of man, life dwells forever
Part of the Cosmic Life, never to die.
Thou shalt not go to the narrow room
When they lay thy body in the tomb;
Lo, how thy soul upsprings
With mighty spreading of its wings!
And it shall mount in its upward flight
To God and the stars and the morning light
And to souls beloved in the days of yore.
They are not lost, they have gone before.
Then fear not, Farer, thy soul upsprings—
For thou hast wings!

The Farer

Oh, sir, your tongue is touched with fire, and when
I hear, my joy has wings and I am rapt
With wonder and intoxicating bliss.
But all too soon the winter chill bites through
My Indian Summer heat and I am cold
Again.
       If gods have love, creative power to put
Their love to test, why do they not devise
A simple way for simple men to understand
And know; to let us speak, perhaps, to those
Whom men call dead? Unveil the face and let
Us see the one beloved—and know—and know!
Make clear to broken hearts and trembling souls
That when the fiercely burning flame consumes
The flesh and turns it back to dust, there still

Remains a kernel from earth's harvesting
To seed new forms of life in realms more fair,
Where souls eternal live in Paradise.
When dust and ashes shall have claimed their own,
And all the earth has been consumed, will life
Have been a dream, a naught from which naught came?
Struck down with grief's foul blow, I vainly try
With lips gone dumb to make my own reply—
But thou, but thou, O seer or friend—if thou
Be real and not a vision conjured by
My fevered brain, I pray thee answer now.

The Presence

I shall depart
If still thou dost not know me in thy heart.

The Farer

Stay, stay, for who or what thou art
It matters not. Thou art my only hope
And I believe—nay more, *I know*—thou art.
Without thee, I were dead, already dead.
Were I to walk the shores of Paradise,
Toward which I yearn, and find thee not, I would
Retrace my steps and search for thee throughout
The void—or hell. You are so much to me.

The Presence

Since you accept on earth the evidence
Of mind against the strident claims of sense,
Should not your soul have equal power to be
Aware in terms of immortality!
Then fear thou not, O Farer, on the way
That leads through night to the eternal day;
For I shall go with you, and there is One
Whose love for you is greater than my own
Who will not leave you comfortless nor lone.

The Farer

Your words of solace are like morning sun
That warms my soul with grateful praise and thanks.

The Presence

The mountain peaks of pure devotion pierce
The dome of blue, conjoining heaven and earth:
The far, the near, the high, the low are one
Where life and light dawn from the Central Sun.

The Farer

But if God loves, why then the pain He pours
As fiery lava down volcanic heights?
Can this be love? How is it that the sons
Of men are scourged by famine and by flood,
By pestilence, by fire-tipped thunderbolts
Of wrath which scorch the shuddering earth that quakes
Beneath man's feet as though itself had horror
Of the scourging lash of gods whose one desire
Is to destroy the earth by ice and fire!

The Presence

Thy words have frenzy as by one bewitched!

The Farer

I do not aim my speech at thee, but at
Almighty Force, Who, if possessed of power
To save, but does not save, seems more of Beast
Than God to me, more worthy of contempt
Than worship. Love and wisdom would not strike
So foul a blow, nor would permit the race
To undergo the torture on the rack
Of human suffering. Should gods not weep
To see the faultless child laid low by foul
Disease, wracked by the pain of festered wounds
And fed upon by inner forces? Which
Like vultures, keeping watch upon their prey,
With ravenous appetites, await the end;

And hovering above the dying form
Make haste to wrest the flesh from off the bone,
While wind and rain and earth claim all the rest.
If this be love or wisdom, let me die
And leave my bleaching bones to lie
Beneath a pitiless, ungodly sky.

The Presence
Not gods but men are authors of their pains—
Harsh though it seems and bitterer to know.
Man has his choice, two paths to him are given
To every goal, a right way and a wrong;
And in each soul there shines a heavenly light
That he may know the wrong way and the right.
No accident occurs by cosmic plan
And heaven itself provides escape for man.
Illumined souls find light before the fire
Which is for blinded eyes a funeral pyre;
An Inner Wisdom shows to them the path
Which skirts the rim of evil and of wrath.

The Farer
But how shall man escape the waiting ills
That spring upon him in unwary hours,
Like jungle-tigers lurking at the pool
Whose cruel jaws do crunch the artless child
And rend his flesh to feed their whining young?
Why is man cast upon the sea of life
With no safe harbor from the storm and with
No anchor that will hold his fragile bark
From breaking on the reefs whose rock-toothed jaws
Devour the stoutest ship?...How answer this!

The Presence
So quickly dost thou seek escape and turn
From him who has alone the answer to
The questions that you ask.

The Farer

> Who then is he?
> And I will scour the world to seek him out.

The Presence

> It is *thyself,* my friend, thyself alone
> In whom the answer lies. All that there is
> Of wisdom, truth or light is found intact
> Within each human soul. This is no wish
> Or idle dream from which you wake to find
> No meaning. Nor is the soul a dream,
> Nor man a dream of gods who rule above.
> For man is substance and not shadow, one
> With Causing Cause, the Primal Cause, That Which
> Is All-Originating.

The Farer

> Whence then the tragedy of life—my life?
> Why have the gods assigned such penalty
> To ignorance? For suckling at the breast,
> Man all but hears the curfew bell that tolls
> The passing of his soul into the vale
> Beyond—if so he pass at all! To *what*
> And *where*—a mystery as great as *whence*
> And *why* he came! The road ahead is blind
> As is the jungle path he left behind.

The Presence

> Man is not cast upon the sea of life
> By deity in mere caprice, to sink
> At length, unmourned, unnoted and alone
> In depths arcane. The sea is man's to sail,
> The stars are his to guide, the winds are his
> To drive his ship against the tide and storm,
> Or run with bellied sails to ports afar.
> How glorious the great adventure of
> The free-born soul where power to him is giv'n
> To *choose* his port and steer to hell or heaven!

The Farer
>But there is pain that is not well deserved!

The Presence
>It is not pain *imposed.* And if there be
>A mystery, 'tis less a mystery
>To find it *self*-imposed than to conceive
>A god who visits pain on good and bad
>Alike and damns the very soul he loves.
>There is no recourse known against the gods.
>But suffering when self-imposed can be
>Deposed. The captive sets the captive free.

The Farer
>If this be so, then must it also be
>In ev'ry evil lies a hidden good
>And man can take a profit out of pain!

The Presence
>The Powers Above await the mind reborn
>By discipline and faith and love of him
>Whose soul has been redeemed, not by their grace
>But by an inner wakening to That-
>Which-Is. Such wakening rests not upon
>The gods but on the *self* that knows at last
>That it *is* soul and cannot find release
>Until the self with self has made its peace.

The Farer
>Is it then true that life but points to death
>And reconciliation with the gods?

The Presence
>There is an end to form of flesh, but not
>To that which truly is, thyself, the seed
>Of life within, which Cosmic Life has strewn
>Upon the earth, as yet not half-revealed,
>But which in time will manifest its being;

Like to a lotus-seed that bursts in bud
And lifts its face in glory to the sun
When morning light has pierced the fearsome dark,
Celestial seeds are planted deep, so deep
That man is unaware they had their source
Within the Garden of the Gods, until
The time has come to pluck the golden fruit
That ripens when the harvest hour has struck.
But all the while, the Higher Power keeps guard;
Nor are men ever lost from sight by That
High Heavenly One Who knows and cares and loves.
The Cosmic Mind can never fail nor does
It make mistakes. The end is sure and He
Will bring the seed to fruit in ripened souls.

The Farer
Am I, O friend, such seed?
                              Can this be true
That I myself am what you have affirmed?
And if there be such self, or soul or God
Why am I then half swallowed up in dust,
And suffer need and feel the adder's sting
Of pain and bear its venom in my veins?

The Presence
The boundless seas, outflung from pole to pole,
Surrender to the will of man; the stars
Are his by which to steer his bark; but each
Must pick his own—Polaris fixed and sure,
Or Algol, "Blinking Demon," often called;
And when his star is set, it is man's hand
Alone that holds the tiller to its course.
Within each man a sacred center lies
Which neither birth nor death can ever change,
And here the self immortal waits the kiss
That wakes and weds him to eternal bliss.

The Farer

    Do you in truth intend to tell me this—
    By freedom man is bound and doubly bound
    Since he has power to choose and is not wise
    In choices made? Far better that his stars
    Or gods should first ordain and then compel
    Obedience to law that, saved from hell
    And suffering on earth, he might secure
    A bliss that would eternally endure.
    From freedom such as this, I pray of thee,
    Whatever Powers-May-Be, deliver me.
    How long, O Life, how long the tragic trail
    O'er land and sea when hopes grow dim and when
    The shadows fall across the weary soul!

The Presence

    Yet souls may sing in darkened solitude
    And peace descend from lofty mountain heights
    From which the waters fall, unseen beneath
    Obscuring clouds which lave the land and serve
    The soil and all the needs of man, and then
    Pass on to join the sea from which they came.

The Farer

    But if we fail in trials of this life,
    Shall we return to bear the load again?

The Presence

    Each soul shall onward go, nor shall return,
    For there are worlds on worlds and seas on seas
    And range on range of mountain heights
    And nebulae that spiral up and out
    Into infinity. Or slow or fast
    The soul moves forward and needeth no return.

The Farer
>Yet some do say that souls are young or new
>Here on the earth and ancient souls return.
>What answer can you give?

The Presence
>   There is no call
>For souls to here return in order to
>Fulfill the purposes of evolution.
>Infinity does not require repeat
>Of birth on earth to thus economize
>On time or place for the unfoldment of
>A soul. Nor does the memory recall
>With surety events of other lives
>The soul once lived upon the earth. (Must it
>Be dead to *self-that-was* for fourscore years!)
>Essential self is 'wareness of the self
>And of that selfsame self that flows throughout
>Eternity, nor can it be unconscious of itself.
>Soul is a stream of consciousness that flows
>Out of the first awareness of itself
>Through time into eternity. Man is
>Himself eternity. Henceforth he shall
>Have memory of his identity.
>If then you fail recall of earthly lives
>Be not distressed. You cannot well recall
>The negative.

The Farer
>   I am by you inspired!
>A thousand deaths were dearer far to me
>Than one return to live my life again
>Here on the earth, were I compelled
>To duplicate each day of it. In this
>Were hell.
>   But why did Powers Above design
>An earth so filled with tragedy and grief

If they have power to build a heavenly place
Beyond the veil?

The Presence
                    Man is not man
Unless to him is given the power of choice
To keep or break the law of harmony;
Which, if he breaks, breaks him. It is by this
He learns and grows. The Powers did not create
His fate nor could foresee the fate of him
In whom the seed of life was planted at his birth,
Save that they knew some day he would awake
In joy and cry aloud, I am a soul,
A living soul—and I am born not of
The earth but heaven! I shall survive the dust!

The Farer
But if he does not so awake,
What then? Will he go on? What good were life
If he does not awake?

The Presence
No one is lost; of this you may be sure—
That life cannot be lost; it will endure,
And that which men call hell will pass away—
And souls go on into eternal day.
Awake, O Farer, be it known
You harvest what your hand has sown.
No god above pronounces woe,
No devil waits for you below.
The gates of heav'n will ope to view;
Look for the key inside of you!

The Farer
I am at once exalted and dismayed
Lest freedom bind and will not set me free.
I long to lose myself in thought of self
That so at length I truly find myself.

The Presence

No failure lies in the eternal plan,
And no mistake was made in making man.
He is no wreck cast on the ocean's side
To be forever beaten by life's tide.
Just as one spark is parcel of the flame,
So from One Mind all things in nature came,
And though the path of evolution wind
And wind before the advent of that mind
On whom the Father lavishes His care,
Still galaxies and souls One Spirit share
And man no more shall prate of "common sod"
For all he sees shall spell the name of God.

The Farer

Why then do children die and aged men
Make painful way down to the dust again,
And why do souls have thirst?

The Presence

In ev'ry drop, the sea; in ev'ry cell,
The universe; in ev'ry soul, the life
Of God; and each contains full power of all.
Life does not give in parts but wholes. There is
No separation, no near nor farther out;
No deeper down nor higher up, no void,
No yonder; and no hopes that cannot be
Fulfilled. The Power-Of-All obtains in all,
And Everywhere is here, and here is There.
Draw thou on *It* if thou wouldst truly be
Complete nor suffer thirst again. Each soul
Is drawn from circuits of the universe
Where life and action have their center and
Where ev'ry point is joined with ev'ry point
And each event unites with each event
In sequence after sequence without end:
And all the seasons of "becoming" are
Unfoldment of events that form a chain

To stretch into eternity; and step
By step man walks among the suns and stars
Consorting with the hosts of beings whose
Existence he had never known until
He struck a higher chord in his own soul
To which they could respond.

The Farer

                    If thou shouldst add
One single word until I still my heart
Of its mad beat, I fear my soul would take
Its flight. Yet would I gladly go if I
Might break the sheath that deadens sound and hear
Such voices speak in accents sweet and clear.

The Presence

Thy soul has kinship in the higher spheres
With beings nobler than the mind conceives,
Both venerable and beautiful in form[9]
And face; and like to gods, are wise in pure
Impassive wisdom; Truth is their bread
And they attain by thought and not by sweat.
All "things" exist in essence and in form
As real; and so are seen in wholes and not
In parts. All "things," that are, are one with all,
And naught on these high planes is hid from sight.
Each soul is loved by every other soul,
Nor is one great, the other small or less,
For each is in the All embraced, the All
Embraced in each, just as the light of suns
Includes the light of other suns, so that
They are one light.

                    Yet each is still aware
Of each, and each is self-aware; as suns
And stars that form the galaxy are seen
In parts and in the whole.

                    And *things* are there
Which serve the needs of souls: for things

Of earth had source from things above; it is
Their native habitat; they are not ghosts
Of earthly things transposed, but permanent
Ideas, the *real* of which the things
Of earth are vaporous counterpart.

The Farer

This is beyond the measure of my mind:
Oh, that I might become a mirror to
Reflect such lore from heaven, to become
Aware of that which is! How can it be?

The Presence

The *mind* is key. For lesser gods, in truth,
Are aspects of the One. In Him the least
Is great; the small, no less; and ev'ry soul
Is more by far than man has recognized
As yet.
             Then do thou, Farer, drink this sweet
Elixir; Wisdom doth embrace within
Itself all qualities. As Truth, it is
The law by which effect must follow cause;
As Good, it is the law of right and wrong;
As Holiness, the choice of good, and so
The freedom from all sin—a choice so wise
That it gives rise to happiness and peace.
As Beauty, it is harmony of all
The diverse parts and blends them into one.
And most of all is Wisdom found in Love,
The soul's desire for good in all its forms.

The Scribe

The Farer could not speak but seemed as one
Who falls into a trance, yet on his lips
Appeared to formulate the mystic words,
"Be still my soul, for THOU ART THAT, and naught
Exists beside."
             He heard or seemed to hear translation of

His vision into words of active faith,
    I gladly give thee all
        Thou aimest at:
    This answer to your call—
        Lo, THOU ART THAT.
    I am thy life within thee,
        Be not afraid,
    Lose thou thy life within Me,
        ONE are we made.
    I am the *good* thou cravest,
        Forever nigh.
    Whenever thou dost say,
        I am, I AM THAT I.

The Farer lay there unaware of time
Or place and wondered at the words that fell
From his own lips, the vision quite forgot.
At length he spoke:

The Farer
    O Presence, if thou be within the reach
    And hearing of my voice, I pray thee now
    Interpret unto me. Didst thou perceive
    Or know by higher means what came to me?

The Presence
    This is a vision far beyond your reach
    Of understanding at this hour; but in
    Due time the meaning shall be given
    Of thy swift vision through the doors of heaven.
    Unto this larger life you shall attain
    And all men shall attain. What spirals first
    Of upward-winding stairs, no man can tell,
    But step by step he mounts to higher planes
    Whereon he stands as on a satellite
    And from this point he sees with keener sight.
    But with the moment's vision not content
    He hurls himself into the firmament,

Unbound by time and uncontained by space,
To seek with greater joy a higher place;
Upon uncharted ethers gladly flings
Himself and dares to trust his wings!

The Farer

O, One-of-Truth, how true! My surging soul
Would break the barriers of earth and air
And soar in realms beyond this human sphere!
I have no fear of death.

The Presence

                    Not death!
Death, so called, is but a myth.
And Time is but the numbering of events,
While space is but a name by which we strive
To make the unknown knowable.
And love and death are but as sequencies
Through which the *less* doth pass along
To form the fullness of a greater good.
All men shall some day reach that greater good
And know the joy of *being* and of Truth.
But he who knows the Truth today shall live
In the Eternal Now and enter peace.

The Scribe

As morning-glories catch the dawning light
And ope their eyes to greet it with a smile,
So did a joy break through the puzzled frown
Upon the Farer's face—and then he laughed—
A clear sweet sound like temple silver bells.
And thus he spoke:

The Farer

Is this indeed what I should understand?—
Proclaim the truth throughout the questing land,
That All-That-Is lies in life's sequencies
And life and death form no antithesis.

The whole wide universe was wrought
By Primal Cause projecting thought;
And so, obedient to laws,
Each new effect becomes a cause.
The stream of life brings to man's door
All that has ever gone before
And he himself has power to cause
A new effect from that which was.
Let him rejoice that "Now" is his
And leave the rest to sequencies.

The Scribe

The Farer's laughter rang upon the air
And found an echo in the universe
As though angelic choirs with harps of gold
Had joined the anthem, singing songs that seemed
Antiphonal with one word, "Joy."

The Farer

                                    In truth,
The words you speak, O Presence, Lord of Light,
Are like the daystar shining in the night,
The perfume of the rose is not so sweet,
Nor lilies at the Galilean's feet.
Only an incense wafted from above
Could lift the soul to such high planes of love.

The Scribe

Yet even as the pressure of his doubt
Was siphoned off, new doubts arose; and on
His face, more eloquent than words, appeared
The age-old suffering, the mark of tragic
Unbelief.

The Farer

            Faith does accept, but reason
Puts to rout, and I am caught between them.
If in the end man's destiny is sure,

Could not the powers that hold his fate in hand
Have mixed the clay with more celestial stuff
So that the bowl would hold more laughter's joy
And less of sorrow's grief and suffering?

The Presence
They could not thus *decree,* or else
The man would still remain the clod or beast
That stalks his prey and knows no moral law
Nor feels the joy of conquest of himself.
The sufferings of human life are pangs
Of birth.
              Though birth be slow, it is not cosmic will
That so decrees, but slowness of man's mind
To learn the lesson that he taught himself
Through pain. The nature of the cosmic mind
Is love, and love is harmony between
All parts. Look on the Milky Way of bold
Andromeda: a hundred billion suns
Do circulate nor ever run amiss,
Sustained by law. But little men collide
Within their little spheres with the belief
They have opposing needs and strive to gain
What all alike possess.

The Farer
                        It is not clear—
Are we not then *compelled* by them to fight?

The Presence
Let man first ask if he himself is free
Of malice, hatred, pride and ignorance;
Let each within himself make sure that he
Has found the central calm. Let him be still
And meditate, rejecting one by one
All things that bind him to a lesser good.

The Farer
What, then is the greater good?

The Presence
                        The Law Supreme is this:
The Law of Correspondences by which
The outer world reflects the world within.
And herein, once again, the secret lies,
The reason why the Higher Powers refrained
From fashioning the world and man in such
Design that he would be incapable
Of pain or grief or suffering.
He must be free to choose and so become
Himself a god, but only by *his* will.
Then seek no more, lo here, lo there,
You shall not find Truth anywhere
Though long the quest or wide or high—
Until with opened inner eye,
Your searching soul shall find revealed
The secret which the gods concealed;
Look thou within, O Soul, and see
The god enveloped in the Me!

The Scribe
The Farer's face was beautiful with joy
As though the finger of an avatar
Had touched his lips, nor did he know that he
Himself had passed beyond the present hour,
And had, a moment, seen the things to come.
Then once again the Presence spoke.

The Presence
The answer to your question then is here:
The greater good lies in the power to choose
The good, nor God or gods designed the course
Or plan for any soul, nor good nor ill
For him. The embryonic stuff of all
That-was-to-be lay slumbering within

The Cosmic Mind. The Powers did not decree
The course of evolution but conceived
Unfoldment of inherent powers until
There should appear a living soul with power
Of choice to give
Or to withhold the passion of his love.

Go back with me along the track to trace
The law of growth, its process and its course
Through endless eons antedating Time,
Until your inner eye shall see and pierce
The cosmic egg and find the embryo
Implanted by the Powers. It must contain
What was, what is, and that which is to be;
In it the germ of protoplasmic life
Must lie—the future form and mind of man.

The Farer

Pray tell me more. I long to know the whole
Great history and future of the Soul.

The Presence

Behold with me in primal fields of space
The movement of a mind! There mist and light
Conjoined in heat and fire which cooled to form
The clod wherein the primal germ of *being*
Could incubate and grow and thus the Fourth
Dimension was reduced to three; and forms
Could multiply by virtue of the seed.
The Higher Powers were patient while the soul
Lay sleeping in the mineral, waved in
The grass and followed with the tiger to
His lair.
            At last! His consciousness awoke,
And lo! a cry! "Behold a Man! a god of earth!
In him the seed of Christ, entelechy
Of Adam Kadmon, archetypal man,
The realized perfection of the ages!"

But he must still *become!* For in him lies
The mind of Him who rules the galaxies
And so his soul shall once again take flight
To spheres beyond this earth, to other light;
Nor seek oblivion in eternal rest
But find new worlds to conquer; going West
Into the void where space has just begun
To view the growth of systems and their Sun
And plot the circuit of their wheeling spheres
In widened arcs and measured by new years;
To test the tensions of the lines of force
And find in Cosmic Mind their primal source;
Describe anew the ancient mystic trine
Where God and man and Nature intertwine;
And from these higher planes again take flight
Into the realms of *other* space and light!
Thus shall the soul of man go on—and never
The cycles cease but will go on forever.
Rejoice that man can share in evolution,
Yet here beware of yielding to illusion
That *primal SELF evolves,* for it was one
With Causing Cause, before time was begun;

Nor need you wait millennia of years
In far-off circuits of the rolling spheres
To find the consummation of your quest
And there at last to enter into rest;
In further galaxies you will but find
New fields to probe with your inquiring mind;
Think not that space remote, my friend,
Achieves the goal and life comes to an end;
The end is *here and now,* this very minute!
And you hold all the keys to knowledge in it;
Not mere pursuit through endless evolution
Of finite things that fail to give solution
To life's enigma, NOW must hold the key—
Not space nor time and not eternity.
If man evades the issue, seeks advance

Through deeper probing of the vast expanse
Of galaxies, he will to his despair
Find failure *Here* presages failure *There.*
Reject outmoded theories of space,
Reject philosophies that seek to place
The source and substance of the wheeling spheres
In laws mechanical. You need no space nor years
To solve the riddle. Discard duality
And let the *truth-of-being* wake in thee;
For what is Now is What-Is-Going-to-Be.
The Now is not contained by time nor space;
In higher consciousness there is no place
Nor time; and space itself is but illusion
That dooms the soul to riddles and confusion.
The age forecast when "time shall be no more"
Stands even now a-knocking at your door.
The whole wide universe invites your soul
To wake and know your oneness with the Whole.
And he who once has felt the cosmic kiss
Will need no sign, no higher proof of this
Than that his soul has fallen into bliss.

You speak the Truth. No doom is sealed,
The reign of hell has been repealed.
At ev'ry crossroad build a shrine—
"The souls of all the earth are MINE."
There is no power that puts to rout
The stalwart mind that will not doubt.

Heaven and hell

The Farer
>   Oh, tell me, Mystic Presence, wise and true
>   Of Heaven and Hell and the hereafter,
>   If so it be that consciousness survives
>   This earthly sphere. Or is there nothing more?
>   Is life a candle-flame snuffed out by death,
>   That like a vanished light has ceased to be?
>   Or does it hold to form like some dead star
>   That whirls through space in neither dark nor light?
>   Or, sadder to the heart of love than this,
>   Do insubstantial netherlands exist
>   Where ugliness and fright and ceaseless grief
>   Hold souls in bondage and eternal fear?

The Presence
>   This is a picture terror-drawn. From whence
>   Did you receive?

The Farer
>   From countless faiths have come
>   These dreadful tales of souls condemned to be
>   In Purgatory, Limbo, or in Hell
>   And suffer pangs of endless pain and grief.
>   Are there such frightful gods as these proclaim
>   Beyond the heated arguments of earth
>   Who thus prepare the torture on the rack?

The Presence
>   If there were chambers such as these described
>   They could be built by gods and gods alone.
>   There are no gods like these, for had there been,
>   They would long since have quite destroyed themselves,
>   Their evil minds reduced to nothingness.
>   Nay, friend, not gods but men with sickened minds
>   And prophets false as hell conceived the hell
>   Of which they prophesied.

The Farer
O Presence, friend of mine and counselor,
How can I thank thee for these words that will,
Through me, be brought to other men to soothe
Their sorrow and to wipe away their tears.
I know not how to bring this home to those
Who stand before the bodies of the dead
Ringed round with grief. How shall I speak to these?
How prove to them that good shall come at last
To everyone and not one soul be lost?
Let me, I pray, become thy tongue; my lips,
Thy lips; my voice, thy voice that I may lift
The suffering from aching hearts and bring
Sweet solace to appease their grief and pain.
What shall I say?

The Presence
                    For ev'ry need of man
There is but God; and hearts that yearn
To solve life's riddle, break the brazen door,
Must see again what seers have seen before:
God is the only Cause and only God can be
The source and substance of eternity.
Time was before man was when nothing was,
When space was thought and thought the only Cause:
No air to breathe, no breathing and no breath,
No light of sun or stars, no darkness and no death:
Yet there was Something, Embryo or Will,
Beyond, behind, within, outstretched and still,
Something that shook the vast outreach of Naught
And, lo, It spoke the word and bodied forth Its thought.
What was, what is, and what shall be is still
Within the care of that Creative Will.

The Farer
I am suffused with light and blinded by
The glory of thy words, and I shall speak
For thee as best I can and so appease

The hunger of those souls whose simple hearts
Ask only that they may find hope and faith
And safe companionship along life's road.
Wilt thou not, then, give words for me to speak
Of heavenly things and of the glories there?

The Presence
Speak first of LOVE for love can never die,
And love itself has wings; with clearer sight
The tear-dimmed eye might pierce the fearsome night
And see the soul upspring all-winged with light.
The REAL is never seen; the Cause, the Source, the True,
The holiness we crave lie just beyond our view.
The high desires, the good, the love that purifies
Cannot be touched nor seen by these too-human eyes.
The faith by which men live, the cause for which they die,
The vision of the saint escape the mortal eye.
Man lives his span and goes, nor ever dreams that he
Lived only in the shade of unreality.
He thinks that changing forms of shadows on the wall
Are real, and stoutly claims that what he sees is all.
Yet just behind his sight and just beyond his eyes
Are minarets and towers of unseen Paradise.
There is the light of Lights, and truth full-blown;
There is Reality and Wisdom on the throne.
Judge not the world by sight: not what *appears* is true:
Your world is thought in form, the only real is YOU.

The Farer
How often have I sought what I so near
Possessed! I lingered by life's temple door
But did not listen to the voice that bid
Me enter in. But now I will proclaim
A fairer temple for the souls of men
Where hurt and fear no longer shall hold sway.

The Presence
Let men await such vision of the truth

Nor leave a single soul without high faith!
Then shall the morn of hope most brightly dawn,
Which noonday sun shall neither burn nor wither,
While evening twilight comes in quiet peace
And lights its star to guide the Farer thither.

The Farer

O friend, you have revealed a truth of life
That will assuage the fears and doubts of men
And gladness bring to dry away their tears.
I know as one who lives upon the earth
The torture heaped upon the hearts of those
Sick souls brought up within the shadow of
Old creeds which have condemned the soul to hell.
I know their fear of sepulchres and crypts
Where ghostly wraiths and phantom forms of fear
Do hover o'er the dead. I share the grief
Of broken hearts that see the fiery pits,
The all-consuming flames that add their fury
To pain-wracked souls in scenes of desolation.

The Presence

To none is given unless he first receive:
Nor can life's wine be pressed from grapes of wrath.
Too oft men lift a down-turned cup and pray
That it be filled with life and love divine.

The Farer

How, then, is this? What meanest thou, my friend?

The Presence

No god could ever join in joyous song
With those who sing a hymn of hate and fear.
Nor can the manna fall from heavenly store
Into the mouths of greed and discontent.
The golden autumn shows no harvest field
To him who plants no seed nor tills the soil.
Life follows furrows straight and sure.

The Farer

> O thou interpreter of life, thy words
> Fill me with awe, but how can I, a man,
> Embrace the meaning of such mysteries?

The Presence

> The simplest soul is heaven-bound and lives
> In heaven *now* whose heart becomes a door
> That opens wide to love. Who pity holds
> For those who faint or walk the road of grief,
> Shall pity find. O blessed peace! Dost find
> In this a riddle far too deep? Faint not,
> Forgive and all shall be forgiven.

The Farer

> The Way is simpler than I thought:
> That man made hell but also makes his heaven.

The Presence

> Be not deceived by prophets hoar whose words
> Do hang like beards of moss to sap the tree
> That lifts its head above the dismal swamp
> Of yesterday. Their gloom has shadowed o'er
> The hopeful heart and bound the minds of men.
> They met the need of savage days and meant
> Full well. Their day is past. So let the dead
> Be buried with the dead and let new sap
> Flow through new limbs and blossom in new fruit.
> The thoughts that ages have believed
> Are written on a secret, hidden scroll
> Which by the unseen law of its own being
> Repeats its error in the minds of men.
> And truth, once relative, is by Tradition held
> Until it is a lie. And from dead stars
> Men take their bearings, spin their compasses
> And hope to sail true course that leads to heaven.

The Farer
>They sail, alas, through typhoons, roaring waves;
>And nights are black with tortured unbelief.
>Is there no other compass and no chart
>By which the soul can sail to heavenly ports
>And over calmer seas?

The Presence
>   The things below
>Have prototypes above, the perfect forms,
>The patterns in the All-Creative Mind;
>And man can so reflect the Truth that he is led
>Into a heavenly glory here on earth.

The Farer
>How can I find this chart that I may spin
>My needle till it points true course for me?

The Presence
>Be still and bring thy mind to rest in peace
>Till thou canst hear the silence speak. Present
>Thy mind as though it were a mirror turned
>Toward heaven and let it be thine one intent
>To know within thyself what heaven knows.
>Then shalt thou know what is to heaven known.

The Farer
>I have so often prayed but I despair:
>For good or evil seems to come by chance.
>Why is it heaven so oft refuses me
>What others boast they did receive, by prayer?

The Presence
>They lift beseeching hands in supplication,
>Appeasing wrath that they themselves create.
>If happily they find release from pain,
>They truly think that God has heard their plea
>And by a special mandate spoke for them,

Bequeathing them a favored providence
Which others equally did seek in vain;
And who, in turn, believed that God refused
To hear or heed. And failing to attain
Do oft accuse and lay the blame upon
High heaven; or grovel in the dust and claim
That God, through love, has chastened them.

The Farer

You reach beyond my power to understand,
For what is Truth—how is it—where is found?

The Presence

In simple words the Truth can be defined:
That good shall come if you in it believe
While forms of fear accursed will fall on him
Whose mind envisions fear and doubt and grief.

Faith is the thought which Truth will bring to form,
Though faith may be in evil or in good;
But Truth itself stands clear, remote from ill.
Truth is the prototype immaculate,
The pattern of perfection never lost,
The Cosmic mold in the Creator's mind.
And flesh is counterpart to symbolize
That which exists above, hid from your eyes—
A crystal mold of unimagined grace
By which Life's Sculptor shapes the human face.
So flesh is soul while soul and flesh are one:
This is the Truth by which a new effect is won.

And he who dares to turn to Truth and Truth
Alone and say, "Thy will be done," will ope
The door to Paradise...
He who denies the Truth must live without
The good that Truth might bring from Heav'n to him.
But Truth itself will suffer no defeat
And like a tree upon the desert's edge,

Wind-blown, sand-scoured and buffeted by age,
Can stand alone against the ravages
Of time and still hold life within itself.
So is the man upheld by Truth. His roots
Run deep and drink their fill from hidden springs.
Yet few there be who claim this heritage,
Discard tradition's blight and choose to live
Free souls! For *one* with Truth is better than
Ten thousand bowing to a golden calf
Within the wilderness of ignorance.

The Farer

Then I who have from early youth
Been bound by creeds, cut off from Truth,
Through ignorance—I see it well!
Myself created Heav'n or Hell.
The nether regions of despair
Are fantasies drawn from the air
By sickened minds held in a trance
Distracted by their ignorance!

The Presence

You speak the Truth. No doom is sealed,
The reign of hell has been repealed.
At ev'ry crossroad build a shrine—
"The souls of all the earth are MINE."
There is no power that puts to rout
The stalwart mind that will not doubt.

The Farer

Then will I put my trust in thee.

The Presence

                              Within
Thyself, alone, and in the Truth, have faith,
For THOU ART THAT and That is what thou art.
I see the light of Truth within thy soul
That throws a cosmic ray to pierce the clouds

Of ignorance and burn away old tales
Of harpies, witchery and imps of hell.
And round about thy light a higher light
Doth gird thy light, as halos crown the heads
Of avatars and saints. This is the Truth.
Toward this let all thy mind and heart be bent
That thou someday identify with it.
And in this quest let no man question thee;
But thou, adorn thyself in robes of faith
In truth. And hold communion deep within.
For intuition is divine tuition—
Who yields to Truth but yields himself to God;
Nor hold a doubt—the harvest is assured!

The Farer

How shall I pray?

The Presence

Prayer is a conscious union of the soul
With God, a recognition that the Whole
Is wholly present in the seeming part
Around, above, below, within the heart,
And in this work—this is of prayer the essence—
The hour-by-hour *awareness* of the Presence.

The Farer

Does this exclude petition for His grace?
That He forgive our sins and make a place
For souls bowed down with shame and grief
In bitter need for pardon and relief?

The Presence

How slow the mind to cast off ancient creeds,
To gain relief by counting of the beads!
Throw off forever the vestments of tradition,
God is not won by groveling petition.
And if it be you have a need of health,
Of friendship, peace of mind or wealth,

Make first your union with the Source-of-All,
Your word contains the answer to your call.

The Farer
O Presence, lead me to those hidden springs
Whose waters bathe the soul and cleanse the mind
And wash away tradition's ancient dust,
And help me *act* upon the truth I gained
From thee, that I may pray, and pray aright.

The Presence
With All-That-Is you are identified
And rule conditions, save in this alone,
You cannot violate the harmony
Of universal law which must obtain
In heaven itself, for heaven is harmony
Whose law is uniform and dominates
All lesser cause and manifested life.
But subject only to the Cosmic Law
Which never binds the wise, you are yourself
Originating Cause and speak creatively
In all affairs that constitute your world.
Out of the Boundless you emerge and hold
The scepter of Its power within your hand,
And in your heart the knowledge of Its Being.

The Scribe
The Presence, overcome, could not restrain
The glory singing in his heart and so
He burst into exalted speech:

The Presence
                              The self,
God-conscious, turns water into wine,
And honey-sweetened manna falls within
The wilderness if man but speak the word;
The sick is lifted from his bed, and those
Who faint with loneliness and fear shall find

A comforter, the Spirit of All Truth,
And friends to walk with them along the way.
The day shall dawn when men shall roll the stone
Across the open grave because there are
No dead nor need to lay away.
The tears men shed in grief shall flow for joy.
Then shall the eye behold no more the slain
Nor death nor crucifixion held in view,
But, looking up, man shall behold the Son
Of God untombed and joined by singing hosts.
And every one He looks upon will thus
Appear as Buddha, Krishna, Atman, Christ, and Truth
Who shall in him again embrace mankind.

Then you must truly turn your song to fact
And realize the One within yourself,
Unveil the curtain drawn by unbelief
And guilt and fear across the face of Truth;
Let love and beauty speak to you of Him
Whose Presence bides within the silence, who
Has covered Himself with the stillness.
You can find and adore Him, He is near
As the breath that you breathe. If your ear
Shall be tuned to the sound of his speaking,
You will find the One you are seeking.

The Scribe
Then was the voice of the Presence
Lost in a sigh of delight
As though to the Greater Presence
The Farer had taken flight,
For he was lost in the wonder
Of listening in his heart;
Enraptured in the silence,
He knew that he stood apart.

The Presence
Your face is bright, you have communed with Him

And heard the Voice of the Stillness. When you
Have ceased to hear the voices of many
Then you can hear the One. And you can see
What was invisible till now. No cloud
Obscures His face when once you know the One.
The highest and the lowest in the ranks
Bear likeness when the inner eye perceives.

The Scribe

It seemed that then the Presence
Was unable to restrain himself
From speech ecstatic and he cried:

The Presence

His glory shines in the morning stars,
The evening sunset proclaims His beauty:
In the stillness of night He is heard;
He is one with the rain, the mists and the clouds;
In all that is formed is His essence.
In whatever is nearest behold Him,
Then watch for Him in the silence,
But not as a shadow without substance,
Nor a dreamer of dreams in a slumber,
Mirage nor a mirrored illusion.
He is substance, not shade of mere seeming;
It is He who ordaineth creation,
Whatever we see in creation is
Manifest presence of God—all is God.

The Scribe

His voice was stilled, yet in the Farer's soul
It still spoke on so that in after years
He never knew from whence the wisdom came
That drew a picture of the paths to heaven,
Profound with warning yet with hope assured
To those who know that love and law are one,
And who through love will reach to bliss at last.

The Presence

 Blest be all paths of worship leading unto God
 And those who point or follow where saints or saviors trod;
   Thrice blest be those with hearts of love
   Who show the way that winds above
 And fix the thoughts of men on heights beyond the clod.
   Hail all the ways from heav'n sent—
   It matters not their sign or name;
   The crown, the Cross, the Crescent bent
   Alike are lit from Central Flame.

 Revere the upward pathways that lofty souls devise
 And all celestial beings whom they idolize;
   But trust no signet and no sign
   That speaks alone of "me" and "mine,"
 For there are many fingers that point to Paradise.
   Nay, hail no dogma and no key,
   However good or reverent,
   That would a *single* faith decree
   The only way of man's ascent.

 Fill up the cup of life with wine from all the ages
 And turn the leaves to read a million pages
   That tell of God and praise His name
   And all His wondrous works proclaim
 Writ down in words of wisdom by the saints and sages—
   But hail no system and no deed,
   Which, lacking wit, would be so droll
   That it ascribes to man-made creed
   The power to damn or save a soul.

 How crude the tale that gods themselves would build a pyre
 And light the faggots of an everlasting fire!
   Is EVIL then a Cosmic Cause
   That turns the course of Its own laws
 To thus consume the soul that sprang from Its desire!
   If Good with Evil *could* comply
   And wrong had equal power with right,

The universe would be a lie
And all that is would disunite.

Nay, what Thou makest, Lord, returns again to Thee
Though it must run the circuits of eternity;
    That which goes forth upon its round
    Is still to its own center bound,
Compelled by its own law and not by a decree!
    No sceptered might shall loose the cord
    That binds the soul back to its Source;
    Its *law alone* is overlord,
    Nor creed nor priest can change its course.

From Primal Fount of Being, love and order rose,
And set up a tribunal which nothing can oppose—
    The Law of Love, the cosmic urge
    Which none can alter, none submerge,
The hand that metes out justice also wrought the rose!
    Not creed but love must hold the scales
    That measure justice round by round,
    Nor love nor mercy ever fails
    To balance justice pound for pound.

There are no gods above, with regents here,
To blast their own creation, rule the world by fear;
    And unto none has power been giv'n
    To arrogate the throne of heav'n
Or doom the seed of life God planted on this sphere.
    Should the Cause of all our being
    Its own integrity blaspheme,
    Then would darkness blot out seeing
    And utter chaos reign supreme.

Eternal Justice has to none assigned the role
To judge the retribution falling on the soul;
    For its escape, no virtue *giv'n*
    Can shrive the soul, assuring heav'n;
Yet each shall yield some day to love and reach the goal.

The scales of Justice balance fair,
And man shall reap as he has sown,
For Love awaits him everywhere
And will reclaim him for Its own.

From Primal Source of Being cosmic star-dust whirled
And on the dome of heaven Love's banner was unfurled,
Proclaiming from the heights above
That law and order follow love
And will bring peace to all the heartsick world.
On life's canvas paint the story,
Drawn with circle, square and chain—
Law and order rule in glory
Where Truth and Beauty safely reign.

The Scribe
Then did the Farer, seized with prophecy,
Join in the chant as in a litany.

The Farer
Life's riddle solved! The quest of all the ages past
Has heard the answer of the silent Sphinx at last—
None shall be lost! Inscribe the scroll
That all are parts of one Great Whole,
And none are damned, condemned to the eternal blast:
Love is the law—this Its decree,
That neither curse nor creed can bind
The soul of him who loving Me
Seeks Me alone, for he shall find!

Who knows in part has found a door ajar
That opens to the Whole. The life of All
Exists within yourself. Be still and know
The Knower and the known. Who finds himself,
Finds Truth; who knows the Truth knows self;
Between yourself and It, naught intervenes.

Truth and beauty

The Scribe
> The Farer woke and wept.

The Farer
>   I am undone
> For I who lost the world of time and space
> Am still shut out from that high sphere
> Which I a moment glimpsed, and I am left
> To swing in vacancy between the two
> And neither now is real. I am distraught.
> I, who have died a thousand times in grief
> Not only for the dead but for myself,
> The living dead, am left to die again
> And yet again and then to die again,
> And joined in pain with those whose souls
> And hearts no longer dare believe, who have
> Foresworn all faith, all final hope of good
> Because the hopes and dreams and loves and faith
> Of yesterday were shattered one by one;
> I find no healing for the broken heart.
> Nor have your subtile arguments sufficed
> To bring to me a fixed abiding peace;
> One moment sure, the next is insecure.
> I awake in the hush of the night
> To a light that is lighter than light,
> And I cry in the still of the air,
> "Are you there, are you there, are you there?
> Are you near, are you near, are you near?
> Do you hear, do you hear, do you hear?"
> But the blackness of night settles 'round
> And I hear not the ghost of a sound,
> And I know and I know it is so
> That I never, no never, shall know.

The Scribe
> A passion of despair had seized his mind
> And sounds of fury struck his inner ear
> As though erupt in dissonance from hell,

Until his body, wracked with agony
Of soul, lay still and numb as if in death.
How long he lay, he knew not; but at last
Became aware of time and place. And then
He heard the Voice,

The Presence

                    Be still and give thyself
To silence and to inner listening.
Surrender grief; no door can be unlocked
By self-inflicted pain nor bleak despair.

The Scribe

So spoke the Voice and then the Farer knew
The Presence had returned. In unbelief
He lay, nor glad, nor sad, but wondering.

The Farer

I hear thy voice again, but I am numb
With grief because I cannot understand.
At times the muddied waters of my mind
Are cleared so that I seem to comprehend,
But straightway I am lost in doubt again.

The Presence

Give time. The fruit must ripen on the tree.
So is it with man's struggle toward the truth.
Impatience will not speed the harvest home.

The Farer

I draw, my friend, some comfort from your word
And all but understand what once I heard.

The Presence

The singing springs of beauty and of truth
Shall rise from depths within and overflow,
And you shall pass through gates of beauty to find

That soul and form are one. I will be guide,
If you will follow me.

The Farer

With all my heart I will attempt. Would that
My mind were equal to my heart.

The Presence

Know this,
There is a *wisdom* absolute from *which*
A knowledge of the truth may be derived
Which opens to the heart by faith; to mind,
By both divine and human reasoning. This
Did the Ancients teach through ages dim—
That Truth reveals itself at every point
In time and space to every man who thinks
His way behind the thing he knows to what
He does not know. For truth self-evident
Exists that all may know and understand.

The Farer

How shall I know or see or recognize?

The Presence

Look to thy Lord, the Ever-Present Me
And turn to Him, the Undivided One
Who is I AM, the center of your knowing;
Where recognized, Truth is and so remains;
Unrecognized, It does not cease to be;
It still remains, the substance of your life.
Look not for revelations from without
But to awakening of Truth that lies within.
The Ever-Present, closer than your hand,
Inspirer, and Beholder, known of old
To those who sought Him in the silence,
Is in your midst and in the Here and Now;
No separated parts can ever be;
No *fragments* of His being can exist;

There is ONE ESSENCE AND BUT ONE ALONE
In God, in man and all creation through,
One Uncaused Being who alone endures.
He is the One Without Who stands and knocks;
Within, He is the only One who enters.
From whence He comes is Undivided Whole,
One Life which does all living things embrace.

The Farer
Outside this One and Only, then, is naught?

The Presence
Since Life is One, there's nothing to exclude,
All things that move must move within the Whole;
And though he seems to travel far from home,
Each must return to that from which he came.
All things refer to ONE, this is the key
Which locks or unlocks ev'ry mystery.
This age-old doctrine still is in its youth,
For few there be who comprehend its truth;
Content to say that deity is one
They leave the greater principles alone,
For monotheism shows us but a part
Of all that lies inherent at its heart.
Conceive of ONE as *substance* and as *law*
Which is to mind a willing servitor.
There is one law of being everywhere
In earth and sky, in ocean or in air;
One law of light, one law of heat and power,
One principle that holds from hour to hour
The galaxies that throng through outer space
And keeps earth's spinning satellites in place.

The Farer
How great my longing is for truth and peace!
This can I understand, at least in part.

The Presence

Who knows in part has found a door ajar
That opens to the Whole. The life of All
Exists within yourself. Be still and know
The Knower and the known. Who finds *himself,*
Finds Truth; who knows the Truth knows self;
Between yourself and It, naught intervenes.
Within a circle perfect and complete,
Which is designed to demonstrate the Whole,
Conceive "self-knowing" as the center point
And from this point draw circle after circle
Expanding to infinity. Observe
Two facts, self-evident: Infinity
Will still remain infinity and each
And every seeming part retain in full
The nature of the whole throughout all time.
Time within the timeless is but movement,
Space within the spaceless is but form.
Where neither big nor little does exist,
No more of one can be than of the other,
Nor from the one can other separate be.
Self-existent *being* is what you are;
In all but outward form, deathless and changeless.

The Farer

Make clear to me what "Being" is, I find
No gain to wisdom by the change of terms.

The Presence

The cause and Causer, form and Former *are*
The same, God's breath congealing in a star
Or in a man; and he who seeks shall find
One master truth, his body is his mind
In action, and all the complex whole
But manifests the movements of the soul.

The Farer
>Whence then springs evil? And what breath from hell
>Breaks down the walls of heaven's citadel?

The Presence
>Evil is a word by ignorance designed,
>To show some *other* Cause than Cosmic Mind,
>Some Devil lurking in horrific caves
>Or masked as "good" to charm men into slaves;
>Yet abstract evil, a thing that lives apart,
>Cannot exist. But when the mind and heart
>Shall violate the law of One Alone,
>In pain or loss man reaps what he has sown.
>The vineyard grows in rich volcanic soil
>Down in the valleys of the sons of toil,
>But if the warnings of the ages past
>Be overcome by greed and, at the last,
>The vineyardist encroaches on the height,
>The hour will come as thieves come in the night,
>When from the hot volcanic mouth is hurled
>Horrific forces shattering the world.
>Here are no dragon's teeth nor flaming jaw
>But the *result* of violating law.

The Farer
>My thoughts are like a whirling pool that sucks
>Me down till I be lost within a void.
>Call Evil by the name of Naught, but still
>It evil seems to me. And ugliness
>And beauty seem to me as *two,* not one.
>How can I see but one?

The Presence
>   *Within yourself*
>Alone lies cause and cure of seeming ill,
>In BEAUTY still the inner self remains;
>Within yourself the perfect whole exists.
>Lo, nothing lies between, for THOU ART THAT.

By Nescience be thou not dismayed, for he
Who does not see the soul cannot thereby
Give any proof there is no soul to see;
Nor can the arrogance of ignorance
Dismay the searching soul who dares believe
He has the gift to see behind the veil.
If you will take a circle perfect-drawn
And with unnumbered radii bisect
From center to the rim, the surface shows
A group of segments, separate as parts;
Yet this is but illusion of the sense,
For each and all will still remain the same
And each the *total* power of all proclaim.

And beauty lurks beneath, within it all,
Since beauty is to see the Whole behind
The parts and merge them into one,
Each held by each in one all-pure embrace.

The Farer

The beauty of your thoughts is unconfined
That man is one with All-Creative Mind.
But this same claim of avatars and seers
Has not been changed throughout unnumbered years.
Once more I ask why evil, pain and death
Pursue the soul until the last faint breath
Escapes the lips? In tears we lay away
The dearly loved within his robe of clay.
The great enigma still remains as deep,
Life turns to dust, man takes a final leap
Into oblivion; on the ocean shore
The wreck of hopes of ages as of yore!

The Presence

How slow is man to recognize that he
Himself is cause and cure of ills, to see
That Law responds to him and pours out treasure
In equal parts exactly to the measure

Of his demands, of faith without pretense;
And he can cure himself of accidents
Or evil; united with the One can prove
There is no wall or barrier to love.
No master dies but by his will; and free
To live or die, survives eternally.
Be thou, O Farer, wisest of the wise
And seek to live on earth in Paradise.

The Farer

How sick am I with sorrow, oh, how slow
To understand the very things I know.
Give me a mind to understand and see
The secret hid behind the mystery.

The Presence

A law of order and a flame of love
Must blend themselves to make the perfect whole
Which neither doubt nor reason can disprove.
This is the mystic marriage, Law and Love
Forever wed, inseparable and One—
And from their union Beauty has been born—
This One and Only is Lord of all.

The Farer

Yet even as you frame this age-old truth
A skeptic voice still lingers from my youth
And asks in scorn, "What will you do with me?
I am a *self*, I am apart from thee;
I know I am; I think, I choose, I will."
How can I know the One? Have you the skill
To make this clear? For though I long to know
I cannot slay the doubts that seed and grow.

The Presence

If God be One, and yet you, too, exist
Then must it be that you are one with Him—
One Life, One Spirit and One Over-Soul

Combining all within the Cosmic Whole.
The One and Only is the central point,
The pivot of the ever-spinning wheel
Whose spokes are souls, but as they swiftly whirl
They are a plane, an undivided Whole.
Within His being, all that is exists;
Or we may liken Him to waters of
The undivided sea in which all forms
Of life are found, from one-celled plants to man;
Yet like the fish, they search the deeps to find
The sea in which they swim. Or like the bird—

The Farer

The mockingbird, I think, who folds its wings
And borrows notes and, melancholy, sings
To yon gray goose who by an inner eye
Foresees the goal to which it dares to fly:
"O goose, in all your journeys here and there,
Have you by faith discovered any air?"

The Presence

You have the gift of humor but beware
Lest you yourself should fail to find the air.
The secret of all being never flows
From arguments polemic, though the prose
Be sweet as verse to him who thus propounds
His thesis in the most sepulchral sounds.
Caught in revolving doors, the systems spin
And disputants come out where they came in.

The Farer

My heart is yearning to withdraw
And find oblivion sweet, or else to merge
In never-ending unity with Life.

The Presence

All souls do yearn for that from which they came,
As though awakening from a night of sleep,

Returning to the Ocean of their Being.
So every heart that hears the Voice turns back,
Turns in and so returns unto the Source
And substance of its being; home, at last!
The Perfect Whole cannot exist in parts,
For ev'ry seeming part contains in fact
The fullness of the Whole, for God is All.
All else is Naught and adding naught to naught,
Subtracting naught, dividing all by naught
Leaves all unchanged; there is no opposite
To Truth; no absolute of evil, death
Nor hate nor greed that can divide the soul
From All.
        Defer not good until another day
Nor dumbly wait until time gives surcease;
There is no time nor place but NOW and HERE;
The past is gone, the future is a dream,
Eternity is drumming at your door.
On those who wake to timelessness will flash
The light'ning vision of the Whole,
And they shall wonder that they held so long
The smoking lamp distorting everything
That fell within its clouded arc.

The Farer
Would that such lightening flash would break on me,
That my small lamp might mingle light with light
In oneness with the beauty undefined
And with those souls who here on earth
Have found their Paradise! Would this were so!

The Presence
Each soul could be to you a string on which
The Great Musician plays and each and all
Would form the Heavenly Harp from which He draws
The music of the spheres whose harmony
Reveals the presence of the Common Soul.
For this, the wise, attuned to higher thought,

Have sought, nor have they failed to find. For this
The otherwise have sought in vain.

The Farer

Who then are these, these otherwise?

The Presence

The "otherwise" are those who have denied
The Presence of the Common Soul-of-All.
He who denies, rejects and plants no seed
Can reap no harvest for his future need.
He cannot use the power that he denies
Nor will high heaven heed his hopeless cries.
Yet all the while Creative Cause is there,
One Knowing-Power that fills the Everywhere,
One Seeing Eye behind the flaming spheres,
One Hand that holds and looses all the years.
From this One Life all living things proceed
And He it is Who meets each human need.

The Farer

Why then do men their systems vast devise
Dividing man from man and soul from soul?

The Presence

They do not comprehend or understand
The Undivided One, the Self-existent.

The Farer

But how could I, or anyone on earth,
Dust-born, dust-bred, and dust-entombed,
Find access to such unitary Cause
And like the monarch moth, on milkweed fed,
Burst from my shell and mount on heav'nly wings!
Your words are winged with hope and I can feel
A joy run through my veins as though I had
Imbibed a cup of liquid beauty and
Become a god-intoxicated soul,

Yet this will pass—so often has it passed
And left me cold and thirsty as before!—
Oh, that I might the perfect chalice find
And drink the wine of endless happiness
Or endless sleep and sweet forgetfulness.
Give me the heavenly wine and bread of life
O friend compassionate, that I may live,
Or give oblivion to me here and now.

The Presence

I cannot give you that which cannot be
For non-existence never could exist;
There is no place where life is naught:
There is no death...

Deathless thou art, and changeless, save in form;
Beginnings endless and endings endless
Mark the sequence of Life's many changing forms.
The Cause is never victim of effects
Of Its own doing, nor bound thereby;
When to one form another has been joined,
It still is harmonized. Arrangement is
In sequence of its number through all time.
Expanding circles still retain the point,
The self-same center of the smaller one.
The union still remains though circles drawn
Expand into infinity and each
Circumference be greater than the last
Through all eternity.

The Farer

I am undone, my reeling brain, alas,
Can apprehend but little of thy speech;
I find myself but mouthing vaporous words:
          In your thinking let the smaller
          Grow at length into the greater;
          Let the greater, still expanding,
          Rise to higher understanding.

Let the circle wider, taller,
Bring me wisdom, soon or later.

O master voice, O soul of wisdom, speak
To me in words I comprehend.

The Presence
All truths are from one Truth evolved;
Unbounded, unconditioned by the past;
The Whole is still intact, though form on form
And part on part appear or are reduced
To Essence once again. That which evolves
Is finite only to the finite mind,
For in Creative Mind the pattern-thought
Remains a sequence in the number and
Arrangement of the parts which but reflect
The order and the harmony that lie
Within Creative Mind. And what to man
Appears as growth from low to higher forms
Is but unfoldment in the Cosmic Mind
Which held the seed and sperm of life within
The crystal. The "Master Mind" is but
The man who reads the mind of God and finds
A *law* in sequence, numbers and array.
Man's freedom lies within his power to know,
And knowing, to conform.

The Farer
                              To what, I pray?
To numbers?

The Presence
                    Nay, for numbers *symbolize*
But have no meaning of their own. 'Tis this:
That man shall know life is complete today
With all he needs to meet his needs today
Though circle to a larger circle grows,
(I must repeat what I have said before)

The point of center still remains the same;
And in the smallest circle are embraced
The qualities of all that future rings
Will manifest in form; the widening ring
Is widened consciousness of That-Which-Is.

Already THOU ART THAT. Expanding rings
Are spirals of your unfolding power
To understand That-Which-Already-Is,
And each ascending grade but marks for man
A step in comprehension of the Whole.
A line is but the movement of a point
And at each point the All will still be found
Whose center marks the All of Everywhere
And whose circumference does not exist,
Save that it be a *name* to comprehend the All.

The Farer
Wilt thou forgive and speak in simple terms
My heart can understand if not my head!
For numbers or for cosmic lore, I have no gift,
But yearn for sweet communion, gentle speech
From that dear Source from which the numbers came.

The Presence
In this, sweet friend, true wisdom is displayed,
For you seek *beauty* through which all numbers speak;
For beauty is the whole and not the parts,
And earth with heaven's beauty must combine
To waken in your heart the sweet delight
Of one who feels behind the face of form
The presence of the Uncaught Mystery.

The Farer
I feel but do not comprehend in full
The meaning of thy speech. My longing heart
Seeks deep communion with the Greater Heart.

The Presence

The paths of love and beauty are the same;
Both have the self-same goal, the secret gate
That opens into bliss; for beauty is
A law of order flamed with wings of love
That lift you high above the world of parts
Until you see the Whole in one vast harmony
And realize the Presence. This is true—
When from the parts the Whole appears to view,
Your singing heart knows Beauty wakes to you.

The Farer

You speak in terms I now can understand;
The world, I think, is saved by love, but not
By thought.
          How then can I and those who live upon
This mortal sphere find such immortal joy
Of union with the All-creative Cause
And drink forever from the cup of love,
Or eat the bread of an Eternal Peace?

The Presence

The boon you ask of life, this greater good
Is open unto all, but Life will give
Alone to him who knows how to receive;
It mirrors back in form what you expect.
This is the circle of life and this its story
Earth is but mirror of a greater glory.

Love meets you on the level where you stand,
Becomes to you what you become to it.
Be thou aware of Love and Love will be
Aware of you, responding kind for kind.
Embrace Him in the silence of your heart,
That He may fold you ever in His arms.
And, lo, the heart that finds itself within
The center of the All-Embracing One
Will find all wakened souls alike aware,

And harmony shall reign and love become
The law that rules your world.
The essence of the All is everywhere,
He gives Himself to each who is aware.

The Farer
Speak more of beauty for thy very words
Sustain an ecstasy so great my soul
Is all but freed from this too-mortal clay.
Why do your words arouse such ecstasy?

The Presence
Inherent in the self all beauty lies,
And memory recalls the whole and not
The parts—the unity which self perceived.
He who sees Beauty, sees the Whole within
Apparent parts; the beauty of the dawn
Is not the sun, nor mist nor spuming sea,
Nor oak-tree challenging the raging wind.
For Beauty lies in him who sees and what
He sees and *how* he sees and what he *feels*.
It is a Whole, and there is naught outside
This One, this ONLY ONE, nor can there be
Some form, some soul, some thing that dwells apart.
All "things" are souls, all souls are one with Him,
From things that crawl to six-winged seraphim.

The Farer
O blessed Voice, interpreter divine,
My infant soul is surging joyfully
As leaps the yet unborn within the mother's womb
As though aware at length that they are one.

The Presence
All things exist within the Cosmic womb,
And in a flash of vision, you may see
Into the heart of things and suddenly

All nature is alive. Each separate part
Is essence of the Whole and thus perceived
The tree has soul, the flower provides the form
In which the Cosmic Beauty is portrayed.

The Farer

This is a marvel and it surely seems
That even I can see a little way
Into the heart of things. For I am stirred
By sunsets and the after-glow that paints
The darkest clouds until they come alive
With fire whose source invisible has sunk
Beneath the rim of earth but still in heav'n.

The Presence

Pure is thy heart, my friend. The lofty soul
In purity perceives the pure, and God
Is visible to him. But he whose heart
Holds ugliness beholds an ugly world.
This is the truth by which the world is healed
Of blindness, war and from all human ills.

The Farer

Who then is right? How can a simple man
Like me, discriminate?

The Presence

Look to the Me:
The All is hidden in your heart. But you,
And every common man who has the power
To think, possess the key, a simple key
That will decode the hieroglyphs.

The Farer

Give me this key.

The Presence
> Between the *faith* and *"form"*
Discriminate. Grant to all men the right
To claim that they have seen celestial things
And have been raptured by the sight; and those
Who give both mind and heart to live a life
Devoid of blame before the eyes of God
And man. For who can find a higher test
Than this, that man be just and merciful
And kind, who gives his heart to God and seeks
To do to other men what he would have
Them do to him. But by this test observe
That such a man has no desire to force
Another soul to yield himself to forms,
Nor to compel acceptance of his creeds.
And when at times you doubt, put love to test.
Within a world by self designed, each lives
In heaven if so he feels the most at home,
In hell, if he has formed a habit there.
Look then within, the Ever-Presence find.
Look not for any life outside the self,
The undivided still remains alone.
He is the All and all that is within
His being is the Presence close at hand.
Inspirer, He beholds and is beheld
By those whose eyes have pierced through Beauty's veil,
To whom the veil becomes a lens to bring
Invisibles to focus and be seen.

The Farer
> Yet oft you have referred to Him as love.
How shall I raise my consciousness of Him?

The Presence
> If love be likened to a string of pearls
And each pearl to the self, then each of these
Reflects the pearl or self that touches it
And each both gives and draws its life from each.

So love, in giving self unto the self,
In all creation thus beholds itself,
And sees itself deep hid within all selves.
The self-unfolding and self-existent soul,
Complete, knows this, that what it gives
It still retains in full, and what it gave
To other living selves, it must give back
Again to that still Greater Self from which
It came. In this I see the meaning of
Redemptive acts—the *willing* self accepts
The sacrifice of lesser self to prove
Its oneness with the Greater Self and thus
It demonstrates that "*I,* if lifted up,
Will draw all of mankind unto my self."

The Farer

I am perplexed.

The Presence

You share with other men
In this, for though 'tis simply said, it must
Be realized. The Christ of Galilee
Upon the cross exemplified the truth,
"Into Thy hand, I now commit my self."
What man is there who can deny that he
Is moved to give himself when he has seen
Another give? Give then thy self to Truth,
To Beauty and to Love but realize
They are not three but One. When thou shalt fuse
The seeming parts into the whole, thou shalt
Attain to everlasting bliss. Thou hast
Returned and found thy Father's house.
The Father manifests as son,
Yet they eternally are One.

The Farer

My admiration is surpassed alone
By bafflement in grasping all you tell,

But what I seem to find is this, that Truth
Is self-revealing and from Nature's book
All secrets can be read, nor do require
Some authorized revealer, heaven-sent.

The Presence
In ev'ry age, in ev'ry place, the seers
Affirmed these truths, that man, unbound by fears,
Might free himself from superstition's yoke
And servitude to those who claim God spoke
Alone to them or to some "chosen folk,"
Or that some angel visitant revealed
The secret of the god to others sealed.
The Artist who has painted all the worlds
Still holds the brush and palette in His hands;
For you He now is painting what you see
Upon a canvas you yourself have framed
And placed upon the easel of your knowing.
Behold the Artist through His art, and feel
His Presence just behind the face of form.
If life be wisdom, beauty is its face,
And Truth and love are just behind your sight.
Life's meaning lies in what you do not see
But can be known through Beauty's form
In which it speaks to you.

The Farer
                              As you know well,
I have accepted what you teach, but how
Can I retain it as a habit of
My mind?

The Presence
                    First lift thy heart in true desire
And love; and pray that Beauty will unveil:
For beauty is diaphanous, a screen
That hides the truth, so thin—or dense—that he
Alone beholds, who, by some alchemy,

Transmutes his baser consciousness of sight
Into illumined vision of the real.
That which these eyes, these all too human eyes
Cannot behold, the eyes of soul reveal.
He sees alone who in the astral light
Perceives that Source from which the *real* must rise.
The heart of Love may yearn but not compel,
And though all sins on earth may be forgiven
And souls released from out the depths of Hell,
No one can be coerced to enter heaven.

The Scribe
In speechless awe the Farer stood awhile
In contemplation of the mystery
By which the essence turns to substance and
Substance turns to essence once again, and how
Through Truth and Beauty, the self can pierce the screen
And view the real and cause the unseen to be seen.
Then in a burst of wonder and amaze
He voiced a hymn all-eloquent of praise.

The Farer
O Ancient of Days, Thou art present; I see
Thou art here, Thou art now, Thou speakest to me.
With ineffable beauty, Thy garments are bright,
Thy face alone veiled by a nimbus of light.
Thou art more than the mind, Thou art more than the heart,
Thou art all of the whole and the whole of the part.
Thou art essence of all and Thou standest alone,
Thou art all of the parts and yet Thou art One.
Thy silver-wheeled chariot thunders afar—
Thou art there, Thou art here, like the light of a star!
Yet soft Thy reply to my yearning for Thee.
"I awaken to him who awakens to me."

So free yourself from the
Illusions of your senses. Sanity
Requires adjustment of the mind between
The thing as it appears and what it is
In fact and in reality.

Reality and illusion[10]

Part I

Truth bears no age, nor can the searcher trace
One line of care, time-chiseled on its face.
Impersonal as Justice, impassively
It binds the false and sets the captive free;
While blind illusion thrusts the Truth apart
And clasps the lie more fervently to heart...
Man, self-deceived, is by himself bereft
When faith departs and only fear is left.
Antiquity, though graced with well-fringed stole
And cassock, chasuble, or priestly scroll,
Cannot compel life's Law to serve the claims
Of superstition lit with candle-flames.
For Truth and Law, though differing in act,
Proclaim infallible the eternal fact
That Life reflects in form immaculate
The image cast by thought. And soon or late
We reap the harvest and we pay the score
For false conception—*or* for Wisdom's lore.

How often men have bowed the knee in prayer
Unto the god whom they projected there
Or gods whom other men have claimed to find!
And ev'ry worshipper doth see behind
The idol's face what he believes he sees
Behind the idol's face.
                              On bended knees
He looks into a mirror, sees reflected
What he in faith or unbelief projected.
All unaware that in himself alone
The Truth is found; the sacred stone
Appears as real and icons on the altar
Reflect the incensed candle and the psalter.

The Presence
>Illusion lies in failure to detect
>The source of Truth and so believes effect
>To be the cause. 'Tis here you find the fusion
>Of superstition wed to pseudo-reason.
>Of all the errors which do damn the race,
>This is the worst, that man has sought to place
>Causation on the outside, not within
>Himself.

The Farer
>>What you call error, some call sin.

The Presence
>I do not speak alone of ethic laws
>But of the false conception. For the cause
>Lies neither in an outraged deity
>Nor in a field of force and energy,
>But in the self and what man thinks and feels
>And what his *thought* about the *thing* reveals.
>You see a shadow when the day is fair
>And say, "I know a man is standing there."
>But that does not describe the man at all,
>If he be stout and short or slim and tall,
>Nor if he be a madman or a seer,
>Nor one we hate nor one we hold most dear.
>We cannot know our world by sense, however keen,
>By what we hear or what our eyes have seen;
>The meaning hidden in a world of light
>Cannot be known except by "second sight."
>
>The world phenomenal is but the face
>Or image of the soul-of-things; we trace
>The forms we see, the visible, and make
>Our judgments by appearances, mistake
>The semblance for the real; but learn that we
>Must pierce the form to find reality.

The Farer

How great thou art! O Voice, how great thou art!
I hear thy speech at last within my heart.
I have no doubt of thee; thy words contain
The song of songs. Yet I have still to gain
Such understanding as to pierce the veil
Of unreality and, without fail,
To rend the tissue of pretense
That binds me to the human sense,
And know the truth that will unwind
The shroud of death from anguished mind.

The Presence

Within yourself the undiscovered truth
Lies hid; in *you,* the very goal you seek!
And though your quest should lead through lands afar
You will return and find truth where you are.
Begin with this—there is within the self
A quality of *being* Absolute;
You are with It identified, for if
You are, and if the Absolute is All,
Then you are one with All. In this
There lies the mystery of *being;* you
May say, "I am, thou art, God is," but that
Does not *define* the Causeless Cause, nor can
It be defined, for to define is but
To limit It, and to be limited
Is not to be the Absolute. It is
At once the Known and the Unknowable.

Do not despair. For though the mystery
Seems great, it is no greater than men find
In their attempt to deal with time and space
And comprehend the galaxies that stretch
Out to Infinity, although from them
Can be attained a partial concept of
Eternity.
            But let it rest;

The finite has no need to comprehend
The Infinite. It is enough to know
The Absolute exists as Source of All
And holds the universe intact, and fills
All space, and ever-present is with all
Its power at ev'ry point;[11] yet is not seen
Nor known save that we feel assured of this—
It IS and It is everywhere. Yet he
Who claims, "I see it," is by himself deceived;
What he has seen is his experience
In individual and finite form.
The Absolute is not removed from time,
Yet is not time; from space, yet is not space,
From energy, yet is not energy;
From ether,[12] yet is not ether; nor void,
Though it itself is not the void. It can,
Perhaps, be best conceived in abstract terms—
The Elemental Principle, to thus
Make real the bridge between the Unknown and
The Known—The Causeless Cause from which proceeds
All things and minds and movements and all thought
Without an end,
                    If, then, as Ancients said,
That it is everywhere, IT IS IN MAN!
In ev'ry age, in many faiths and in
The minds of all the seers, this was the key
To the Unknown and otherwise Unknowable,
"He knows who knows himself"—the voice of MAN
Becomes the voice of God, and man is thus
The inlet and the outlet to the one
And Only God whom he can ever know.
"Man is the key"; the voices of the sages
Became the voice of God to all the ages.

The Farer
  I oft have heard the words, "Man, know thyself,"
  Yet truly found no meaning clear to me.

The Presence

> He knows himself who finds within himself
> The *being* who upholds the self,[13] and knows
> Him as the One Supreme, Eternal Being.

The Farer

> Such concept of myself seems far too deep
> For me but gladly would I welcome it
> Were it to open doors into the Real,
> And give me sight to penetrate the cloud
> Of my unknowing and bring to light the cause
> And cure of my own ignorance; for what
> I see *seems* real, and I do not discern
> Between the false and true. My eyes behold
> The ever-moving forms that come and go
> Where ceaseless change of scene portrays to me
> The movement of some power invisible,
> Hid in a mystery. Reality,
> It seems, is veiled through all creation.
> What is this veil?

The Presence

>   No mist or cloud by gods
> Designed doth veil reality, but you
> In ignorance of cause and of effects
> Give substance to the world of form and call
> It matter, thinking it to be a thing apart
> From mind because it has another name.
> And when you have conceived it thus, you hold yourself
> As subject to *its* laws, conditioned by
> A force extraneous to yourself, although
> Your "so-called matter" is extended mind
> And is itself conditioned by your thought.
> For nothing can exist apart from it.
> There is no so-called thing.
>   So free yourself from the
> Illusions of your senses. Sanity
> Requires adjustment of the mind between

The thing as it appears and what it *is*
In fact and in reality.
                              The tree
Beside the road as you pass swiftly by
Appears to move, but in your mind you make
Adjustment to it, contradict the false
And so arrive at truth.

The Farer
                              This I perceive;
Self-conscious life must ever look for cause
And mode of motion in the finite world,
But whence did the *appearance* come? From what?
How is it that a something is construed
From nothing in itself?

The Presence
                              Nay, friend, all things
Exist, but they exist in mind and are
From mind derived, for mind itself is all.
A common error speaks of "matter" as
Some substance on which Creative Mind is
Said to "move" or that the Cosmic Spirit
Moved upon a nothing and from a "naught" evolved
Objective substance and from this substance
Created form. This is a sweet illusion,
Fit for childlike minds, compelled to think of
Endings and beginnings, who measure out
The universe in terms of time.
                              But he
Alone can understand who knows there is
No "First" Cause but Eternal Cause alone,
And that all manifested "things" exist
Within the Absolute in prototype,[14] yet
Invisible to unaccustomed eyes,
But visible to wakened consciousness[15]—
For matter is but spirit visible.

The Scribe
> The Farer's eyes were brilliant with desire
> To argue or to contradict. He spoke:

The Farer
> If "forms" be replicas or shadows of
> Reality they must possess some value
> For our daily living! Does that not make
> Them real?

The Presence
> Across the plane of relativity
> The transient shadow moves; but what is *that*
> *Which moves the shadow?* What is permanent?
> All that we know or will in future know
> Is this: Creation *is,* it *was,* and *shall*
> *Exist* forevermore. The universe
> Does not possess a history and what
> To finite minds appears as ends or as
> Beginnings are unknown to Absolute.
> Creation IS, life IS, God IS and We
> Are IN Eternity, nor less, nor more!

The Farer
> Are not the things I see and touch as real
> As what they seem to me?

The Presence
>   Phenomena
> Are but the symbols of reality;
> For what we know is only known within
> Ourselves, and what we know in mind is quite
> Unlike the order and events we say
> We "see." We "realize," "infer," "become
> Aware," but what it is of which we are
> Aware the senses do not tell, for it
> Is noumenal within the Absolute.

The Scribe

                                     Tears filled
The Farer's eyes. He wept because he could
Not understand.

The Farer

                          This, then, is why the seers
Of old proclaimed the Absolute to be
Unknowable!

The Presence

                        They spoke this only of
The intellect. Yet even here they showed
How understanding leads to wisdom that
In turn will open doors through which
The ardent soul can pass to find reality.

The Farer

    I feel the chill of reason, cold as ice,
That freezes all my veins. Is there no way
By which a simple Farer like myself
Can feel the warmth of verities and by
Some inner knowing find assurance of
The real and comprehend the noumenal?

The Presence

    "Truth does not rise from outer things"[16] but in
The deep recesses of the mind wherein
Phenomena and thought are reconciled
And unified. This is the purpose and
The goal of earthly life—the final growth
Of cosmic consciousness. You must evolve
To this, though slow and painful be the path;
Learn to interpret all phenomena
Into the terms of mind, *but freed* from all
The misconceptions of the past. For such
As these do color and deform the thought

And suckle error at the breast so that
It passes down from one age to the next.

The Farer

We are then heirs to error and illusion?

The Presence

Men tend to imitate what they have seen
And to conform to ancient ways of thought,
Interpretations true or false of those
Who lived before. The cloud or mist men see
Is in themselves, though they are but the heirs
To ignorance as great or greater than their own.

The Farer

It is no easy thing to extricate
Oneself from habit-thoughts, from the world-mind,
As to my sorrow I have found. By what
Strange quality or fantasy of thought
Must we pursue the endless circuits of
The past or weave new garments from rav'lings
Of a worn-out past?

The Presence

                Your error, Farer,
Is found in that word "must." There is no "must"
In reasoned thought. No force compels, no God
Demands the blind acceptance of the past.

The Farer

Yet all events and all traditions seem
Unbroken links in one great endless chain
Of ever-growing panoramic scenes
That bear the record of the past and so
Impress themselves upon the mind that man
Cannot escape the dominance of ancient thoughts.
Are we not victims of our fathers' faults
And bound thereby as though they were our own?

I do with vigor curse the past! Oh, that
Some star of hope might shine for me from out
The black abyss of the unknown and the
Unknowable!

The Presence
Self-pity is illusion in itself
For it proclaims the inescapable.

The Farer
But I see that which you of purest mind
Do not perceive. By some strange inner sight,
I view or seem to view a vast abyss
Or field of essences wherein the acts
And thoughts and even forms of living things
Are so impressed upon a moving screen
That past and present seem inscribed upon
A cosmic memory. I see the beasts
Of prehistoric times, the slow advance
Of primate man, emerging from the clay;
I see the races move across the land,
Led by the lords who are in turn led on
By other higher Lords who speak to them
Through clouds. Clouds! Clouds! Always the mist and clouds!
The whole scene seems to turn, revolving like
A platform on a stage where the same play
Repeats, rehearsing endlessly, and where
The dead, like Pilate, wash their hands of blood!
Or, like the Christ, are slain and offered up
Again and yet again.
                    Is this illusion
Or the real?

The Presence
                    It is the memory
Of nature that you read, nor good nor bad,
But you are not the victim of the past,

Nor subject to a spell. Illusion lies
In this, that you accept the patterns of
The past as auguries of things to come;
Effect is thus accepted as a *cause*
Which you project into the present and
The future. It need not be; there is no
Fate, no god proclaiming that you "must."

The Farer

But I can dimly see the future on
The cosmic screen! Am I not bound to live,
To suffer and to die as fate decrees?
Am I not victim of the universe?

The Presence

You have the power to choose from out the past;
Reject the evil and with the good stand fast!
There are no barriers to him who knows
That all he seeks from Spirit flows;
In Pure Causation perfect good exists
And he who faithfully persists
In calling on the Higher Source alone
Will find the kingdom and the throne!
Illusion lies in this, that man accepts
Conditions as the *real* though they may be
But consequence of antecedent thought
And can survive no longer if ideas
Be changed.

The Farer

Why should Celestial Powers
So hide the real that none can view the truth
That what they seem to see should be illusion?

The Presence

This is not part of a creative *plan;*
The growth of knowledge must depend upon
Man's own awakening to what he is;

He learns to read the mind of God and to
Translate what he has read in terms of law
Or principles. The Unseen Cause itself
Must then await for man's awakening.
The mask or mist that seems to cloud
The truth is not on Nature's face but on
Our own. Some day the eye will penetrate
The mystery and will reveal there is,
In fact, no mystery and no illusion.
Then shall we find that what "things" are is but
Symbolic of reality which waits
For our perception.

The Farer
                    O glorious day,
When I shall rouse from my long sleep and see
The light of truth! My soul is anguished. I die
To learn the meaning of it all.

The Presence
                         Perhaps
It is more simple than you think. Restore
Your childhood's attitudes of mind, before
The clouds of doubt closed in and hid from view
The *living* things whose voices spoke to you,
The roadside roses, the birds that seemed to say,
"Be of good cheer, this is a happy day";
Go back, I say, to those half-pagan days
Before reality was hid in haze.
Learn once again to view the airy wings
Of conscious life, the very souls of things.
As artists see the aura which they paint
Around the head of master or of saint,
So he who penetrates the outward screen
Shall view the unseen hid behind the seen.
God speaks in thunder; His tender voice is heard
By tiny nestlings of the hummingbird.
He laughs with children playing on the beach;

The sea is His, the spuming waves His speech.
Behold Him as the Cosmic Mother-Love
In ev'ry mother's face that leans above
The infant nursing at her ample breast;
And it is He who gives the child its rest.
The whole wide world is whispering his name
He is the altar, offering and flame.

The Lord is present, the single and the Whole;
When least aware He floods the seeking soul.

The Farer
I have not been unmindful of the world
Of things and I have often seen behind
The "form" some sentient spirit lurking, but
It mocked at me and seemed to speak, "We all
Are creatures bound to time, we flourish for a day
And then fall into dust. None can escape
His rendezvous with death."
                                          And even as
He suckles at the breast, the babe is doomed
And in his sleep he but prepares himself
For that long night which waits him at the end.
The matin bell commingles with the curfew bell
That tolls the passing of departing souls;
To where and what, who knows? For who can know
Who does not know the *whence?*

The Presence
                                  But have you not
At times beheld another plane or sphere
Of consciousness behind the face of sense?

The Farer
It brings no hope that I have seen the past
In astral light nor does it prove to me
Survival of the soul. I cannot tell
What fantasy of mind unrolls a scroll

Or if it be but vagrant images
Of flitting thought across an inner screen.
What is illusion? What is fact? I ask
Myself.
      And more than this I seek to know:
Am I the victim of relentless fate
That I can never know the real from the
Illusion, nor in fact if there be "real"
At all? Am I so chained by ignorance
That I must be a passive mirror which
Reflects unwittingly the phantom forms
And faces of the past and *even thoughts*
That one time passed across the minds of those
Who lived and died so long ago?
           Or can
It be that, by some inner sight, my mind
Has pierced the future and the past alike.
If this be so am I so bound by fate
That I must endlessly review the screen,
Caught in events beyond my own control?
Or is there still some freedom of the mind
That can transcend the written scroll and write
A fairer one more close to my desire?

The Presence
Man's life would be a hell beyond the hell
Created by mythologies of old
Or theocratic prophecies
Designed to drive the frightened soul to heaven,
If he retained no power of choice or will
To turn his eyes away from pictures that
Appall. He lives in happiness whose eye
Is fixed with steadfast gaze upon the best
He knows; and if his mind be full of love
He will attract still other "best," set free
From dwelling on the ugly and the false.

The Farer

Ah now, you touch upon the problem that
I face. What is this false, I pray of you?

The Presence

With face turned toward the sun, no one can see
The shadow cast behind; and he who looks
Upon the beautiful will see the true.
The memory of nature must reflect
As in a mirror all events alike
Of present, past and future, good or ill,
Portraying heaven or a hell or both.
This gloomy cloud or mist, reflected on
The mirror-mind, becomes the substance of
A new creation. Since man has the stuff
Of which new hells are made, he makes a hell
Which will endure until he turns his eyes
To view the good, the beautiful and wise
And with this stuff he builds a paradise.
The common mind, alas, does not perceive
The Real. To such a mind, "things" will exist
As they *appear* to be because it puts no strain
Upon the intellect. Convenience lies
In seeing them as "matter" in itself.
His knowledge, then, is knowledge of that which
Does not exist. To such a man the seer
Is mad, unbalanced, living in a cloud.
But when at length his own eyes are unstopped,
He knows the cloud lies only in himself.
Man is not victim of the universe...
Let fall the seeds of thought, beloved friend,
And they will germinate and grow until
Your world reflects the object of your will.

The Scribe

They parted then but on a certain day
Communed once more and on the Farer's face
A look of questioning.

The Farer
                    I pondered much
Upon your words that man can build his world
Of insubstantial stuff. If such be true,
Could men long dead project their forms upon
The screen of present time in this our living world,
Becoming visible to us?

The Presence
                    There are
No dead. No barriers exist between
The "There" and "Here." Among all "faiths" the seers
Have taught a conscious contact made between
That "other world" and "this." He who deletes
From sacred scripts the heavenly visitant
Would rend his "faith" apart. We are at times
Aware of that great "cloud of witnesses,"
And even see them clothed in silver white.

The Farer
I would behold such visitants. And once
I thought I heard the voice of one who died
Long, long ago.

The Presence
                    How long is long ago?
And what is death but change of vehicles
Which bear the *self* to realms of light beyond
The present scene. Behold, the self
Or "*me*" is free of time and space, unbound
By age, unfettered, unattached. The self
May build a vehicle again and yet
Again, whose pattern lies in Cosmic Mind.

The Farer
But is the self immortal, will it not
In ageless time come to some final end?

The Presence
>   Immortality is but a name, a mode
>   Of counting up or measuring the time
>   Of birth and death of personality.
>   Here illusion lies, for time is thus
>   Confused with the Eternal. For in the
>   Eternal nor time nor age exists and we
>   Can enter it today. Here we escape
>   Illusion of division and of time
>   And the illusion of the "we" itself,
>   And realize our oneness with the All
>   And know that we are "THAT" and THAT ALONE.

Part II

The Farer
>   To minds like mine you speak in riddles
>   Your speech does not accord with what is taught
>   By masters sacrosanct.

The Presence
>   Truth is not bound
>   To make accord with error. Conformity
>   To creeds does not assure their truth.
>   Another day is dawning and new light
>   Is breaking through the mists. Man stands upright
>   Before the God of Truth; with willing mind
>   Casts off old creeds and leaves old gods behind;
>   And as his universe expands he too will grow
>   And find the greater God whom he can know.
>   He joins with Truth against the world's illusion.
>   And fears no evil and no retribution.

The Farer
>   I have such pressing need to realize
>   The truth, and to escape futility of life,

What profit lies in going on across
A trackless waste? I have no will to wait
The slow uncertain growth of some far day.
And if survival of the self demands
That I must build myself a soul[17] for life
Beyond, I have no will for *that,* since I
Have found this world so fraught with pain.
What matters it to me that all illusion lies
Within myself, not in the universe; a pain
Whatever be its cause, is still a pain.

The Presence
If you with equal eloquence should plead
The cause of truth to satisfy your need
As now you plead for error and illusion
You would escape from terror and confusion.
Truth does not yield itself to prejudice,
Nor is it bound by unbelief like this.
The finger writes, the mirror still reflects
The good or evil that the mind projects,
And he alone has harmony who makes
His own adjustment to it, and who takes
The time to grow and with enlightened sense
Permits the truth to give its evidence.
Illusion of itself cannot exist;
But false projection through the mist
Of man's own mind is image of his thought,
His form of misconception...
                                        Its stress
Lasts but a day and then in nothingness
It disappears in pure confusion;
Nor can reality become illusion.

The Farer
I am engulfed in my own ignorance.

The Presence
>   Be not dismayed, my friend,
>   You grow by reaching up. The virtue of
>   Such truths as I unfold for you lies in
>   Assurance giv'n that *mind alone is real.*

The Farer
>   Must I forever wait to know the truth?

The Presence
>   The mist or cloud that veils reality
>   And hides it from "the wise and prudent" will
>   Be dissolved before the face of innocence
>   And love of good, of beauty and of truth.
>   If darkness were essential to the soul,
>   Then Paradise itself could be accused.
>   The mind attuned to cosmic harmony
>   Becomes a mirror or a quiet pool
>   Which will reflect the prototypes above—
>   Thought-forms to be impressed upon the mind
>   Spontaneously.

The Farer
>   The meaning, then, of prayer
>   Seems here implied. For though the conscious mind
>   At present does not know, the deeper Mind
>   Should know and so impress the truth upon
>   Receptive attitudes.

The Presence
>   You can become
>   A mirror to Creative Mind which will
>   In turn help you discern the path of truth
>   And guide you to your longed-for goal.

The Farer
>   I vow myself to this: I will become
>   A willing vessel to contain the life

And essence of reality and bring
It forth in form. This is, at least, my aim.

The Presence
You will become the master of your fate
If you will yield yourself to the divine
And inner knowing; though your body be
By sickness racked and all your limbs are weak,
The healing power, God-consciousness shall lift
Your wasted frame and free you from illusion
That you are formed of dust and clay.
And heal you from infirmities.
                              The Me
Indwelling all is all-indwelling. That
Which thou art is all and THOU ART THAT!
Know this: Man stands perplexed between two[18] worlds,
Nor can he orient between the two
Until he knows that there is only one,
His body one, his members many more.
If, then, each part attempts to live apart
It suffers waste and pain and even death;
Unless the master in his house of clay
Shall contradict illusion and shall say,
"I am thine inner lord, thou shalt obey;
Thy life is God, be thou made whole today."

The Farer
O Master, Presence, Lord of all my being,
Give me thy light, thy wisdom and thy seeing.

The Presence
There is one Source from which all Being flows
Through all your veins with healing as it goes;
As water turns to juices on the vine,
And thence becomes the sacerdotal wine,
So shall the body from the spirit sup
The blood of life within the cosmic cup.
That which is REAL within your soul has power

To meet your needs and in your highest hour
You feel the Presence. Strengthened by His hand
You dare stand forth and give your stern command
For ev'ry need; the doors are opened wide
And *good* pours forth in ever-swelling tide.

The Farer

If, as you say, the mist that hides the face
Of truth is in myself, what arguments
Against appearances can I devise
To melt the mist and clear away the lies?

The Presence

Denial of the false does not affirm
The true. The false appearances dissolve
Before the light of truth. Analysis
Is of the human mind, but the Divine
Beholds the whole, not fragmentary parts.

The Farer

If wisdom be the judgment wrought by years,
Why has the mist persisted and the tears?

The Presence

The thoughts and deeds of men survive within
The racial mind like some vast pool in which
All streams converge; the like attracts the like
And so the ignorance and prejudice
Of men from ev'ry age—aye, too, their sins
Or their delight in sense desires; and all
The idol worship and the fears that damned
Their earthly lives—all these create a vast
And steaming reservoir of psychic force
In which the unenlightened mind may dip
Till it believes the evil and the good alike
Are real; and oft the worse appears more real,
More reasonable than good itself.

The Farer
> How hopeless is the fate of man—my fate!
> Not one sustains more wretchedness than I!
> For ranges of ages untold run back
> Into the mists of time and not one soul,
> One avatar appears to dissipate
> The clouds nor empty out the reservoir
> Of this conglomerate of human sin
> And evil memories of fate bedamned!
> What monstrous fumbling with cosmic clay
> Is this that He who molded man should form
> Him with so many flaws that he becomes
> Not only victim of Creator's faults
> And of his own, but heir to wretchedness
> And all the wickedness piled up through all
> The ages and held intact for ages yet to come!

The Scribe
> Distraught by his own speech he brooded on
> The hopelessness of fate. The Presence spoke.

The Presence
> Though you have reasoned well there are two flaws
> In all your arguments.
> The first is this: GOOD, too, accumulates
> And cosmic memory retains the love
> And wisdom of the past and all the songs
> Of hope, the music of great deeds, the prayers
> Of all the saints, the speech of martyrs who
> Through their faith have drawn men nearer God.

The Farer
> You lift my soul to hope again. What else
> Have you to give? What is the other flaw?

The Presence
> There still is the *redemptive*[19] *act* of Truth
> Itself, the miracle of revelation

By which the light shines on the soul with such
Clear rays that darkness disappears and to
Such soul there is no reservoir of hell.

The Scribe
    The Farer mused upon these words and in
His heart the warm, sweet glow of love and hope
Was richly stirred as though he were possessed
For one brief moment by the soul of faith.
But then he cried,

The Farer
              No light so shines on me!
Still does an empty void repeat my cry,
My eyes have never pierced the screen!

The Presence
                 The eyes
Of seers and avatars have pierced the mist
Of unreality and they become
Your eyes until you see and know the truth—
Take heart in this—the world we see is not
The Real. Man feels this true although today
He sees by others' eyes.
                Thus is he "served"
By revelation[20] and is assured the real
Exists. Yea, more, he comes to understand
That *what he is* conditions what he sees,
That faulty seeing and acceptance of
Akashic negatives creates the cloud
That hides Reality.
             The poet sees,
The singer feels, the lover knows, the seer
Reveals directly from the Light of light,
Which suddenly breaks through the darkness thick,
And the Eternal is realized by you;
No more you isolate yourself in "time"

Or "space," no more you prattle "me" or "we,"
For Thou Art That—THOU ART ETERNITY!

The Farer
    I do not understand.
    I see, but do not see, I hear but do
    Not hear; for even with the truth in view
    When I would make myself a bowl to hold
    The treasured wisdom, both the new and old,
    That very moment is my vessel shattered
    And all of Wisdom's brilliant gems are scattered.
    Why did the All-Creative Mind conceal
    The power to know the real from the unreal:
    And by what chance, what strange mirage of sight,
    Should desert wastes transform the very light
    To spires and domes and mosques and minarets
    And pools and gardens flanked by parapets
    (Like Mecca's well whose waters murmuring
    Praise Allah and the prophet as they sing!)
    Yet as a farer hastens toward the gate
    They disappear: he always comes too late!
    What are these phantom forms that come and go?
    The sea appears as mist, the mist appears as snow.
    Is life itself illusion? Is the mind
    The falsely seeing eyesight of the blind?
    Do not, I pray, resort to sophistry.

The Presence
    You could not ask what you have posed to me
    Without a mind to frame the questions asked,
    Nor could the great enigma be unmasked
    Save that, behind the conscious mind, the soul
    Contains in embryo the fullness of the Whole;
    For Cosmic Consciousness is everywhere
    And so in you. Awake, and find It there!

Untouched, supreme, unvexed, the Great Alone,
Beyond the reach of doubt, sits on His throne
Awaiting man's awakening from sleep
And gently rocks the cradle of the Deep.
There is beyond the range of human thought
A benediction for the soul, upcaught
By Love Divine which man cannot destroy.
Destined to life and to eternal joy,
The sons of earth shall find at last the goal.
And enter peace in oneness with the Whole.

The Farer

A dream most beautiful but still a dream
Of some dim goal, part of a cosmic scheme
So far removed from this life's daily breath,
It is to me beyond the doors of death!

The Presence

Eternity is NOW, it is the habitat
Of him who realizes THOU ART THAT—
The Past is shadow cast across the way
That leads through NOW to the Eternal Day—
A lengthened shadow stretched around the spheres
Which will fulfill by sequency of years
The pattern of creation's need for action,
An outlet to provide the satisfaction
Of livingness, to thought with act relate
And so to *be*—to be is to create.
Else all of life itself would be ungrowing,
All unfulfilled, unknown and all unknowing.

The Scribe

Caught in a sea of dark bewilderment
And tempest-tossed by raging waves of doubt,
The Farer lost his bearings so that he
Could neither make his headway nor retreat
Lest some terrific force of nature should

Submerge him in a sea of nothingness.
The Presence brushed aside his sympathy
And opened up the treasures of his thought.

The Presence
Invisible behind its cloak of clay,
Eternally alert but silently,
The power that guards man's evolution waits
Unmoved and motionless within its depths,
As waters of the sea; but it is still
The Substance of the waves, the tides, the ebb
And flow of finite forms of life. Within
All things and yet containing all within,
It permeates the whole; and frictionless
Within Itself, it offers violence to none,
Though like a rock-girt shore, *appears* to cast
The raging waves back to the angry sea;
Yet moveth not; for motion is in truth
But concept of the finite mind. Without
A form, It giveth form to all;
Devoid of time, It is the source of time;
Its center everywhere is found, and yet
It is without circumference.
Individual but universal,
Universal but individual,
It present is in Its totality
At ev'ry point with Its infinity.
Within the atom hid, but not confined;
Behind the atom in a form too small
To bear a name, It still exists, remains
The perfect and the undivided whole.
And he who would infinity conceive
Needs first to know infinitesimals.

The Farer
                                    Your words inspire
An agony that lacerates my soul;
I feel their truth but cannot understand;

Yet long with all my heart to cheer the sad
And soul-sick world with comfort such as you
Have given me. Alas, I cannot change this wealth
Of gold into the coin of speech.

The Presence
                                        Do not
Despair. The journey of the soul is flight
Of the alone to the Alone,[21] and each
Absorbs into himself such truth and such alone
As he is ready to receive, no more, no less.
Your words are jewels to the hungry mind,
But chaff and dust when cast before the blind.
Truth is abstract and man cannot receive
Save in a mind conditioned to believe.
It comes by revelation from the few
Or wakes within as it awoke in you.
Yet I would make your measure overflow
With wealth of truth beyond your power to know
The fullness of it now; you will expand
And grow the power at last to understand.

The Farer
I welcome ev'ry challenge, for I fain
Would go beyond the boundaries of brain
Into the realm where truth outreaching ken
Is verified by mighty minds of men.

The Presence
The world we say we "see" is known by means
Of our sensations of it—something that
Has happen'd in ourselves. (We do not see
A star but only light from which we may
Infer a star.) Sensations may give rise
To true or faulty inf'rences. The real
Or the illusion rests upon the power
To know, interpret and to classify
The so-called facts which incubate in sense.

By logic we can verify that time
And space are properties of sensuous
Receptivity, graphs by means of which
We picture an external world. To this
Extent the world appears to each in shapes
And shades conditioned by his consciousness.
While one acclaims the perfume of a rose,
Another claims that poison from it blows;
What is for one a visitant of light
Is for the next a ghost that haunts by night.
The world that seems so foul or exquisite
Becomes to you what you become to it.

The Farer
If this be true, each man would find that he
Lives in a world of subjectivity
And that he lives alone! Dread to relate
Would be the tragedy of such a fate!

The Presence
More tragic he who has presumed to find
Some power beyond the magic of his mind.
Be not distraught, thine errant soul
Is anchored in the cosmic whole;
Nor seas of doubt, nor waves of wrath
Can drive thee from thy chosen path.

The Farer
If I accept the thesis you have laid
How can I find a unity of fact
Between my mind and other minds like mine?

The Presence
There is a common ground on which the minds
Of thinking men are met.

The Farer
                    How can this be
If naught is real of what we seem to see,
Or touch or taste or measure by our sense
How can we know the how or where or whence?

The Presence
The measure of all knowing lies within
The consciousness and we can well assume
That each responds in equal terms with each
To equal stimuli. Space is inferred
By naturalist and by idealist
Alike, the one by direct knowing, while
The other cultivates the consciousness
Of space by his reflections based upon
The evidence of what he deems his sense-
Experience.[22] Space is the *form* which MAN
Conceives to understand his universe.
He thinks in terms of form and so invents
What he calls matter, conceiving it as real.

The Farer
He limits the Universal that
He may thus conceive and comprehend its
Universality?

The Presence
                    He uses three
Dimensions to reach the fourth, and from
This peak he leaps with his new wings out on
Infinity. Thus he arrives at last
To concepts of existence beyond
The range of "things," and so at length acquires
Abstractions of the intellect.

The Scribe
                    Such as?

The Presence
    Ideas, or that which must exist apart
    From form. Let us take anything—
    A book, perhaps—and analyze it as
    A whole. We first may measure it in terms
    Of thickness, length and breadth; then open it
    To find a fourth dimension, printed there
    Upon the sheet; the "meaning" makes a fifth;
    While sentiment awakes a sixth; and so
    The soul may penetrate still other fields
    Of consciousness.

The Farer
                How is the limit reached?

The Presence
    Dimensions fail to measure out the bliss
    Of cosmic consciousness. It is to this
    That all the hopes and dreams of men aspire,
    A flying goal which draws us ever higher,
    And as we pass the posts that mark the way
    We sense in each succeeding circumstance
    The joy of the pursuit, the sweet romance
    Of union with the Whole, and hourly prove
    Love is emotion and emotion then is Love.
    Love is the mystic cord that binds the soul—
    Linga Sharira—forever with the Whole.

The Farer
    Some scientific minds, I know, have claimed
    Discov'ry of the last and final key
    To unlock nature and the mystery
    Of life itself within magnetic fields.

The Presence
    Let them reflect that they have found but this—
    A *principle* of unity, abstraction

Of the mind, and have dissolved their world
To energy composed of units which
Are *metaphysical.* So give them thanks!

The Farer

I would most readily give thanks were I
To understand the meaning of it all,
Yet I in faith do share *your* larger sight.

The Presence

Matter absolute does not exist, by
And of itself in any state in which
It can be known in independence of
The substance of a given thing in which
It doth appear. It is as abstract as
Conception of the principle of truth,
Or metaphysical hypothesis
Of good or evil, sin or punishment.
The hypothetic particle or stuff
Of which all matter is composed is an
Electric charge of energy. But charge
In *what?* In nothing! Or a vacuum!

Be not deceived by those who claim that you
Are victim of some hoax of mysticism;
They are more mystical than you when they
Make claim that from insensate "nothing" blades
Of corn boil up mechanically, take form
And string their beads of pearl beneath the husk.
Less mystical was He, the Master, who
Made use of corn to symbolize the life
That rises from the grave.[23] Resurgence
Or resurrection demonstrates that life
Is CAUSE and it can build and then rebuild
The mansions of the soul.

False seeing breeds false knowing; it misleads
And feeds upon the litter that it breeds.
Only by revelation can we know

The *real* from which the revelations flow.
All explanations are efforts to make plain
Reality, but it will still remain
Unknown save through the inner sight;
And intuition is the final light.
Yet you to reach this end need not deny
The intellect; for you must still apply
The checks and balances of conscious mind
To clarify the findings and inspect
The data of your consciousness to show
The meaning of your vision and to know
The occult from the pseudopsychic flow.

The Farer

I do agree. I would not change one world
Of unreality for still another.
How can I know when I have reached the true
Conclusion?

The Presence

You must attempt to unify
Your total consciousness, so that no line
Is drawn between the reason and the inner sight,
And body, mind and spirit are agreed;
Then you will know and know you know.

The Farer

How can
I best attain this higher consciousness?

The Presence

Identity with Being must be found
By him who seeks the high and holy ground
Of untaught wisdom. His a triple goal
Who would essay to unify the whole!
Let him deny the lure of base desire
And seek the *good*. Then let his mind acquire
The sense of *beauty* till it fills his veins

And in his heart no ugliness remains.
Let *love* be sought, in an ascending scale,
Then *truth* stands forth and gladly will unveil.
When you have reached a sense of rightness in
Your inner self, so pure, so crystalline
That you will feel a oneness with the universe,
You will escape from error and immerse
Yourself in Cosmic Consciousness, and so
You will find peace because you know you know.

The Farer
If it be true that history repeats
Itself, may it not be that future man
Shall swing across the arc of cosmic time
And on a higher plane of consciousness
With deeper understanding view the Real?

The Presence
Not intellect but *inner sight* reveals
This truth to you. For men already on
This planet have attained through evolution
Psychical and through their contact with such men
As have already reached attainment, the plane
Of cosmic consciousness. The eyes of soul
Possess the second sight.

The Farer
How can I learn—

The Scribe
The voice was still; it seemed that even he
Who was the Voice, the Counselor of Light,
Had need of time the deeper truths to trace;
Reflectively he gazed into the Farer's face.

The Farer
I gain some insight on the plane of thought
But I have need to *feel* and to be caught

156

Up to the plane of *lasting* ecstasy
And walk with God and hear Him talk with me.

The Presence
There is no need to leave the world of men
Nor to retreat to some high cave or glen;
Search deep within if you would truly find
The springs of life in the Eternal Mind;
Look in yourself and you at length shall view
Creator God who hid himself in you.
Within this precious bowl of alabaster
Is found the secret of the hidden Master.
Too long a dying world has longed to see
The God that man and man alone can be.

The Scribe
Upon the room fell silence, deep, profound,
As though the world itself were stilled of sound;
The Farer stirred; and these the thoughts that ran
Through mind exalted—

The Farer
                    I will be that man!

The Presence
You set a goal above all goals and yet
Fulfillment of the goal that God has set
That man should find himself, grow and expand
Until he is to God another hand,
Another eye, to see and bring to birth
New forms of beauty chiseled here on earth.
The god-like soul must art and artist be
Through whom mankind perceives reality.
The world of wonder just behind the screen
Can through the eyes of higher souls be seen.
And he who would, by paint or sound or stone,
Reveal the values seen by him alone,
Must learn to live beyond the present hour

Behind the field of sense, and see the flower
Within the seed, the fruit within the bloom;
To him the *finished* work is but a tomb
In which old visions once so warm and tender
Have lost their lure, their glory and their splendor,
The fleeting glimpse of that reality
Which lies behind the things the eye can see.
Before the canvas dries, the artist turns away
And brings a new bright vision into play.
So must it be for him who would unseal
The blinded eyes and higher truth reveal.
He first of all must know beyond all speech,
The inaccessible, impossible to reach
Save by the mystic vision of the soul
Which does not see in parts but sees the Whole.
This is no call to sainthood nor to art—
The secret lies alone within the heart.
There is one goal which lies *beyond* but near,
Though unattained it is both *there* and *here*.
It is not joined to any time or place,
It has a million eyes, a million faces—
It is the REAL behind the things of sense,
It is the ME; nor need you question whence
Nor where nor how nor what nor why it came;
Forever changed, it still remains the same.

The Farer
End and beginning seem to me alike,
Why then the quest if this be truly so?

The Presence
The goal is *understanding;* not to *know*
But rather be *possessed* by That-Which-Is,
And to be unified in consciousness
With Being Absolute; no more content
With shadows but with creative light;
No more the mirror nor the parallel
But full identity with prototypes.

Each soul with each, and *all* with each, and all
With all commingled in one consciousness.
The future man shall be so far above
The race that walks the earth today he would
Appear among us as a god, yet he
Will be the common man; nor will there be
Such selfish aims as now divide mankind;
Illusion of false values will dissolve
Into their native nothingness and things
Ephemeral and transient of this earth
Shall pass away, and by the second birth,
The field of consciousness shall so expand
All sons of earth shall reach the Promised Land.

The Farer
I will not wait for such a distant morn,
I enter NOW, for I have been reborn!

The Presence
Glorious the day and wondrous the might
That brings all men into this cosmic light!
And none shall judge and none shall be denied,
And none condemned and none be crucified.
Coldness and hate and ignorance long passed,
Man shall transcend his lesser self at last,
The Buddhist light of calm untroubled love
Shall blend with Atman and the Christ to prove
That Eden was no fantasy of old;
The tree of life shall bear its fruit of gold;
Among its leaves the hawk and sparrow nest;
And none bear need and none shall be distressed.

The Farer
What then of life's pursuits, can man survive
Or even realize he is alive
Save that he struggle and meet the issues of
Uncertainty of life and death and love?
How then shall *life* be known

Unless the soul be grown
By chances taken and with evil blended?
By conquests made in fight
In name of God and right?
Will not the joy of victory be ended?

The Presence

The joy of victory dies with the fight,
It scarce survives a balmy summer night;
And when the tale is told by winter's fire
The hands are cold upon the stringéd lyre.
Nay, Farer, nay, the all-enthralling bliss
Lies not in conquest but it lies in this—
Creative thought, creative plans and acts
That bring rewards in action and in facts
Of high achievement of the goals thereat;
To be and to become—for THOU ART THAT.

The Farer

My soul is set aflame
By this the Nameless Name;
I look upon the world of form and view
What the Creative Word alone can do
And vow myself to Thee,
Creative Trinity.[24]

The Presence

You have arrived at meanings and have heard
The song of songs and the Creative Word.
So shall it be for all who live on earth
When the millennium shall have its birth;
The symbols then to substance shall be turned,
The hopes fulfilled for which the ages yearned,
That Truth once hid behind the veil of sense
Should be revealed in its magnificence;
One God be recognized behind the veil
Of Isis or Osiris and the pale
Moon-goddess Ishtar, Kali, Mithra, all

Who served as windows through the wall
Of nature, who revealed the deity
And opened doors to show the Trinity
To be in truth but One, the Primal Cause,
Known once as La[25] or Ra or That-Which-Was.
The mirror of the Sea of Darkness will
Be broken and its illusion turned to nil;
The bondage of the law will be the token
Of freedom through the law which, never broken,
Shall be to all mankind a guest and friend,
To serve man's needs until his journey's end.
In joy, O friend, uplift your eyes and see
The *life* upon the cross, and *death* shall be
No more the gate to some *far* Paradise.
And look around you, see the good and wise;
Behold the miracles of daily living

And all the things creative thought is giving—
The loaves and fishes multiplied,[26] the wine
From water drawn—yes, all of this is thine.
The Everlasting NOW, *today* shall be;
The future from the past at length set free;
The rose of life shall bloom in gardens fair
The noonday sun shall never wither there,

The Scribe
The Farer, overcome by feelings taut
Was wrapped in bliss beyond the reach of thought,
And for a while he gazed into the sea
Of cosmic life, *became* infinity.
Then from some depth beyond the human mind
Drew forth these words as one who might unwind
A hidden ball of threaded pearls in wonderment
Of whence they came or what was their intent:

The Farer
Awake, awake, the trumpet notes are sounding
The hour of dawn is marching up the earth,

The Voice of Day proclaims in tones resounding,
"I am the heir of Time who gave me birth."

Behold the gleaming eye of the anointed
Who offers challenge from the lofty height;
The bows are strung, the long bright arrows pointed
At yon gray moon and shadows of the night.

How swift the march! Lose not this hour of wonder,
This glow and glory filling Everywhere;
The morn so soon is passed; the noon, like thunder;
The eve draws on; your day dissolves in air.

And even now the western skies are graying,
The twilight soul will soon be laid to rest;
The world be stilled, no single sound betraying
That life still slumbers in the Cosmic Breast.

Such is the fate of man; and Time, unceasing,
Gives birth to day; and like the shifting tide,
The waves of life now wane and, now increasing,
Show naught is fixed and nothing will abide.

What matter, then, if springtime turn to summer,
Or that the warmth of summer soon shall fade,
Or that the winds of autumn leave us number?[27]
We still may face the winter unafraid.

The things of life are changing, shifting,
From substance of an unseen essence drawn;
From star to dust all things are ever drifting,
Day turns to night while night gives birth to dawn.

The span of human life is left unmeasured
And all its transient seasons swiftly pass;
Like autumn's harvest, for a moment treasured,
The evening shadows fade upon the grass.

Time's ebbing tide draws back into the Timeless,
No more the waves shall break upon the shore;
And all the world, unreasoning and rhymeless,
Shall have no seed, no harvest, and no sower.

Yet is this death and final desolation,
Or is it but inbreathing of a God?
Is there no mode of transubstantiation
That life shall wake again in sky and clod?

Will life go on, the wheel forever turning?
Will it remain when form has passed away?
And will there be an answer to our yearning
That we see beauty and another day?

In vain we search the musty tomes of sages
And scan the circuit of the wheeling spheres:
We listen to the echo of the ages
And hear the empty moaning of the years.

No flesh nor blood nor senses can reveal it—
The answer to the what and when and how.
Can That-Within-Us yet unseal it?—
What is, has been, and what has been is now.

'Tis man alone gives nature all her beauty,
Outside of him, there is no light of Truth;
Apart from him, there is no sense of duty;
While age is but the ripened fruit of youth.

These are persistent things, beyond all dying,
The overtones that never know decay,
The Voice Within that evermore is crying,
"Life will endure and never pass away."

The mind that seeks the Higher Revelation
Shall come at last into the Realm of Cause—

A CLEAR DESIGN that, running through creation,
Proclaims a Law above all lesser laws.

This is the Law: One cause goes on forever;
This is the way by which man can foretell—
For *form* must follow thought, nor can we sever
The *pattern* from its earthly parallel.

Let it be known that flesh and bone and sinew
Are but the leaves we fashion in a wreath;
They are but chaff, and when at length we winnow,
We find the seed embedded in the sheath.

The soul will spiral upward; and, ascending,
The ring into a larger circle grows
Until it merge into the life unending
And he-who-knows is One with Him-Who-Knows.

This is the ripened fruit of incarnation,
The flowering of the less into the Greater.
The journey's end and final consummation,
THE SOUL IN CONSCIOUS UNION WITH CREATOR.

And yet
The light is even now about to break
Upon your soul and you shall see beyond
The sight of earth.

Illumination and intuition

The Farer

    O Presence luminous, in radiant light
    Attired; too bright to see, too lustrous
    For me to look upon; I shut my eyes
    But still thy *being* penetrates my own.
    I am in wonderment, Celestial One,
    That thou dost come again and yet again
    To one of humble life and low estate
    Like me.
              I do confess no one could be
    More lifted up nor yet bowed down than I
    By his unworthiness.
                   But I have heard
    How God once sent a messenger and raised
    A shepherd boy to be a king and turned
    A humble maid into the mother of
    A god or avatar. I will not stress
    My own unworthiness, for Thou hast come
    Of thine own will and I am born again.

The Presence

    Men pray for *good* but when it comes, the door
    Is shut by self-abasement or by doubt.
    They had the faith to ask; but not enough
    To quite accept the gift—Here one accepts
    And his deep wounds are healed; God hears each call
    But cannot force your hand to take the gift
    For which you prayed. Another asks for full
    Supply for daily needs and streams of plenty
    Swirl around his door. And some do pray
    With hope but no expectancy and they
    Do not receive. "Ye must believe ye have
    Received.[28] (I promise you) ye shall receive."

The Farer

    Through thee, O friend, I am already raised
    From hell to closer heaven. Beyond my reckoning
    Have come events above my conscious willing.

As eastern skies at early dawn awake
In radiant glory from the ghostly night
To paint their beauty on the wooded hills
And lift the silv'ry coverlid of mist
Along the stream where meadow daisies sleep;
Just so, it seems, from upper air there breaks
On twilight-souls like mine, supernal light
That lifts the mists and spreads new life abroad
Until the common soul is full awake,
Aware of self at last. In hours like these,
O blessed one, the stars bend low as if
To draw the twice-born soul into the sphere
Of their own galaxy, and radiance lend
To raise the shadows cast by age-old fears
And light the path for souls as young as mine.
But tell me, O Illumined One, just why
The whole wide world is suddenly transformed
And everything is animate with life.
All Nature seems awake and I can see
Into the heart of things and hear them speak.

The Presence

Of *waking* soul, this is the evidence;
And that soft glow which breathes from everything
Is astral light from which all Nature springs.
The first creative word is "LIGHT" from which
All things are made and molded into form.
He who awakens to this light beholds
The *real* behind the things of sight and sense,
And with enlightened eyes, he apprehends
Directly; knows true from false, the right
From wrong, the path to take, the friends to choose,
The words to speak and how to heal the sick,
Turn thoughts to things, create new forms
And move men's hearts to peace and faith in God.

The Farer

    I see the light but still I know that I
    Myself am weak of faith and will. Make clear
    To me the source and substance of *this* light;
    And if it dims or wastes away through use.

The Presence

    Light IS and that is all that can be said,
    Save that It is the primal stuff of which
    The universe is made; it changes form
    But still remains the same. Its radiations
    Like waters of a river flow, but flowing
    Still remains a river. Unlike to snow
    That drifts and banks upon the outer crust,
    It penetrates, transfusing all around;
    Yet still flows on full-brimmed, nor does withhold
    Its sparkling draughts from thirsty suckling mouths
    Along the meadowlands and pours itself
    In foaming falls into the sea below.

The Farer

    It is too vast for me to comprehend.

The Presence

    Think not on vastness of the streams of light,
    Compare them to a crystal pool
    Whose waters fed by springs invisible
    Sustain the desert isle and save from death
    The thirsty caravan. So from within
    Illumined souls eternal truth upsprings.

    The Me is pool! Become aware of Me—
    For THOU ART THAT. By constant effort hold
    Thy mind to this: I AM. Maintain this truth
    Against the siren call of doubt, against
    Old doctrines shutting out the light by
    Defamation of the soul's divinity.
    Who comes to self will surely come

To Me, Indwelling, Indivisible,
Invisible, the Highest and the Best.
If thus you set your mind to realize
The Me, you shall attain and find at last
The answer in yourself. The goal of light
Is reached when you at length affirm, "I *know*
Because I see it deep within myself."
For knowledge is unfoldment from within.
The conquest of illusion once achieved
Removes the film of sense that sullies o'er
Inherent truth that lies within the Me.

In science, and invention, or in arts
Of poetry, of music or religion,
The process is the same—to enter in
The object and to find *by sympathy*
What is its meaning as a whole.
                              The steps are four. [29]
Prepare by conscious search. Your concept, next,
Must *incubate*. It grows, ye know not how,
Beneath the wing of Mother Mind by faith.
But on a coming day it bursts its shell
And suddenly a sound! a cry! Behold!
The birth of something new! And this is called
Illumination. Such has come to you.
And in due time the fourth and final step
Will *verify* and prove in fact and form
That faith and love and light and life
Alone are real—the one and only real.

The Scribe

The voice was stilled. The Farer's face in awe
Was lifted and it shone with inner light.
Celestial vision shut him deep within
Himself where he was one with All. Time was
Forgot, and hours skimmed past like homing birds
And winged their way into eternity.

The Presence

As progress rests
On Inspiration and the swift perception of
The real; as evolution rests not on
Mechanical unfoldment but by new
Mutations swiftly come about, as though
Some principle of life had waked at last—
So does *illumination* come in one
Great dazzling flash of light which bursts
From minds made ready by those who have prepared
By incubation.

The Farer

Long have I dwelt on this.
How often in the watches of the night
When stillness spread like mist across the moor,
Have I in sacred silence brooded on
Reality until its meaning fell
Away from me and I seemed lost upon
A sea of nothingness. How then can you
Declare that incubation holds the key?
I might with equal value ask myself
This question, "Who am I, oh, who am I?"[30]
Until I lose all consciousness of self
And vaguely wonder who it is who asks
Of whom.

The Scribe

He seemed as one distraught and for
A while the Presence waited, seeming not
In haste. But finally he spoke.

The Presence

And yet
The light is even now about to break
Upon your soul and you shall see beyond
The sight of earth.

The Scribe
Then, even as he spoke,
The Farer's eyes seemed fixed upon some scene
Beyond the human sight and he became aware
Of That Deep Inner Light of Nature which
Unites all things in one as though each gave
Its light to each and each to all and none
Lost anything because it was itself
The source and substance of the light
From which it drew.
Yet these are not
My words but his as he in after years
Has set it down. For now he cried aloud,

The Farer
Teacher of teachers thou!
The light is streaming now
Through spaces measureless...

The Scribe
His tongue was still; he was possessed by some
Strange ecstasy that took away his strength
And in a moment's time enveloped him
With light ineffable...Of this he speaks:

The Farer
I feared my feeble light would fail the air
And leave me in the blackness of despair
When suddenly in vision most intense,
I broke the spell of blackness and suspense
In which I seemed asleep to all around—
Nor death itself could be more stilled of sound—
And found myself aroused, awake, aware
That Something I had never known was there;
And in such ecstasy there was no night,
But only light and light and light and light.

The Scribe
>It was only in the after years he knew
>That this was truly Cosmic Consciousness.

The Farer
>Light comes when we are least aware of it;
>We suddenly look up from sameness of
>The everyday and there it is, unasked
>And unexpected. Indifferent to our acceptance
>Or rejection of it, the light is there
>And that is all we know! Impersonal
>As is the beauty of a sunset!
>
>We are bathed in it at all times;
>It does not move from place to place;
>It is just there, always and forever.
>At once its brilliance dazzles us and yet
>A film of softness seems to shade our eyes.
>Its beauty lies beyond the power of speech;
>It seems to flow into our vision, then
>Out of it once more.
>   We cannot know
>This mystery; it lies beyond
>All explanation. But it is not illusion,
>It dispels illusion. It is a solid fact
>Of our experience. All things are seen
>Within this light and none shut out,
>And every part has equal brilliance
>With every other part like facets of a gem.
>One cannot say *his merit* brought it forth
>Though he has long invited it. It comes
>To none by concentration or by will.
>It seldom is the fruit of effort, and
>Not reward of virtue dearly paid.
>It is its own excuse for being and never
>Does it seek to reason or explain.
>It was not brought nor was it sent,
>It was not planned nor was it purposed,

It neither was coerced nor heralded.
It is not found as though it were absent; it merely is.
All theories and faiths will neither make nor obscure it;
The reality is that it exists.
Whether or not we are aware—we are in it without need of proof.

Like tides from an invisible ocean of life
Bringing messages to the shores of time,
Eternity presses upon us.
It belongs to the present moment;
Occasionally a door opens,
Eternity enters and brings the light to the shores of time,
Messages from the unknown mystery of being.
Seldom are these messages articulate to consciousness,
More often they are swept back into the stream
Or ocean of their being, unrevealed.
We stand on the shores of this larger life,
We hear its tide.
O Life of Life, O Ocean of Being,
To me revealed!
                    I stood upon the shores of
The Larger Life, I heard its swelling tide,
I felt its lapping waves upon my feet.
Uninvited, the unknown became the known,
The invisible was seen. A voice spoke
And I heard it. Beyond all reasoned thought,
It spoke a language that feeling and only feeling
Can interpret...but *real*, oh, so real!
Illusive, fluidic but substance of
All substance, Illumination came!

The Scribe

He was submerged in seas of consciousness
But from his lips there fell half-uttered thoughts
Which carried sequencies from time to time:

The Farer

    We shall never again be the same,
    We shall never forget...the mark is left
    Upon our being...We have felt its spray...
    Plunged at times into its depths...All doubts
    Dissolved,
    Fear...only a word!...
                The universe alive!
    Totality, one cosmic livingness...
    A whole, no fragments and no parts, but in
    Itself united and continuous...
    Containing variations endless from
    The Infinitesimal to the Infinite,
    From mind of mineral to mind of man...
    Ranges of consciousness unlimited,
    Outsweeping and outstretched without a bound...
    Cohesive, eternal, yet expanding
    From specks of dust to systems planetary,
    From the heart of a bird to the heart of Christ,
    And on and on to that Great Heart that beats
    In rhythmic lovingness in everything!
    O heart of Christ, O heart of God, O Light!

The Scribe

    That warm first glow he never could recapture
    And only part explain. His consciousness
    Had been enveloped so completely that
    It seemed detached. In retrospect he could
    Recall the memory but not the deep
    Emotion which had held him so enthralled.
    Yet it had given him such deep perception
    Of reality that his intellect
    Awoke to higher power of thought and speech.

The Farer

    I saw the real, I knew the truth at last,
    The days of half-blind sight for me were passed;
    I understood how senses had deceived

And in one flash of vision I achieved
An insight that reason cannot fashion
From sense experience and human passion;
The world I knew or thought I apprehended
I found conditioned, relative and ended
In unreality. It was made plain
That sensuous perception gives no gain
To knowledge but it only verifies
Our ignorance and proves reality
Must lie beyond the bounds of what we see.
Whatever good there is in life—in hopes,
In dreams, in loves, in knowledge of the real,
And ALL the joys to which the heart aspires—
Shall take on body and a soul in life
Beyond this life.

The Scribe

               No word the Presence spoke
The while the Farer was engaged in mystic
Contemplation. Yet like to haloes seen,
A something flowed or glowed between,
Each seemed by each entranced as one,
Yet did the Presence seem more like the sun
From which the moon draws light.
                     The Presence spoke,

The Presence

From stone to star, from dust to Betelgeuse,
From plant to man, from man to Seraphim;
From insect brain to Cosmic Consciousness,
There is but One Eternal Light of Lights;
Yet ev'ry candle lighted on the earth
Is seen by Him who brought it into birth,
And one small flame devoted to the Me,
May light the way through all eternity.

The Farer

> May I fulfill this dream nor lose my way
> Through fear and doubt of my own worthiness!
> How can I keep the path? Ease my distress!

The Presence

> Be like the wingéd bird who would fulfill
> Its destiny. It first prepares
> A nest where it may lay its eggs and then
> It broods with half-closed eyes and meditates
> Until, the incubation done, the chick
> Breaks through the shell. Dwell on intangibles
> Until they shape themselves to visibles.
> As artists sense the soul of things
> Like visions hovering on wings,
> Be thou aware of light and give it birth
> In beauty born immaculate on earth.
> The door swings wide and in the Me
> Is light through all eternity.
> One Light there is and ONE ALONE,
> One Lord of Light upon His throne.

The Farer

> What are the steps that lead to intuition?

The Presence

> Turn first and last and ever to the ME,
> For THOU ART THAT: the knower and the known
> Must meet within. With mind unwandering
> Proclaim within thyself the fact of Heav'n,
> Declare thy reverence for the Inner Good,
> The True, the Holy and the Beautiful.
> Think on the nature of the Truth and say
> "Thou art the Light, Thou art the Way, Thou art
> The Untaught Teacher of the Truth.
>   I would see only Thee;
> For where Thou art is wisdom. Be to me
> The candle and the flame, the star that shines

And light that streams therefrom. And let me walk
With Thee. O Light Eternal, guide my steps."
One beam of light can put the dark to rout,
One truth affirmed will drive the evil out.
For ev'ry problem that you face there is
One way by which it can be solved. Turn to
The Light Divine. Declare Its Presence and
Affirm that you are ONE with It and that
You do not walk alone. Nor will your path
Wind back into the shadows of despair,
If you will hold to Him and let His hand
Hold yours. And though your eyes be closed, you still
Will see the Light Divine. Let it be guide.
He who shall send his word before his face
To mark the trail and clear it for the race
Shall reach the goal to which his mind is bent,
Untouched by fate, unharmed by accident.

                         If thou shalt meditate
On light and light alone, it shall not dawn too late.

The Scribe

Then spoke the Presence of lamps whose wicks
Were wet in Eden's oil and whose clear flame,
Unquenched, had lit the age-old paths of men,
Which, although dimmed by lusts of earth, still burned
In secret while the times were dark, and then
Were passed along to races still unborn.

The Presence

Whoever comes with lowly heart to God,
Be he of Krishna, Buddha, Moses, Christ,
He will not fail to see! How sweet the words
The lamp of love for man is lit,
And *man* walks in the light of it;
From here to the Eternal Shore,
The circled beam will go before.

The Farer

    Would that my eyes could see this light!

The Scribe

    The Presence spoke no more. It seemed that he
    Himself was one with all eternity,
    And that perhaps he lingered there until
    The Farer's heart united with his will.

    At last the Farer roused and from his throat
    There burst a song of rapture note on note
    Until he seemed some angel in disguise,
    Upon his homeward way to Paradise.

The Farer

    O Light Divine that shineth on my way,
    Supernal light that radiates from heaven,
    Thy glance has pierced the sepulcher of doubt
    In which I lay entombed, and brought to life
    The seed of hope...
              And let my soul
    Be bathed in light so that I shall be whole
    In ev'ry part and way. O Light of light,
    Divine illumination, I have set
    A vessel to contain thy holy oil
    That I may pour myself into the lamps
    Of unenlightened souls whose smoldering wicks
    Bedim the light of life. Thou art the oil,
    The lamp, the light, the giver and the gift.

The Scribe

    The Farer seemed himself to be aflame
    With exaltation like Mithra seated on
    His throne within the sun, reflector
    Of the Absolute.
              He peered beyond
    The stars into infinity as though
    His ear had caught some far off note divine.

The Farer
 I cried unto Thee and Thou didst give reply;
 I sang unto Thee, and Thou didst hear my song.
 I besought Thee and mercy has been shown;
 My prayers no longer echo in a void.
 I brought burnt offerings of my heart
 I laid them on the altar of all being,
 And Thou didst welcome me.
 I who had died found life in Thee again
 O Immensity, O Fathomless, I have fathomed Thee!
 The shield of Thine indifference has been shattered,
 The coldness of Thine isolation has been melted,
 The armor of Thy silence has been pierced.
 O Vastness, O Timeless, O Infinite,
 Thou hast shown cohesion in Thine endless cycles
 And healed the loneliness of separation.
           My heart has found its peace
 At last I rest in Thee in pure inclusion!
 Not in Thee as One who stands astride the spheres
 Too high for mortal thought,
 Remote and unapproachable;
 Not in Thee as One who spins the worlds
 In space and leaves them there
 In soulless evolution!
 Nay, but *in* Thee, in perfect union
 And inseparate. In Thee, In Thee, In Thee,
 In Thee alone, O Uncreate, in Thee!
 Here only is fulfillment found!

The Scribe
 He paused bemused, in wonderment that he
 Had voiced such words so fraught with mystery.
 Transformed by awe and suddenly aware,
 He knew the Presence once again was there.

The Presence
 'Tis this alone can solve the mystery of fate
 That men shall find the Whole in each,
 And each the center of the Whole.

The Scribe
> Then to the Whole as to a deity
> The Presence rendered an apostrophe:

The Presence
> Yea, each the center of the Whole must prove
> To solve the mystery of life and love.
> In themselves deepened to Thy depth, O Creator,
> In themselves expanded to Thy vastness,
> In themselves encompassing Thine immensity,
> In themselves embracing Thine eternity.
>
> In a flash of timeless Time,
> The passing fancy of a moment;
> In themselves, the Infinite Formless;
> In themselves, the Uncreated[32] Possibility;
> In themselves, the Imagery of the Uncaught;
> In themselves, the Undivided, Cohesive, Inseparate;
> In themselves, the fusion of Time and Timeless;
> In themselves, the Formless and the Formed.
> For only in themselves shall they find Thee;
> Only in themselves shall they find union
> Of the apparent fragments in a Whole
> That certifies the Indivisible.
> Only when eons have passed through the moment
> Can time be found and eternity encompassed
> Only until Thy vastness comes to a point
> In the Omnipresence of Thine Infinity
> Can Thy Center be discovered.
> Only as the point expands to Infinity
> Can Thy circumference be found.
> So shall time and the Timeless merge and fuse
> With the Caught and the Uncaught,
> With the Created and the Uncreated;
> For only in union is wholeness found
> Only in Thee can Unity be gained.[33]

Then suddenly the Farer seemed to be
The earth, the sky, the mountain and the tree:
And he became to each the music and the voice
That sang for them as though they must rejoice
In being earth or mount, or tree or stream
With each a soul tuned to the cosmic scheme.

Praise and thanksgiving

9

Like birds escaped from winter's chill, who feel
The first warm draughts of summerland and pour
Out melodies that fill the upper air
And echo back again to thrill the earth with praise,
So did the Farer's thoughts arise on hope's
Bright wings and from his lips there burst a song:

The Farer

O hope reborn, O truth from heaven brought
That gladdens all my being; I, who sought
In vain amidst the bleakness of despair,
Awake at last to find assurance rare
That gives me peace. And I can hear
The voice of Truth so comfortful and clear.

I am once more a child untouched by doubt
Who joins his mates and running all about
Is free from thoughts of ill through happy hours,
His face aglow amidst the springtime flowers;
And oft we find him at the angelus
In play with friends invisible to us,
As though his pure young eyes prepare to see
The Father's face within Eternity.

O why should man dig his grave in the slime
And dull his ears to the joy and the rhyme
Of life that sings in the sea and the air
And songs that arise from the Everywhere?

The Scribe

He mused in wonderment, then in a voice
Of rapture cried aloud, "Rejoice, rejoice!"

The Farer

I have captured the hum of a homing bee
And the lisp of the leaves of the maple tree,
And I leaned my ear to the sibilant sod
And heard it singing a song of God.

I plucked high C from the blazing sun,
And the deep, deep base of Aldebaran;
And I soared on wings to the topmost heights
And caught the tune of the Northern Lights
And I shook the notes as I sped along
Over my shoulder in waves of song.

The Presence
Through praise you have unloosed the thongs of doubt
That bound your faith and you have put to rout
The armies of your fears; and by your song
You lead all men of equal faith along,
For he who flings his song upon the air
Will draw the people to him everywhere.

The Farer
                    I hear thy voice
In everything and I am so transformed
I seem not I but thou; thou art my life
Set loose from concept of duality
Which chained me to a double mind, like twins
Ingrown, inseparate of movement, which
Yielding to the one must thwart the other.
Thanks, thanks to thee, Celestial Visitor,
My world is *one,* all-glorified, alive
With consciousness, and everything I see
Is palpitant with joy that seems to sing
A song of praise as though each living thing
Responded to the melodies above
Which float to earth attuned to cosmic love.
At ev'ry dawn when earth and heaven meet,
My inner self goes out with flying feet
To join the chorus and to greet
The Soul-of-Things.

                    Praise rises from my soul
Like incense wafted from an altar-bowl,
As though the winds of morning gently blow

Across the garden of my heart, and so
Do gather perfume for me to offer Him,
Who fills all space out to the farthest rim
Yet still is here in me and I in Him.

The Scribe
Then it was the Farer chanted
With a vision so possessed
That his conscious thought supplanted,
Freed his soul to speak the rest.

The Farer
Inner Presence, Great and Mighty,
Inner God that undivided
Is the Truth that is the Me;
Inner Peace that has provided
Inner Calm that comes from Thee,
Inner Life that lives completely,
Inner Truth that never fails me,
Inner Love that gives so freely,
Inner Eye by which I see,
Inner Ear that hears me always,
THOU ART THAT-I-AM IN ME.

The Presence
Yea, THOU ART THAT, born not of molded clay
By gods who made thee for a summer day;
For even as I looked upon thy face
The mortal disappeared and in its place
The silver-whiteness of celestial grace,
Soul-substance of the deathless self to be
Enshrined within the temple of the Me.

The Farer.
O heav'nly visitant, I am so full
Of joy, I lack the words to say...

The Presence

    Give gratitude for truth already known
    And in due time a greater shall be shown.
    Who renders thanks for truth already given
    Shall open still another door to heaven.
    All songs in heaven sung are hymns of praise,
    And thus they sing unto the Lord of Days
    Since there is nothing else for which to sing,
    Because they have no need of anything.

The Farer

    I am with gratitude so filled,
    So thrilled, so overcome, so awed,
    Amazed and glorified,
    I am as one beside
    Himself. And I am willed to build
    My soul a temple of my God.

The Scribe

    The pain of other days had vanished from his eyes;
    He seemed as one who had by miracle apprised
    The answer to the mystery; his quest
    Was solved. He had at last found rest.

The Farer

    He knows as he knows his own, that He is my all,
    My earth, my sky, the substance of my world.
    I see not, but through His eyes
    For He has lent me His vision.
    I breathe not but by the breath of His life!
    I love not save in the ecstasy of His affection!
    Truly, Thou livest in me, my All; truly as I live in Thee.
    No earth surrounds me
    But that which Thou hast set before mine inward eye.
    All good springs before—clears my path—for I walk with Thee.
    O Star to the very stars! Thou shinest me!
    Radiant I, with Thy pure radiance beaming!
    O Livingness! O loving Tenderness!

I breathe, and breathing, drink Thy splendor.
I live, and living, mirror Thee back.
I love, and all-embracing love answers in love undying.
King Thou art. Soul of my life!
Mount Thou the throne of my being
And reign, clothed in Thy celestial splendor.

The Scribe

Then silence fell the while the Farer sought
To drink into his soul the love he voiced,
As though the icy mountain range that had so long
Obscured his vision began to melt and flow
Away; and new horizons broke upon
His sight. Thenceforth, though oft in doubt, he seemed
To ponder more and question less and to
Withdraw within himself and listen for
The voice that spoke to him, though unaware
Of whence it came—from God, or from himself,
Or from the Presence.
                    Yet oft he paused,
Half-turned as though to nod and give consent
To what the Presence said, as friends are wont
To do in fair exchange of thought and love.
This did the Presence know and so he spoke:

The Presence

Be not afraid to look for truth within;
No avatars nor "shade" nor "guide" nor soul
Returned from astral planes to haunt your room
And give you sage advice has wisdom to
Impart what equals that which you can find
Within, when once you listen to the Me.

Enlarge, expand awareness of thy cosmic self;
Not God made small but man made great doth solve
The riddle of the universe, for
THOU ART THAT.

The Farer
>You are, O Living One, my very Lord,
>And but for thee I would be lost in that
>Dark pit of ignorance wherein I stared,
>Nor ever found an answer to my quest—
>The age-old search of man to solve the black
>Enigma—whence did he come, and why and
>To what end.

The Scribe
>Silence fell between the two.
>And then the Presence said:

The Presence
>It is not I
>But thou. He sees alone who turns his eye
>To that bright light that shines within the mind
>Of him who looks within. There unconfined
>The Whole is found, the Me is ever shrined.
>Search for the Me; *there* must the Truth be sought,
>Look to the self—for *wisdom* is untaught.

The Scribe
>New joy suffused the Farer's face. He spoke
>And seemed at once to challenge and invoke
>Awareness deep of ev'ry living thing
>From star to clod, from birds upon the wing
>To galaxies that course through outer spaces,
>And back again to little loving faces
>Of gentle things that peer from hidden places.

The Farer
>Of life I sing, of everything that lives;
>I sing to the earth that gives its suckle
>To growing grass, to trees, and to the beasts
>That feed upon the verdure of the hills.
>I praise the sunrise on the mountain tops
>And sunsets that leave a lingering touch

In promise of another day. I praise
The shadows cast across the earth to give
The peace and soothing solitude of night.
I praise you, rose-garden, spilling fragrance
Upon the air, and jasmine blooming in
The dark and breathing softly by my bed.
I praise the rain that falls to quench the thirst
Of parching grass and flowers and trees.

                                    I praise
The bosom of the Holy Mother Earth
Cradling the world in all-embracing love.
I sing to you, I sing to you, O all
And everything that falls within my sight;
And *forces* that I cannot see which yet
Enfold the universe and hold it fast.
I praise you, ocean, with your vibrant life,
The turmoil of your ceaseless stirring and
The teeming multitudes that suckle at your breast.
I sing to you, ye spuming waves and
Racing tides. You bear a thousand thousand
Ships that thread their way around the Seas
To spin the warp and woof of commerce to
Encircle all the world and knit in one great
Brotherhood the races of mankind.

I sing to Holy Mother-Marys, all who bear
Within their wombs the embryos of those
Who will be saints and seers to point the way
Of truth and life to that new race of men
Who will appear. Rejoice that now the morn
Of that new world is close when even those
Who seem to be the least shall nonetheless
Be most; for they shall know that ev'ry man
Is born of God, one with the cosmic span.
I praise you, then, ye mothers of the race,
And with prophetic vision, view the place
Where men shall shrine you in deific grace.

The Scribe

> Then in a swift transition the Farer turned
> To praise and gratitude for little folk.

The Farer

> I sing to you, all children at your play,
> Whose sweet young voices ring across the way.
> I praise your faith in what tomorrow brings,
> You are to me the song-thrush as he wings
> His way above the madness and the strife
> That holds the earth-bound soul to lesser life!

The Scribe

> The Farer paused and lost himself in thought
> Of all the ills that fear and hate have wrought.

The Farer

> My soul is tall above the wall
> That separates by hate;
> Come search my mind and you will find
> My heart an open gate.

The Presence

> Thou hast well said, for all tomorrow's good
> May rest today upon your gratitude,
> For he who gives his thanks before the wine
> Is pressed from grapes still clinging to the vine
> Has shown a faith above, beyond the present hour
> And his thanksgiving holds the future flower.

The Farer

>   O Presence, I do hear
> With gratitude.

The Presence

> O Farer, thou of noble souls most wise,
> Look to the Me and enter Paradise.
> Nor think that Paradise must lie somewhere

Beyond the reach of time, nor here nor there;
God still is One from Alpha to Omega
And earth will be no nearer Him in Vega.[34]

The Farer

Then shall I see Him in all earthly forms,
In nature's stillness or the thunderstorms
That peal among the mountains where the roar
Flings down a challenge to the valley floor.
And on the quiet days, I gaze on peaks
That tower cathedral-like or helmeted
With ice from which the steaming vapors rise
And stream out brilliantly like plumes
Of giant knights who march in serried ranks
Across the rim of Time into Eternity.
I praise you all, ye forms and forces shown,
I find in you the known and the unknown.

I praise the sun-faced daisies drenched in dew
That mirror back the brightness of their god.
I sing to lights and shadows on the earth
And leaves of trees with worship-palms upraised.

The Scribe

He seemed to listen and to see what was
Invisible, at one with Causing Cause;
Then like a priest behind the altar blaze
He raised his voice in chanted prayers of praise.

The Farer

I praise the Magi of Chaldean lands
Who crossed the desert and the burning sands
Responsive to the ancient prophecy
That One would come to set the captive free
From superstition and ignorance that damn
The souls of men, proclaim the Great I AM
And prove that man draws life from God's own breath
And cannot die. Thank God there is no death.

I sing a song of praise; (let go the past),
I sing of life that will forever last.
Forgotten now, the shadows fade away,
Praise God for dawn and for the endless day.
I sing the joy of sunrise and the morrow
Which will dawn clear of hopelessness and sorrow.
I sing of new horizons and the rim
Of heaven, and light that shines from Him
Who Is and Was and Ever-More-Shall-Be,
And spreads His glory through eternity.
I sing to ev'ry light of earth or heaven,
And ev'ry altar lamp or candle given
To cheer the heavy-hearted and to prove
He serves the most who gives himself in love.
O human heart, I praise *you* when you share
Another's need, another's grief and care
Of him who faints and falters in despair.

I am aware of you, all living things
For I am you and something in me sings
As though I were immersed in life and life in me,
I am the sap within, the leaves upon the tree,
I am the cataract that leaps from lofty steep,
Down, down and down into the deepest deep.
I am the eagle soaring gracefully,
I am at one with him and he is one with me.
I am the majesty of mountains and rejoice
That it is I who echoes to my voice.
I am the light that pierces through the mist
And turns the dark to day, the cloud to amethyst.

The Scribe
It seemed to him he was a satellite
That swept around the earth, in swiftest flight
Nor could his piercing eye be brought to rest
Upon some line dividing East from West.
And ev'rywhere the lands and seas were bound
In one great whole and ev'rywhere the sound

Of singing rose as though the earth canorous
Were harmonized to join the cosmic chorus.

The Farer

I praise you, vast Sequoias, flung so high
Your bridal veils seem wedded to the sky.
Sing, sing to me, ye mountains! Yea, I hear
Your thunder-notes upon the atmosphere.

The Scribe

Then suddenly the Farer seemed to *be*
The earth, the sky, the mountain and the tree:
And he became to each the music and the voice
That sang for them as though they must rejoice
In being earth or mount, or tree or stream
With each a soul tuned to the cosmic scheme.
More swift than sound his psychic satellite
Passed the Sequoias basking in the light
Where Nature's temples, first to serve the race,
With granite walls were cut in splendid grace
With porticos and naves; and in the glade
Vast columns crowned with abacus of jade,
A Parthenon upreared of stone and trees
With worshippers who bowed upon their knees
To chant in praise the great Magnificat,
"We thank Thee, Living God, for THOU ART THAT."

The Farer

O world of beauty, spread before my eye,
Thou art the real, this I can verify—
Behind the form I see reality.
Thy shapes and shades, thy changing landscapes seem
Like strains of music in a dream;
Perhaps the pipes of Pan convert the "thing"
Into its soul and give it voice to sing.

Those fields of corn and wheat that circle 'round
As I pass swiftly by convert to sound

And in their place I hear the voice instead
Of grateful people thanking God for bread;
I skim by mines and smelters and the blaze
Of founderies; and, piercing through the haze,
I see the workers joying in their might,
Their strong-limbed figures glowing in the light;
And from their lips the toilers' songs arise
To join the harmonies of Paradise.

The Scribe

So did the Farer from the heights look down
Upon the plains, the wilderness or town
And everywhere he heard and gave reply
To everything that fell beneath his eye.

The Farer

I praise you fishermen; full be your net
That you may thrive, and may your loins beget
Still other fishermen, nor Christ forget.
I praise the great leviathans that sail
The foaming seas in calm or in the gale.

O happy I! How gratefully I hear!
Thou art, O Presence, father, mother, seer:
Thank thee that all my doubts are laid at last,
Thank thee for raging rivers over-passed.
I give my praise that I can be a voice
That bids the world once more to sing, rejoice
That all shall pass into the Promised Land
Where fruits of Eden grow on every hand
And where the tree of life shall shelter be,
And where each soul shall ever, through the Me,
Be one with God and man eternally.

The Scribe

A far-off organ with pipes of fluted gold
Pealed through the clouds and as its thunder rolled,
A melody burst through the open gate,

With trumpet-notes to sweetly syncopate:
Soft on his ear there fell a heav'nly voice
That bid all men rejoice;
And then a chorus, opening soft and slowly,
Rose in crescendo, "Holy, holy, holy."

Love is expansion of the self and he
Who centers thought and heart upon the Me
Becomes aware of cosmic unity.
Man is to God what moon is to the earth.
What earth is to the sun; and in the birth
And growth of love, the secret force is found
By which the soul to Over-Soul is bound.

Love and friendship

The Scribe

    He heard a bell, a quick impatient bell,
    That sounded an alarm within his brain
    And bid the Farer breathe once more,
    So that he woke and, breathing, wept that he
    Must leave the world of light and take his way
    Through utter darkness back to earth again.
    A voice quite strange pursued him out of sleep
    Or death and speaking still, it said,
                      "You have
    At last come close to the Eternal Real;
    It is not knowledge of the One, nor Truth,
    Nor is it Beauty, nay, nor Holiness,
    But Love when love in truth is understood."

    The Farer cried aloud:
                  All this I knew.

The Presence

    But, knowing, did not know; for each must make
    The journey to the center all alone;
    Another's torch will not dispel the dark,
    Nor can the traveler returned describe
    The solitude, the vastness and the light
    Of that mysterious realm wherein the soul
    Is fused with All, yet individual;
    And all the contradictions of his selves
    Have found a synthesis as though from each
    An essence of some good were merged with all.

The Farer

    How true your words, O Presence, for I did
    By some strange miracle of consciousness
    Withdraw myself until I stood away
    And saw the whole of me, my present and
    My past, my body and my mind, my thoughts
    And their pursuit in endless circling.

The Presence
>Until you soared above
>The transient world and from the mystic plane
>Beheld the universe compressed, embraced
>Within a single moment of earth's time.

The Farer
>I had no thought nor consciousness of time
>Nor was concerned, but only that I felt
>No longer incomplete nor self-divided
>Nor farer in a foreign land. I was
>At home.
>   I was untutored, unprepared;
>Like Mithra's acolyte of ancient time,
>"A kid, I fell into the milk." And I
>Awoke reluctantly as though my soul
>Were loath to habitate my flesh again.
>This is most strange to me. I know not where
>I went nor how nor why returned, nor whom
>It was who spoke to me of love.

The Presence
>It is by such device man overcomes
>His mortal sense; and so the sage or saint,
>The prophet and illumined ones unfold
>The hidden god; for in the deeper self
>The lesser god and Greater God are one.

The Farer
>Your wisdom is as dark to me as is
>My ignorance. Forgive, and make more clear.

The Presence
>There are times when logic seems to choke
>The mysteries that we invoke;
>Yet darkest clouds at time unfold
>And pour out showers of dripping gold;
>And from the labyrinths of mind,

The hidden mysteries unwind.
Man treads the mystic path alone
But if the "what" and "how" is shown,
He can develop wisdom till
He comes and goes as he shall will.

The Farer

O Precious Friend, O angel of my soul,
Who looks into the face of God unveiled,
It is enough for me that I reflect
Thy glorious countenance...It is enough!

The Presence

Be not content until thou shalt thyself
Stand glorified and consciously aware
Of *being;* neither self nor selfless but
A *whole* wherein there are no parts and no
Division, where different ages meet and
Co-exist and there is neither far nor near
Nor height nor depth.

The Farer

                              Stay, stay thy words for I
Long since have lost myself in wonderment.

The Presence

I but repeat what I have said to you
Again and yet again. The world is *found,*
Not lost, by visions such as yours: you leave
The dual world and find identity
With highest consciousness, the Infinite
In you, for THOU ART THAT.
                              But only he
Can know THAT ONE who knows Him in himself.
This is the GREAT AWAKENING.

The Farer

                              How sad
The lot of him who lies asleep, nor knows
He is asleep, nor dreams; or, if he dreams,
Does not awake; or, if he wakes, he fails
'To know the meaning of the dream.
                         What then?
How can the soul be liberated? Who
Can build the bridge or span the gorge that lies
Between the finite and the Infinite?
Must there be one who meditates?—*Logos,*
Perhaps, or is some other way designed?

The Presence

Most aptly do you speak; but there is still
A better way,[35] a way quite native to
The soul. This is THE WAY OF LOVE.

The Farer

                              The Way
Of Love is little understood, I think,
And few there be who can define the word,
Much less find love or give it unto man.
What then is love? I know not what is meant.

The Presence

Love has a thousand names, a thousand ways,
But in all forms resolves itself to this:
Love is the union of two kindred things[36]
Each with each and all with each, and all with all.
When you shall see your self in every one
You meet and *feel this union,* and care
For him because he has a need which you
Can fill, you have become a lover of
The Me, a self devoted to the higher self.

The Farer

You give new understanding, better hope
That I may find in human love, the Love
Of Loves, that he who shares his love will find
It grows by giving and thus expands himself.

The Presence

Whose heart is fixed upon the good because
It is the good shall fill his soul with good,
And he who revels in the beautiful
Because he sees in it the beautiful
Shall grow a soul as beautiful as well.
So he who loves all things that live and breathe
Shall know the Love of Loves within the Me.
Where love is felt, there unity is known,
And all the woes that damn mankind have flown,
While he who serves but *one* has served the Whole,
God loves them all and knows them soul by soul.
Man's love is instrument of something higher,
A cosmic love to which he is the lyre.
And vain those men who in the name of faith
Exalt him most who seeks to put to death
All human love for mate or family.
For he who cleaves in purity to love, loves Me,
Unlike the sadist soul who cannot scent perfume,
Till, crushed the flower, he robs it of its bloom,
Love, like a goddess moves in mystic splendor
And with a queenly voice bids all attend her.
Obedient to love's compelling inspiration,
Man dreams, designs and builds some new creation.
From love comes sculpture and the painter's art,
The poet weaves a phrase that moves the heart.
For love the soldier bares his breast in strife;
To love, in blood, he dedicates his life.
Through love of God the martyr braves the pyre
And proves his *will* imperishable by fire.
Reject the claim that earthly love is sin,
And that ascetics only enter in

Celestial gates; each birth is virgin birth,
And each has come immaculate to earth.
Be not deceived by those who seek to prove
That virtue lies alone in flight from love.
Retreat from life to cave or hermitage
Does not convert a man to saint or sage;
The solitude in which thy God is shown
Is in the mind and in the mind alone.

Yet love gives proof of something higher still,
Than sense delight—beyond the human will.

The Scribe
The Farer softly entered bliss,
With face upturned he felt the cosmic kiss.
Time passed upon the earth, but unaware,
The Farer knew it not. Still waiting there
The Presence stood and then at length he spoke.

The Presence
The deepest caves will yield their secrets to
The soul who bears the torch of love,
For love identifies it with the Me.
One thing alone can heal the wounds of sorrow—
To know the Heart that beats through all creation,
The Love that sees all others in relation.
Love's essence lies in its own givingness
And naught is whole without this blessedness.
The healing balm is love and not the mind
To soothe earth's heartaches, for love alone can bind
A farer's soul back to the source again;
For love is union and all the sons of men
Who wander like the Prodigal afar,
Through love, return to where the Blessed are.

The Farer
But hearts estranged by sense of guilt! How can
Love reunite, give peace again to man?

If it be true, as true it seems to be
That guilt divides the heart, rejects the Me.
How can the wanderer make a safe return
When all the fires of guilt within him burn?

The Presence

God gave Himself when He gave life to all
And givingness itself must answer to the call
Of need, and givingness to be complete
Includes forgivingness. Who at the feet
Of Love shall fall, with love concurring,
Shall find his circuits clear and without erring.
This all the great and good and wise have known,
He who forgives shall have forgiveness shown.
Clear thou thy heart from grudge against another,
Act toward thy foe as if he were thy brother,
For curse or blessing ever is reflected
In equal kind to that which is projected.
Look long and earnestly upon each man
Until you pierce the outer shell and can
Behold in him the hidden soul and see
How like he is to God; seek for the Me!

Exalt the soul of man although no trace
Of God appears today upon his face.
Hold reverence for *that* innate in him
Which doth relate him to the Seraphim.
Go to the street and watch the children play
In innocence. The *self* you see today
Will not be lost though some may take the path
That breaks the Law, and suffer from its wrath,
Each child is *born* immaculate on earth.
Nor need await some mystic "second birth."
See in that child the offspring of your heart
And like your *own* let him be counterpart;
For love grows rich the more it is expressed,
And love for one can never rob the rest.
They all are children of the Cosmic Whole

And you the foster-parent to the soul.
A man, love-filled, is God fulfilled, the dream
Of Love Divine. When love flows like a stream
Into the hearts of men, it wider grows;
The cosmic springs expand it as it flows.
And at your work or when you kneel and pray,
The more you give, the more you take away.

The Farer
O, let such love
Be mine that all I see
Shall but confirm
Thy presence in the Me.

The Presence
Through eyes of love the world is born again
As at creative dawn God had a dream
And brought it forth in form. He still remains
Within the form, His Presence everywhere;
His beauty rises with the sun at dawn;
His glory lingers on horizons dim,
His peace is in the desert and the stars,
His majesty within the smallest thing!

The Farer
The wind has spoken to the sea,
It speaks to the waves also;
And every grain of sand upon the shore
Is dancing to its tune and each grain shares
Alike the ever-present sun.

The Presence
Most true. He is in all for He is all,
It is through love his presence is revealed.
Breathe deep the fragrance of that love, a love
That heals the broken heart and will renew
The flesh of him who has awakened to
His presence. Love is Spirit's alchemy

And Love transmutes the less into the more,
Proclaiming heaven here upon the earth.
Love frees us from the past. Eternity
Is not the slave of time; awakened man
Stands free from ancient cause and he
Can change the sequency of its effect
By virtue of the streams of love and truth
That pour the clean, fresh waters of Today
Into the muddied karmic stream and so
Create a new clean life that lies ahead.

The Farer

I had been told that man is victim of
The Law of Cause and its Effect and that
We shall tomorrow still be slave to what
Our past has been.

The Presence

New thoughts, new love, new faith
Can make the future clean, so clean that you
Will all but think the law of sequencies is lost;
Yet the effect is measured by *new* cause.

The Scribe

The Farer was bemused by doubt because
He had accepted karmic law until
He was imprisoned by the self-closed door.

The Farer

Though you affirm that love transcends the law
To bring new cause to bear on old effects,
Is it not true that law is thus reversed?

The Presence

The seeds of love implanted on the earth
Contain their counterpart in realms above
And they are flow'ring *there* and even now
The fruit is setting on the heavenly tree.

The substance of the heaven yet to be
Is love, and in this love man shares with God,
For love is fruit of union of two hearts,
The Heart of God, the heart of man; and man
Shares equally with God in bringing forth
The stuff essential to this Paradise.

The Farer

What more is there, I pray? I would do all—

The Presence

There is a blindness deeper than these eyes
Which often look, but looking do not see.
Teach men to see what inner sight reveals,
He knows things best who seeing also feels;
Though born with eyes and with the gift of sight,
Man walks the earth all unaware of light
And beauty; or the loveliness that could
Be *heard* if he gave ear and understood.

Is it enough to classify a tree
Or to portray biotic energy
As "force" within the acorn or the seed
Which causes growth, yet fail to give due heed
That growth itself is fourth-dimensional?
If rightly taught, the merest child can see
That mind and soul are hidden in the tree.

The Farer

I do agree; where life is, there is mind,
Where mind is, there is soul; where soul is, there
Is God with arms outstretched to welcome me.

He paints the blush upon the rose,
And from his brush, the color flows
That rainbows show when cloud and sun
Are all aglow and day is done.

At such an hour I often see
Where storm clouds lower, He speaks to me.

The Presence

He comes in beauty and he comes in storm,
But in them both the Presence is revealed
To him who is attuned, and he
Who loves will hear the voice of love.
It is through love that God reveals Himself,
But each attracts from Nature only that
To which he is in pitch, as one harp string
Will echo to another harp in tune
With that same key.

The Farer

      I would to Him be harp
Or string that I may be His instrument
And let the key be love.

The Presence

        The lover knows
What the belovéd feels. Love overflows
The banks like singing waters caroling a hymn;
No sweeter song is sung by Scraphim.
The power of God sustains in harmony
Those who through love have found their unity.
Too oft in fear man looks at God as Force
With Whom there is no mode of intercourse,
Yet all the time this perfect Love stands by
With outstretched hand behind the darkest sky:
Some day the clouds of fear and doubt will lift,
And you will see God's face there in the rift.
The gift of love is freedom under law:
God knows no pain because he breaks no law,
In harmony with love. But giving man
The power of choice, He sets him free
To keep or break the law of harmony.

The Farer
>This you have taught and now at length I know
>That while the Cosmic Love will never let man go,
>It leaves him free to seek or spurn the clod
>And grow a soul[37] until he acts as God.

The Presence
>There is no knowledge that reaches higher ground
>Or goes beyond this wisdom you have found,
>That love is keeper of the law and he
>Who lives in love will live in unity
>With law; he who obeys the law is freed
>From pain and failure, loneliness and need.

>What I have said to you, I say to all,
>Love waits for you and answers when you call,
>Not by a miracle nor by some ruse
>Through which some lofty seer sets up a truce
>Or mediates between the souls who sin[4]
>And God to break the law and let them in:
>Nay, not by some disruption nor some flaw
>Through which the soul escapes by breaking law
>But by keeping of the law to prove
>That he is free who serves the law of love—
>Saved from commission of the act or thought
>For which a pardon otherwise were sought.

The Scribe
>The Farer pondered deeply on these words
>As though he measured them against his own,
>And then he spoke:

The Farer
>   I do confirm your words
>And I, like you, would be a voice to say:
>O, you who have been bound, as I have been,
>In bonds of superstition and of doubt,
>I cry to you; ye bear false witness to

The power of that which non-existent is;
Ye have but made a *law* of accident
And chance, of fallen man and angry gods
Who send offending souls to purgatory
Or buy them back again. How strange the story!

The Presence
The God whom I proclaim is not such God,
But Being Absolute, from Whom outflows
A ceaseless stream of wisdom bathed in love:
For *being* is both essence and a state
Of consciousness or mind in action which
At all times has harmony within itself
And cannot know the feeling of revenge
For sin, because it knows no sin; for sin
Is but a name for states of consciousness
Of those who fail to harmonize with law.
The river will not make you drink though you
Should die of thirst; it does not leap the banks
To lave the parching fields nor force the roots
To drink, yet rushes joyously to fill
The channel or the reservoir when once
The gate swings wide to let it give itself.

The gate to God is love in prayer sincere.
The sweetness and the joy of love is all
But pain, so high the ecstasy of him
Whose soul is ravished by awakened love!

Say not, "I search, how can I enter in?
I know no way to free myself from sin."
From what you seek you are so swiftly fleeing,
When deep within, you are, *already, being!*
No more of BEING can there ever be
Than that which is this moment in the Me.
From this deduce the truth—NONE ELSE can view
Or state the terms by which Love comes to you,
Nor can he give the verdict "No" or "Yes"

For entrance into cosmic consciousness;
And love alone reveals such unity
And soul by soul it wakens in the Me.

Most wisely do you speak and wise the soul
Who heeds; for consciousness of God alone
Provides a way for mind to unify
And synthesize all fields of knowledge in
A comprehensive whole, where opposites
Converge to form a perfect round and where
All faiths will be dissolved into a flux
Of direct knowing. Frictions disappear
Where harmony is found—and love is key.
No one can doubt that in the Over-Soul
No conflicts can exist between the fields
Of knowledge nor the laws of things or thoughts
Or of religious faiths. The truths in each
Are true in all and in the cosmic mind;
Untruth cannot exist.

           The Over-Soul
And lesser self are one, and he in whom
The union is complete must share with God
In freedom from the conflicts that divide
Mankind and rend their hearts and lives.
Once more I say to you, you need not wait
For heaven, for heaven waits for you, and it
Is Now. Immortal life is *here* and he
Who has through love found life within the Me
Resolves all doubts and solves life's mystery.

The Farer
This I believe, who through the bitter years
Was rent apart because I saw in part
Nor did I find in any of the paths that wind
One single person knowing how to say,
"Many are the ways of looking at truth,
There is one only Truth at which to look."

And it remains the same from ev'ry point
Of view. So let us say that love reveals
Because it unifies.

The Presence
                    He has the gift
Of knowledge who has found its source within
Himself enfolded in the Me and dwells
Therein embraced by cosmic love; who holds
A steady rein upon his heart and mind
And brings himself to feel the Presence of
Immortal Love until so filled that he
Will live in consciousness of Him while still
At work and in the midst of daily life.
God waits to feel your hand in His, that He
May give you strength and guidance in affairs,
But most of all because of His own joy
To know the oneness of *your* fellowship.
He waits complete surrender of the self
That melts in union, heart with heart as one,
For essence of each is essence of all.
Trust as the rose divides its heart to spread
Its sweetness on the air,[38] yet still remains
The rose, so does the Cosmic Lover give
Himself in love to His creation with
But one desire—that it be channeled back
To Him through other hearts to whom it has
Been passed. For love is giving of the one
Self to another in endless circling.
Love is a sea of Cosmic Consciousness
Upon whose surface ride the swaying waves;
And as each breaks in foam, it takes the form
Of woman (or of man) whose streaming hair
Flows backward in the sea, whose eyes look out
To other eyes across a narrow space,
Whose voice cries out in liquid melody,
"I love you and I long for your embrace."

The Farer

How sweet the thought that human love is one
With Cosmic Love and that beneath each wave
The boundless ocean of eternal life
Is the Eternal Bosom for mankind!

The Presence

When men have fully waked to unity
And each to each is linked in conscious love,
Then will a new and different race of men
Appear (and some there are who like yourself,
Are on the planet now) who have survived
The concepts of a dying age in which
All things were based upon or measured by
Material force and dualistic thought—
A universe mechanical; with man
A captive, slave to instinct, and the laws
Evolved therefrom to regulate the race
By stern taboos in morals and in faiths.

The Farer

How will the new age then replace the old?
By what shall it be known?

The Presence

       Look to the Me,
For in the Me the world is born again—
A sense of spaceless space and timeless time,
The measurement of things by a new scale—
A *direct* knowing, cosmic consciousness,
A world alive, a breathing universe,
Soul-knowledge which transcends the intellect
And codifies its own morality
And proves its faith *by living*, not *by laws;*
Which sets its compass by soul-star light,
And not by charts of ancient mariners.

The Farer

> The son of man shall then find place where he
> May lay his head?[39]

The Presence

> It is through love the revelation comes,
> For love bears witness to itself, nor does
> The lover need a proof he is in love.
> And love cannot exclude; it spreads beyond
> The one beloved. Encircling all within
> Its reach, its never-ending ripples run
> To timeless shores, embracing all and by
> The All embraced, For where love is, God is.

The Farer

> It was through love I understood; through love
> And thee I have been reconciled with life,
> And all its seeming contradictions have
> Been harmonized. Henceforth when doubts assail
> I will within the crucible of love
> Dissolve them all; and welcome each demand
> On faith, however stern, for thus I grow
> Through trials met and overcome by love
> Into the likeness of the Love Divine.

The Presence

> Then are you near the hour of revelation
> When you shall find that you are unified,
> With all your selves into the total Me.

The Farer

> I give thee thanks, O friend and more than friend
> That I have found my over-self, the end
> And final consummation of my quest;
> It was from thee, O friend so wise, so good,
> I found the way of love, and understood.

My love for thee is like a fountain spring
Remaining full though laving ev'rything.
In ev'ry Farer who shall pass my door
I shall see thee and know we met before.
He shall in me find shelter, warmth and light,
Though my heart crave for thee throughout the night.
I yearn for thee and on the altar-stair
I long to place some priceless work of art,
But I can only offer thee myself
And give thee all the love within my heart.
Oh, that myself would grow...

How dark the day would dawn, how black the night
If I should lose thee, Presence, from my sight!
Yet shouldst thou vanish from the inner eye,
I still would feel thee somehow standing nigh.

The Presence
Love is expansion of the self and he
Who centers thought and heart upon the Me
Becomes aware of cosmic unity.
Man is to God what moon is to the earth,
What earth is to the sun; and in the birth
And growth of love, the secret force is found
By which the soul to Over-Soul is bound.
Nor earth nor man upon the Void is tossed
To whirl in space, and in the vastness lost;
But, bound by ties invisible to sense,
Both are sustained by love's omnipotence.

Take time to know, take time to care and feel
The relaxed power of the Eternal Real
Whose unstrained strength is like to that of steel.
Your body holds the cosmic force and fire
With which God molded earth to his desire,
And in your heart the motivating force
Which holds the spheres in mystic intercourse!

Look not to distant times and far-flung spaces
To find fulfillment in heavenly embraces,
Nor to some age Unwisdom has projected
Wherein the soul must still be resurrected,
But look to NOW for Love's fulfilled reward
And find in Love your Master and your Lord.

The Scribe

The theme of love was music to inspire
The Farer's heart; he seemed himself a lyre
Whose singing strings the leitmotif began—
The key of life God used to fashion man.
To this refrain love acted troubadour,
And he was lost in ecstasy once more,
His soul enraptured and still serene with peace,
Like that high world where earthly strivings cease;
And knowledge, love and beauty blend
In happiness and union without end.
He seemed to pass beyond the bounds of this
Soul-searing world into a world of bliss,
An ever-circling river in whose tide
The past and present pour and there abide;
Where all the opposites of a world of space
Unite, nor conflicts find a dwelling place,
But each absorbed in each, and each in one,
Through love are merged, and life in heav'n begun.

Second Book

Then could I clearly see the ALTAR OF
THE AGES, object of devoted love
Of untold millions of the human race
Who rendered worship in this sacred place.
Behind the altar in rainbowed arcs of light,
I saw a priest, arrayed in silver-white...

The altar of the ages

The Farer

Let him but *dream* of heaven whose eyes
Have never *viewed* the spires of Paradise!
Or let him search as I myself have done
With fainting heart—how pitiless the sun,
How dry with age the skin-embalméd scroll!
In fevered search for light upon the soul.
But I need *dream* no more, for I have seen
With my own eyes behind this mortal screen
Into that realm where cosmic memory
Preserves the past; and it was given me
To see and hear the masters and the sages
Who walked the earth back through unnumbered ages.

I was in meditation and I fell
Too deep into the mystery to tell
In words coherent save to those whose sight
Has pierced the veil that screens the astral light
And seen into another space to wit
Another world and enter into it,
And like myself beheld the ether shake
And souls appear with bodies so opaque
That we can view the harvest of the years,
The life and works of masters and the seers.[1]
And find the proof that what doth seem as past
Is the eternal present and will last.
The panorama of the ages would
Have been but mist had I not understood
Through thee, O Presence, true and good,
Who pointed out each scene and each event,
Each soul-form of the master, what it meant.

I was enrapt and passed from forms of thought
Until I was in vision so upcaught
I entered into super-self and knew
The ecstasy of *being* through and through.

A mist went up and spreading fold on fold
Condensed to clouds that caught the white and gold
Of some far sun and, piling mass on mass
(In huge escarpments cut by wide crevasse),
Seemed like a range of mountains great and high
That pierced a dome of blue that crowned the sky;
And on their crests translucent clouds, that spun
A veil to shield the eyes from cosmic sun
Too bright to look upon, but setting free
A rainbow arch that bridged eternity
With time. Along the rugged slopes, the steep
Ascent was cut by canyons deep on deep
And rushing rivers leaped in foaming falls
Into a sea that lay beneath the walls.

Before me stretched this vast and crystal sea
Between the shores of time and of eternity.
Down to the bridge that spanned the gulf I saw
The saints and sages, keepers of the law,
Lead bands of pilgrims out of every clime,
Freed from the burdened slavery of time.
Across the sands the master highways ran
Thronged by the souls who formed the caravan;
And everywhere, from south and north, from west
And east the pilgrims crossed the crest
Of mountains sloping to the sea; and on
They came, the multitudes who from the dawn
Of human day had through the troubled ages
In serried ranks been led by ancient sages
Who marched beneath the banner, LORD OF KINGS,
And all of whom bore gifts and offerings
To place upon an altar which was set
Beside the sea where earth and heaven met.
It was permitted me to view the past
And prove as *fact* what I believed, at last.
Space turned to minute form in astral lights
And from afar beyond the towering heights,
(Borne on the winds, that whirl in space

217

From the Eternal Dwelling Place,
As thunder rolls when lightning speaks aloud)
I heard a great voice crying through a cloud,
"The tabernacle of God is with men
And God Himself shall dwell with them
And He shall wipe away all tears from eyes
That weep, and pain shall be no more; not one
Shall sorrow for death no more shall be.
I am Beginning and the End, and he
Who turns his heart and thought to Me
Shall never thirst but ever is my son."[2]

Then could I clearly see the ALTAR OF
THE AGES, object of devoted love
Of untold millions of the human race
Who rendered worship in this sacred place.
Behind the altar in rainbowed arcs of light,
I saw a priest, arrayed in silver-white,
Melchizedek, eternal priest and king
Of righteousness and peace, outrivaling
All priests of all the altars of the earth,
Who could not die nor had he second birth
But wore the miter placed upon his brow
By LIFE and not by LAW[3] and took the vow
Of fealty to God from all the saints and sages
As he had done throughout the endless ages;
Not Jesus only but every seer to wait
Before the shrine had been initiate
Of the Order of Melchizedek. This
Master sage and priest whose genesis
Is hid among the stars whence he acquired
The teleois[4] measurements which inspired
The temples and the pyramids that show
In human frames and in a flake of snow.[5]
Then first appeared Great Rama to my view
With poets and singers in his retinue
Who joined in Vedic hymns of the creation,

The first of all the faiths of correlation
Of men with God; and I beheld the morn
In blazing light where Eastern faiths were born.

"...The Vedic Hymns you hear, which tell the tale
Of First Creation's dawn, are echoes from
Millennia of chants across the hills
Of India, which rolling out for all
Mankind became the source of all great faiths."

The Vedic hymns

2

Of First Creation's Dawn

The Farer

    I roused within myself and heard a voice,
    "I will translate for you, for wisdom lies
    In thought as well as speech, and Veda means
    The knowledge[6] of all things, all Cause and
    All effects; and the initiate sees
    Through Nature's veil the moving forms of Truth.
    The Vedic Hymns you hear, which tell the tale
    Of First Creation's dawn, are echoes from
    Millennia of chants across the hills
    Of India, which rolling out for all
    Mankind became the source of all great faiths."

    I could not tell who spoke but listened well.
    "Behind the tales of gods and metaphors
    Of nature, you can hear the sages speak
    Of Him Who dwells apart, the One Alone.
    And He was THAT, and neither Being nor
    Non-Being—*then* He breathed and from his breath
    The substance of the spheres began as space
    And taking shape appeared in varied forms.
    'Yet who He was or what He was, who knows?'
    They said, 'for how can finite comprehend
    The Infinite?' It is enough to know
    He is the All. From Him the world has come,
    In Him contained, to Him it will return!"[7]

    These are but terms to fit the finite mind,
    For he did not *create*, but he *became*,
    For He is Brahm, Eternal Essence, who
    Has never changed but He made visible
    That which He is; nor can aught be destroyed
    For He inhales and forms will disappear.
    The Real is never seen and it is well;
    "Our sense deceives," said the interpreters.

They further said that that which first appeared
To human eyes is formless, and was known
As *Agni,* sacred fire, or Spirit pure,
Eternal-Masculine: and *Soma*[9] is
His mate, Eternal-Feminine, the soul
Of Nature, womb of worlds invisible
And visible alike. And from these two—
These aspects of the One, a third appears,
Which Krishna called the Word and which the scribe
Called John proclaimed as Logos to the world.
This cosmogonic act, the Vedas teach
Is *sacrifice,* the One *divides* Himself
And manifests as Mother and as Son.

From this the great redemptive faiths were born,
Wherein the disunited soul is brought
Through Krishna, Buddha, Dionisos,
Osiris, Christ, to union once again
With the eternal consciousness of Truth—
That there is One Alone and that the Fall
Of Man is his belief in Two—of Good
And Evil.
              Once again the voice was low
But gaining strength it quoted from
The ancient manuscript: " 'Fear not, the day
Of Brahma cometh to an end.'"
                              I may
Not understand, but this it seemed to me,
Time will dissolve into Eternity.

And everywhere his teaching spread across

The mountains and the seas—equality

Of Races, of victor and of vanquished,

The end of human sacrifice, respect

For woman in the home, belief that souls

Survive, that men should venerate their dead

And tend the sacred fire in reverence for

The Nameless God.

                And thus his message came

To ancient Egypt and to Eastern lands

And circled back to Cythia again.

Rama, founder of faiths

The Farer

 I saw thee, Rama, stalk across the dawn
 Of history, along Caucasian slopes
 With all thy vast array of Cythians[10]
 Into the fertile valleys of Iran.
 The ethers shook again, and there you stood
 Before the sacred fire against the moon.
 On Holy Night when the Night Mother gives
 Rebirth to sun and year, I heard thee speak:

 "Within this sacred fire behold with me
 The symbol of the unity divine
 In which the visible is ever one
 With the invisible. I do proclaim
 That Light is Life and Life is deity.
 And at this Yuletide I do consecrate
 The newborn child to Nature and her god.
 And I do make the law of God the law
 For men; and woman shall no longer be
 The priestess of the temple, but shall tend
 The sacred fire upon the hearth of home."

 I saw him yet again withdrawn and lone
 And watched him plot the stars and fix the twelve
 Signs of the zodiac beginning with
 The Ram, the constellation of the fire
 Or Universal Spirit which confers
 Upon initiates the knowledge of the Truth.
 The panorama moved and I once more
 Beheld the great lord Rama with his eyes
 Of lotus-blue that smiled into the eyes
 Of men, a father-mother soul who bound
 All beings with the chains of Love.[11]

                              And they
 In glowing faith took up the march with him
 Along the mountain path to India,
 And here his faith subdued the magic arts

Of priests of devil-gods whose temple shrines
Were foul with serpents fed on human flesh.
For he appeared among them with a torch
Of light of Truth and they were stupefied
With awe and crawled into infernal caves.
And when at length his work was done, with his
Elect he disappeared in his retreat
On Mount Albori where he taught to them
The secrets linking Nature to her god.

And everywhere his teaching spread across
The mountains and the seas—equality
Of Races, of victor and of vanquished,
The end of human sacrifice, respect
For woman in the home, belief that souls
Survive, that men should venerate their dead
And tend the sacred fire in reverence for
The nameless God.
                    And thus his message came
To ancient Egypt and to Eastern lands
And circled back to Cythia again.

My eyes half-blinded by the radiant light
That shone around the altar, I could see,
Surrounded by his priests and acolytes,
The white-robed prophet, Mithras' sacred son,
The soul-pure Zoroaster, sainted one
Of Persia's golden age, who taught and lived
For centuries before the advent of
The prophet of Judea who taught as he...

Zoroaster, Mithras' priest

The Farer
My eyes half-blinded by the radiant light
That shone around the altar, I could see,
Surrounded by his priests and acolytes,
The white-robed prophet, Mithras' sacred son,
The soul-pure Zoroaster[12], sainted one
Of Persia's golden age, who taught and lived
For centuries before the advent of
The prophet of Judea who taught as he:
Yes, I saw him who first of all the race
Gave concept of a conscience to mankind—
Which like an angel moves with man throughout
His life, remaining pure from evil and
Accompan'ing to heav'n the home-bound soul.

So sweet the romance of the soul, which as
It passes o'er the bridge Tchinvat, the bridge
Of Retribution, sees a maid advance
With welcome on her lips! Astonished by
Her beauty and her grace, the soul inquires,
"Who art thou? thou who seemest unto me
More beautiful than any daughter of
The earth." To which she makes reply, "I am
Thine own good works, the incarnation of
Good thoughts, good words, good actions and good faith."
Yet if the life be bad and evil thoughts
Have entered in, then shapes horrific meet
The soul—and it is thus *by conscience* judged,
The final arbiter of its own fate.

So was I taught and told that evil is
The negative of good but need not be.
And I perceived that Zoroaster showed
A harmony behind the dual face
Of deities: that evil is not absolute—
But absence of the good, as darkness is
The absence of light; and that the Light
Is God, the universal Word, the Real,

Which will at length absorb and dissipate
The mimic god; and that Ahriman will
Be swallowed up by Ormuzd.
                              This I knew,
But now the *ignis subtillissimus*
Revealed the astral forms of acolytes
And priests of every land and age who moved
In long processional each on a line
Or path which ran unerringly into
The cosmic center—and there a shrine
Majestic—THE ALTAR OF THE AGES!
And each religion bore a banner bright
With its own crest against a field of light,
And then I saw that all lights were the same,
The Light of Lights, known as the Nameless Name.[13]

The scene was swiftly changed: it is not giv'n
To look too long upon the light of heav'n.
For suddenly the moon was full, a great
Illumined shield that caught the rays of some
Far cosmic sun; and Zoroaster came
Accompanied by his priests, the sainted twelve
Who bore each one a censer in his hand.
And on the altar I beheld the spheres,
A replica of our own galaxy;
And when the sun of day came forth to shine,
These orbs became inflamed and each revolved
In its own circuit 'round their central sun;
And clear and sweet, a singing sound was heard,
A music real but seeming magical.[14]

But now the rose of dawn announced the day
And on the eastern rim the sun began to rise,
And Zoroaster spoke, "Behold, He comes;
The Mighty Mithras, the messenger of God,
Protector of the Truth, the enemy
Of evil and of falsehood, Holy Fire
Which purifies the soul of false desire.

Behind this veil of flame, for eyes too bright,
Is Ormuzd, God of gods and Light of light."
Then kneeling there in humble ecstasy,
They chanted, "God in Light, we worship Thee."

"Bright, bright, bright is the path of God,
Light, light, light is the way of Truth,
Warm, warm, warm is the flame of love,
Holy, holy, holy is the eternal light.
The sun and stars all sing Thy praise,
The sky is filled with Thy presence,
Divine is the holy Son of Light,
Wondrous the pathway of peace,
Holy is the Eternal Word,
Blessed the manger of Truth,
Holy the Child of Love,
Warm are the Mother-arms,
Divine the offering of Heaven."

Then suddenly the ether seemed to shudder,
The *ignis subtillissimus* grew dim;
And all the figures faded from my sight,
Save that I saw a child, an acolyte,
Whose face stood out, still luminous at night.

"If so it be, as I believe, that He,
Our God is hidden in the heart, and yet
Man loses sight of Him and plunges once
Again into the depths of ignorance,
How then will he awake to primal truth?"

Prophets of India

5

Krishna, the Radiant

The Farer

The Past is by the Past so overlaid,
It would be lost save that one radiant face,
One form supreme shines through the mists of Time,
One voice reveals a newborn truth and gives
New vision to a race of half-blind men.
And it was so with *Thee*, thou son of heav'n,
Thou first of all the avatars sprung from
A virgin womb, thou child of cosmic love,
Whose valor slew the serpent-headed beast
Of aged ignorance and the devil gods.

I saw thee seat thyself upon the sward,
Beneath the cedar trees; the autumn moon
Fell on thy Brahmic face and thou didst pluck
The vina's strings and tell the raptured throngs
The tales of gods and heroes and the wars
Of Rama the divine...And seeing them
Too far entranced by thee, thou taughtest them
To sing the glorious deeds of heroes and
Of gods, in tune with thee, with beating drums
And cymbals; and with arms and hands
And rhythmic step, to execute a dance
Which showed in pantomime the majesty
Of Brahm and passion of the hearts of those
Who served or suffered in His sacred name.

Time passed, and Krishna lived in forest depths
With anchorets who saw in him the son
Of Mahadeva, Divine Intelligence
Or Father of all beings; and son
Of Devaki the virgin, faultless soul
Who formed with them the Sacred Trinity.
And here it was he taught those truths divine,
The very sound of which is so inspired

That beauty floods the listening soul
With such delight it overflows in tears
Of purest joy; while yet the inner eye
Beholds in clearer light the sacred face
Of Krishna and the devotees of Truth,
Of whom each one could, word by word, recite
The Vedas, all by heart.
                              I see thee, now,
The seven-knotted staff within thy hand;
The sacrifice of fire to Agni is complete
And thou hast bent thy loving look upon
The noble face of young Arjuna, king
And heir of the Pandavas, descendent
Of the solar monarchs who with Rama
Fought and overcame the worshippers of
Luna gods and goddesses whose shrines were
Consecrate to serpents and the devil gods
Of evil, ignorance and lust and fear,
"And I have come to earth again as once
Before, to turn men's hearts to knowledge of
The soul, invisible, impond'rable
Immortal and divine[15]...Man is triune,
His soul must find its place in *Sattva,* with
Wisdom and with peace, but the passions,
Or Rajas dominate, intelligence
Is lost and Man is spun upon a wheel
From which is no escape; and if it be
He yields to body-sense and its desires,
He into *Tamas* falls, in ignorance and
Temporary death."

The Farer (continues)
                              "How can we then escape?"
My self inquired it of my deeper self,
"If so it be, as I believe, that He,
Our God is hidden in the heart, and yet
Man loses sight of Him and plunges once

Again into the depth of ignorance,
How then will he awake to primal truth?"

I heard reply: "Man does not *lose* his soul,
But loses *sense* of soul until a soul
Like Krishna or the Christ appears so bright
With consciousness of God that he inspires
In other hearts the longing for the good,
And thus he mediates his god to man.
Divinely human, humanly divine,
Such souls are seen and heard and so become
To us the voice of God. How dazzling is
The vision they inspire! Yet tragic oft
Their fate, misunderstood alike by all—
Condemned and persecuted by the race,
Their mission misconceived by those who wish
To chain the seeing soul to monstrous creed
Of fallen man redeemed by suffering.
The Masters made no claim to pay for sins
To angry gods for other men, but to
Provide a knowledge of the way whereby
Man might redeem himself from lust and false
Desires, and step by step unfold the god
Already hid within. It is their word
That THOU ART THAT, a god concealed within.
Revere each avatar for what he was—
A soul who lived as you yourself can live,
A soul who knew what you yourself can know,
A soul who was what you yourself can be."

Akasha quivered once again and I
Perceived on Mount Merou the seated form
Of Krishna on whose face the light still glowed
From his transfiguration when he saw
His Virgin-Mother and the angel hosts,
And was aware that he was son of the
Divine Intelligence, the Father of
All beings.

236

Stretched out before the prince
A happy valley lay and forests of
Great cedar trees and mangoes blossoming.
A placid pond drowsed in the sun, strewn o'er
With wheel-like lotus blooms that tell the tale
Of cycles of existence. Ardent bees
Profanely pierced their treasury and bore
Away the golden loot; while drowsy storks,
In reverie, gave them no heed nor to
The shrilling cries of pheasants amorous.
The holy Rishis, mind-born sons and heirs
To wisdom of those seven seers who heard
The Vedas sung by cosmic choirs, came from
Their hermitage to listen glorified.

.   .   .   .   .

Three thousand years it was before the Christ
Of Galilee would once again affirm
Lord Krishna's words of love of man for man:—
"Just as the earth forgives the trampling feet
And plough that rend her bosom, so ought we
To render good for evil. The evils we
Inflict upon our neighbor follow us
As does our shadow...Works of love are best
And will outweigh thy faults...If thou dost keep
Thy company with righteous men alone,
Thy good example bears but little fruit;
Fear not to live among the wicked men
To bring to *them* the light...To *know* is not
Enough...Good deeds are all in vain until
The humble heart, in love of Him, has laid
Them down at Brahma's feet...Search for
The Me...who seeketh Me, vowed to the Me,
That man I love." Such were his doctrines new.

Then in a voice exalted, Krishna sang
Of Him Who Is and Was and Is to Be:

Ageless He, unborn, undying,
From Whom all things have come.
In Him they live, to Him return.
He is the Source of all,
The light within the soul of man;
He is center and circumference:
Those who dwell with Him find peace,
Those who love His Presence become one with Him,
All-pervading, over-dwelling and imminent;
He is the Lord of Life,
The glow of dawn, the gleam of day;
He is the midnight darkness,
The moon, the sun, the stars;
He is the song of heaven,
The dancer of all dances,
The weaver of all music;
He is the Lord of all earthly life,
The Wayshower and the way that is shown,
The whirlpool and the wind.
He is the life beneath the ocean's surface;
He is the sight of the eye, beholding all;
The hearing of the ear, hearing all;
The speech of the mouth.
There is no speech beyond His saying
Or words He does not utter.
He is the writer of all hymns of Faith,
The substance and the shadow.
He is action and reaction,
The law, the seed and the deep silence.
Nothing exists outside Him,
He is both formless and the formed,
The unadorned and the adorning,
The worshipper who lives upon the earth,
The whispering of prayer.
He is the One who answers,
The altar before which all worship,
He is the prophet, seer and sage,
The teacher and the teaching of the ages.

He is the earth, the skies,
The rainbow in the mists of heaven.
He and He alone has life,
All within Him live forever.
He is the Ancient of Days,
The nameless and the named;
The calm within the storm,
The voice speaking from the silence.
He is That Which alone is Real—
The unreal has no existence.
He is that which never came to birth—
The unborn; He is the birth of all.
Undying, He is transition;
Uncaught by time, He is the timeless.
He is the self within all selves,
The changeless in which change takes place;
He is beyond all space and time;
Time and space are his garments.
He is the Atman of man's being,
The overlord of all the parts.
Concealed in everything, pervading all,
He is the soul of all that lives,
The permanent, eternal and self-existent.
Of all effects, He is the essence.
He is the begetter of all begotten,
The Father of the Sons of life,
The Mother who conceived their being.

Brahma, Lord of all creation,
Lord of Wisdom, Lord of Right,
Lead us from the paths of folly,
Lead from darkness into Light.
Brahma, joy of all creation,
Life of life and love of love,
Gently lead us to salvation,
Lead us to the heights above.
Thou within all things, around them,
Brahma, Light of Life Divine,

Shatter all our days of dreaming,
Change our being into Thine.
Rob the mind of its illusion,
Strip the ego, naked, bare,
'Til the waiting heart within us
Finds Thy Presence hidden there.

Let the soul awake to Brahma
That it no more separate be;
That the life that seemed divided
Be not lost but found in Thee.

The Farer

Arjuna sat as one entranced, and love
Enveloped him as in a cloud. And he
Who wills can read in the Celestial Song
Of him on whom the light of Krishna fell,
Of how he understood the mysteries
And dared to pit his sun-god strength against
The lunar gods and devil-worshippers—
A history set down in script in after-years
In that same century[16] when Moses heard
Jehovah's voice proclaim the Unitary God
Whom Krishna had made known.
                                    How Great
Thou wert and art, O thou whose beam of light
Celestial falls across the pages of
All faiths; who reaffirmed the Trinity,
The Manifested Word, assurance of
A life beyond the grave and spoke these words:
"Know then, that soul which has found God is freed
From death, rebirth, old age and grief."

Of Krishna I can say no more save that
I saw the primal substance, weaving, form
The pattern of his death, which he forecast,
And so designed, a sacrificial act
To set his seal upon the doctrine of

The soul. Beneath the cedar tree he knelt
To pray. The archers of the king and of
The lunar priests fell back abashed and filled
With fear when they beheld his raptured face,
But when at length they bound him to the tree
Insulting him and casting stones, he made
No effort to escape, and when at last
An arrow pierced his flesh from which the blood
Gushed forth, he cried out words of victory.
Transfixed again, he called to Devaki,
"My radiant Mother, grant that those who love
Me enter with me in thy light." And at
The third, he cried out with a single word—
"Mahadeva" and with the name of God
Upon his lips, fell into bliss."[17]

Through you, O Buddha, Light of Asia, we
Behold the law that binds or sets souls free...

Ascription to Buddha

Through you, O Buddha, Light of Asia, we
Behold the law that binds or sets souls free—
You who through reason's higher vision saw
The ever-turning circuits of life's law;
Yours was the offering of celestial light
That pierced the darkness of the veil of night.
You saw the souls incarnate on the earth
Bound endlessly in fear of death and birth
By black belief that in the soul is hidden
The faults of former lives, and that unbidden
It must return to suffer; yet it then
Will sin once more and must return again.
You saw the wheel of life go round and round
On which imprisoned souls of men are bound—
You who believed lives come and go
To pay to earth the karmic debt they owe.[18]
You showed the way of wisdom by which men
Escape the chains that bind them back again
And proved to them that from the timeless shore
Enlightened souls need to return no more.
If they be free from fell illusion's blight,
They pass from darkness to Nirvana's light.
The soul evolves, nor e'er again returns,
But finds the peace toward which it fondly ycarns.
Man is self-bound and by himself set free
When he shall take the Path, O Buddha, set by thee.

He sat himself to meditate within
The shadow of a fig or Bo tree where
In agony he wrestled with his doubts
Until he won to victory and for
Himself attained Nirvana from that day.

Buddha, the enlightened

The Farer

> How can I, being man, describe the scene
> When Buddha came, a demigod, to place
> His gift upon the Altar of the Ages,
> How it seemed the great Melchizedek himself
> Was moved: and what the Presence said to me?

The Presence

> From prince to pauper, from mendicant
> To god, the romance of a soul who claimed
> No soul, no primal entity, yet taught
> As none so well has taught *the way to grow*
> A soul![19]
> In this is all of Buddha told; who knows
> It not, knows naught what Buddha gave mankind.
> How dread the fate of faiths, how dead the soul
> Of India until he came! The Song
> Celestial and the Vedic joy in life
> Snuffed out by witchcraft and astrology—
> The ancient Brahmic lore degenerate!
> And then he came! Gotama's son was heard
> "Beating the drums of the ambrosia."[20] Yet made
> No claim to be the Buddha nor was called
> As such by them until he passed beyond.

The Farer

> Then I beheld the panorama shake
> And scene by scene I read his life and works;
> I looked across well-watered fields of rice
> To peaks of the Himalayas against
> The clear-blue Indian skies; and on the banks
> Of the Lumbini, flowing quietly,
> I saw a garden under satin-trees,
> And there had Matna Maya[21] stopped to rest
> And there she brought a raja's son to birth,
> Heir to Gotama's wealth and royalty
> ...The shifting scene portrayed a buoyant youth,
> A charming sportsman, living handsomely,

With his beloved wife and infant son...
Yet sore distressed by unsolved problems of
Existence and the sight of suffering
And broken age, disease and loathsome death...
Then came the day he saw a Wanderer[22]
Who walked serene and dignified amid
The throng..."I, too, will be a Wanderer,"
He thought. That night he bid his servant go
Prepare a mount; and, giving soft
Farewell to sleeping wife and babe, he rode
Away to Anoma.[23] And here took pause
Upon its sandy banks, cut off his long
And waving hair with his own sword, bid
His servant Channa take it with his rings
And jeweled ornaments back to his wife;
Then seeking out a jungle-cave, he lived
For six long years in penitence and pain
In hope of a deliverance from grief
Of mind and tortures of despair that spring
From ignorance and doubt of human destiny,
Until his fame was spread "like to the sound
Of a great bell hung in the canopy
Of Indian skies."[24]

       But it did not avail.
One day his frail and weakened frame collapsed;
He fell as dead amidst the wreckage of
His hopes of a deliverance by way
Of suffering...Then he began to eat
And straightly his disciples fell away!
In full despair of learning life from death
He turned his thoughts toward home but, rallying,
He sat himself to meditate within
The shadow of a fig or Bo[25] tree where
In agony he wrestled with his doubts
Until he won to victory and for
Himself attained Nirvana[26] from that day.

The Farer (continues)

I was in vision once again and, lo,
Before my psychic sight appeared in view
The Altar of the Ages and I saw
The Buddha standing there surrounded by
A host of witnesses. I knew him not
At first among the sacred throng, for I
Had seen him only as a prince or in
Squat figures cast in bronze or carved from jade
Or ivory; false images of some
False god, I thought, and passed them by, though I
Was vaguely touched by their serenity.
I heard him speak, in deep and bell-like tones
Which mark the avatar, discoursing on
His concept of the soul—his one sure key
To open wide the door and simplify
What might have been complex..."To sum it up,
My doctrine of the soul is this—there is
No soul, no fixed, unchanging entity,
But embryo unfolding endlessly.
It is not "being" but "becoming" like
A river's flow, a changing stream
Of consciousness[27] which deepens and expands
And moves through time into eternity.
But since it is in change, "becoming" leads
To difference and differences must lead
To dissolution. Both thought and form
Are in a constant flux so that no moment's "Me"
Can e'er repeat itself. Impermanence
Exists in all and in thyself.

                    "Then is
Man doomed?" Inquired a follower: "For if
All things at length dissolve and if
The wheel of change forever spins, there can
Be no escape from karmic law, I think."

Buddha

 Man cannot change the law but he can change
 The sequencies. The Noble Eightfold Path
 Will lead to his emancipation, for
 He who fills the stream of consciousness
 With Noble Truths and Love shall cause its depth
 Of waters to run clear: he shall be held
 From pains of guilt, which dying out will set
 Him free to enter in Nirvana.

The Farer

 Then did I hear such truths as Plato taught
 In after centuries.[28] For Buddha first
 Conceived and gave the Science of the Mind—
 That source of good or ill lies in the heart
 And in the consciousness; and joy or pain
 In "life to come" rests in the purity
 Or guilt of each who lives. Man has his choice!

 How wondrous were thy words! I thrilled to hear
 Thy deep and loving tones and gave a prayer
 Of gratitude that I had learned the law
 And so could understand.

Buddha Speaks

 There are three basic sins—"sense" and ill-will
 And worst of all, stupidity—the sin
 Which cannot be forgiven. Between the two
 Extremes—"sense" and asceticism—lies
 A Middle Path which leads to wisdom, peace
 And to Nirvana, named the Eightfold Path—
 Right Views and Aspirations, Speech, Conduct,
 Mode of Livelihood, Right Effort and Right
 Mindfulness and last of all Right Rapture.
 I do not teach suppression of desire
 But of a mind unwavering and free
 Of evil thoughts and speech, void of offense
 While everyday suffusing vicious men

With rays of loving thought; and from this plane
Include the whole wide world with thought of love,
Far-reaching, great, unmeasured, void of all
Ill-will and anger.[29]
                    He who cultivates
A heart of love toward all the world is wise;
To fail, is sign of his stupidity,
For love will hold him to Right Conduct
On his path and he can meet each change
And all vicissitudes with mind serene—
Such are but phantoms, shadows cast by his
Own ignorance—wise is the Eightfold Path!
To this I now make known Five Hindrances—
A lust for worldly things; corrosion of
The mind through wish to hurt a living thing,
The sloth of willful ignorance, and, fourth,
A fretful worried consciousness which finds
No place for peace; and last a mind that, like
A boat at sea, is pitched about by waves.

Once more I say, YOU are the cause that chains
You to the wheel, the rounds of birth, decay
And death; but karma is not endless pain—
It CAN be endless bliss and start today;
Nirvana is the dying out of false
Desires that lead again to suffering.
You need no more return upon the slow
Revolving of the circuits you create
For your undoing.

                    He who seeks to find
Some Greater Soul to pay his debts will still
Remain a debtor, but he can free himself who
Will destroy the power of ignorance
Through knowledge and pursuit of Truth.
Break through the dream of nescience which doth
Breed illusion, since Mother Maya is
The womb in which it generates, for thought

Is germ and it takes form for good or ill
By patterns you have set. Nirvana waits
The hour, the day, or the eternity
When you shall cast aside false knowing and
Through enlightened mind shall free yourself
From bondage to the whirling wheel.

Disciple

                              Of all
Thy precepts which is most to be desired?

Buddha

This have I oft defined: That man should seek
For others happiness he seeketh for himself.

The Farer

I sensed the trembling of the screen as though
The stage were being set for the last scene.
I seemed to hear the Pali poets' songs[30]
Of love raised to a cosmic plane yet soft
Attuned to harmonies inspired by
The seer who made no claim to deity,
But Arahatship, a state of worthiness,
Of which they sang:

                         "O island midst the floods,
O Holy City, farther shore, O Home
Of peace, the end of suffering, O joy
Supreme, this is the goal of goals."

                              And then
The last great words of Buddha softly fell:
"Be lamps unto yourselves and seek ye not
A refuge in that which lies beyond yourself;
Hold fast to Truth and go ye forth to teach
The Way; set out the higher life in all
Its fullness and its purity. Teach men
To seek salvation where alone it can
Be found, within themselves. Behold now, I

Exhort you, brethren, that you yourself
Work out your own salvation with all your
Diligence."[31]

"All things on earth," so Hermes said, "all forms
Are patterned from above, the Source is One
In essence, substance. Only He exists..."

8

Hermes, Egypt and
the law

All history begins within the mind
Of God. The story of a nation or
A race can best be read inscribed upon
The brain of one great seer or avatar
Who reads the cosmic scroll, becomes enthused,
With God intoxicate.[32] His vision is
The matrix of his race, its battlecry,
Its order and its laws. In Egypt first
Of all, the rule of kings was by the will
Of temple-priests. O mystic land, I stood
Beside the Sphinx[33] and heard its silent speech
Of untold centuries ago and of
Those seers who read the movements of the stars
And told in stone[34] the tale of evolution.
Thrice-Greatest-Hermes[35] might have read thy lips,
Priest, scholar, king, half-myth, half-man—but mind!
And it was he whom now I saw before
The Altar of the Ages, mighty soul
Who was the first to clarify the Law
Of Correspondences,[36] so long hermetic,
But now a commonplace among all schools
Of thought. Did you perhaps cross over land
From Mayas[37] in the West, intent to teach
The youthful Egypt the secrets learned
From Quiche priests ten thousand years ago?

I know this not but this believe, that you
Were first in history to show to mortal man
What he could know of God, Who cannot be
Defined and is invisible and
Without form, Source, and Causing Cause of All;
Who speaks and outer worlds appear...

                                        This wisdom, known
By priests, did Moses learn and write
Upon the scrolls the Levites later bore
Within the Ark with manna, rod and Law...
"All things on earth," so Hermes said, "all forms

Are patterned from above,[38] the Source is One
In essence, substance. Only He exists.
Sole generator, He Himself is Cause,
The only Cause, yet He is manifest
As Three—Nu, Tum and Phtah, a Trinity."
Age hid itself beneath the mists of time,
The Sphinx crouched on its granite hill
And kept its watch beside the Pyramid
Of Gizeh where initiates were shown
These cosmic mysteries—the Sphinx whose eyes
Were fixed upon eternity the while
The waters of the sea below filled up
With silt, and desert wastes engulfed it in
The sands of time.
              Yet had those lips a voice,
They might recall some seven thousand years
Or more when first was seen the brilliant light
Of Rama shining from the east, and priests
And seers conjoined their streams of Truth[39] and
Ammon-Ra became the solar god of Thebes,
And Menes, first of Pharoahs' priestly kings.

The Farer's Query
    "What is the secret key that will unlock
The mysteries of Egypt?"—This did I ask,
And softly heard—
              "There is no mystery
For him who knows the Mysteries. Hid in
Himself the answer lies, for none but *self*
Can find or know the self; the goal is not
To *know* but *be,* for knowing leads thee to
Becoming. Thou art soul and now possess
Those buried qualities, that hidden sense
Which can be brought to life and consciousness."
This is the object of the mysteries,
And the initiate can enter here
On earth into the knowledge and the life
Of God.

The pageant of the mysteries
Portrays the journey and provides the keys
By which the soul can reach Amenti's shore:
The bold initiate must pass the door
Where Isis sits, "whose veil no mortal hand
Has ever raised"; escape the burning brand,
The fiery furnace and the stagnant lake;
And lured by singing harp-strings, he must take
The path that skirts the bower wherein lies
A temptress whose beauty, fit for Paradise,
Conceals a peril deeper than the pit,
The promise of fulfillments exquisite.
Though willed his step, his eyes are backward turned
To that fair form for which his senses yearned.
But fairer still the vision in his soul,
He lifts his eyes and gazes on his goal.
He wins! he comes at last to his release
And at the feet of Isis finds his promised peace.

. . . . .

This is but part and having passed the test,
He is prepared by gods to be possessed.
Through passages of stone the priests now bring
The candidate to Chamber of the King;
Where in a stone sarcophagus he lies,
Outstretched as on a cross, with open eyes;
A hierophant exerts his dominance,
Inducing sleep; he falls into a trance
Yet hears the voice that straightly charges him
To leave his body and, through the passage dim
To find his way to Light and Life that lie
Beyond the tomb beneath an open sky.
"Today is resurrection and thy *Kou*[40]
Becomes aware that it is ever you.
The mysteries possess a torch to light
Thy path through death and fearful shapes of night;
Thy genius holds the secret past, and can

Unfold the future to immortal man.
One Only Soul is All—that One gave birth
To all the souls, the mortal gods of earth.
Thy soul is His, thou knowest this at last,
Go, take thy way, 'THY JUDGMENT SHALL BE PASSED.'"

He finds himself, soul-farer, on the way
That leads from death down to the Judgment Day
In deep Amenti's land confronted by
The Law, Maât, the goddess in whose eye
Calm justice shines; she is his advocate—
True justice comes not early nor too late.
She pleads his cause before Osiris who
Sits on his throne and calmly hears her through.
Upon one scale an image of the law
Is placed, of Maât, acting monitor,
And on the other scale is laid his heart
And he is judged according to the part
He played in life on earth, good works or sin—
His fate decreed by what his past had been,
Not by the god; he knows the fault is his
That he has made himself just what he is.

The Farer
My mind bedazed with glimpse of things I thought
Unknown, unknowable, I listened, caught
My breath in fear of judgment and my fate:
The Voice went on, began to correlate
The Laws of Manu[41] and the Maât Law—
Each seemed to each to be the creditor.

The Voice
The streams conjoin in Egypt, each alike
Proclaims one law of conduct, and the soul
May not attain Nirvana nor the bliss
Of its absorption into God nor can
Return unto the Father's House until
It pass the test imposed upon itself.

257

If good outweighs the evil of his days,
If he has been a father and a friend
To those in want, he need not dread the end;
He cannot enter to a world of bliss
Unless he first begins it here in this.
But if his works were good, then he can claim
Identity with God and take his name—
"Known as Osiris, he has become as He"
And enters life throughout eternity.
The soul which by its works is purified
In Brahma's[42] bosom ever will abide.
The *names* of God and gods shall pass away;
No more the need of rites or "Passion Play";
Old Night shall yield to the Eternal Day.[43]
Not death but life—of gods, shall be but One;
Look deep into the West when day is done
And you shall see the East, THE RISING SUN.

The Farer

The diorama moved as though I were
Enclosed within a wheel and saw its spokes
All centered in myself, yet running out
Into infinity; each spoke, a god,
Each god, an attribute of One, and I was one
With One and had no name, nor had God name.
The priests of Egypt, ev'ry one appeared
And bore an image of a god who had
A name but ev'ry priest bore in his heart
The knowledge of the Nameless One and laid
His gift upon the ALTAR OF THE AGES;
Then drew his robes apart and sank to earth
Upon his naked knees. The High Priest bowed
His head crowned with the white tiara and
The horns[44] of Rama while from his breasts
There flashed the fire of the symbolic stones.

The pontiff lifted up his hand and then
I heard the sweet voice of an acolyte:

Acolyte

Speak, O Sphinx, and break the silence
Of the age-old mystery;
Why the horror of unknowing,
What has Time revealed to thee?

The Pontiff

Speak not to wood or stone but give thine ear
To hear the voice of Him that speaks in thee.
When thou hast crossed the bridge dividing light
From darkness, time from eternity;
When thou no more shalt haunt the ghostly world
Of unreality and feel no more
The loss of that which seemed so tangible
And real—then shalt thou be afraid no more;
Nor doubt. As Shepera, the Father of
The gods did by his word create the worlds,
So dost thou draw from Him the power
And so create *thy* world. If now amiss
It seems, dark and illusory and full
Of pain and suffering, it is because
Thou hast not crossed the bridge into the real,
And still are subject to the laws of earth.

The Farer

I heard a voice but did not hear a voice—
Or did I hear? and if I heard how did
It speak? Was it to me or was it to
The acolyte? I do not know. IT SPOKE:

The Voice From The Altar

From sorrow and the horror of
Unknowing, be set free—
Self-knowing, known and knower
Are one with Changeless Me.
I am He, the Truth Incarnate,
Light of everlasting day,

It is I that speak within thee,
Life to each, the Truth and Way.

He who seeks and sees Me only,
Holding Me his heart's desire,
Finds the flame of life within him
Lighted at One Altar Fire.

All the paths of worship reach Me,
All the shrines to Me belong,
Hymns of praise in all the ages
Parts of My celestial song.

I, the end and the beginning.
And the bridge that lies between,
I am Father, Son and Mother,
I the Seen and the Unseen:

Clothed in Nature, garbed in spirit,
Hid in seed and air and stone,
In the sparrow and the nestling,
In the sower and the sown,

Smaller than the tiny atom,
Larger than the Cosmic Sea,
I am force that moveth in them—
Pageant and the pageantry.

I am Source, the Cause, the substance
Dark of earth and light of stars,
Of the sun and moon the variant,
Light of dawn, Aurora's bars.

I am root of ev'ry being,
They the branches, I the tree;
Seed and fruit, the past and future,
All that is revolves in Me.

In My hidden life, though formless,
I am form of all on earth,
I am Way and Life and Spirit,
I am present in thy birth.

I am both the life immortal
And as mortal bear a name,
I create though uncreated—
I the fire, the ashes, flame.

Splendor of the light supernal,
I am wisdom of the wise,
Giver, taker and the keeper,
I thy doom or paradise.

Flame of uncaught cause in heaven,
Seed of seed which passes on,
I am action and reaction,
Infant, age and breath withdrawn.

I am hid in evolution,
Silence, beauty, vision, will,
I alone revolve the cycle—
I, immovable and still.

He came to Sinai and the Great I AM
To claim the promise made to Abraham
And to himself, still unfulfilled. No tears
Had dimmed his eyes through all the tortured years,
For most he grieved for stubborn souls and cruel
With whom he waged a never-ending duel.

Moses and the great I Am

The Presence
Man is not born of dust but faith and fire,
Now burning low, now flaming high and higher
Until the brilliance challenges the sun,
And through such soul a new age is begun.
So was it then with thee, thou Moses, flame
From whose volcanic depths explodes the name
IEVE[45] and from this Father-Mother God
A son is born, the living Word, the Od.[46]
A lightening flash inspired the soul of him
Who first had known his God as Elohim,
The God of gods whose breath proclaimed the light
And formed the worlds from Chaos and Old Night.

The Farer's First Vision
The wheeling centuries spun slowly through
The arc of time and thus they brought to view
This man of iron and flame, this cosmic Jew.
Yes, I beheld the youthful Moses now;
How stern his face! and yet his lofty brow
Bore awe, that awful awe before his God
Which lifts the soul above the clay or clod,
So much exalted that the lesser eye
Cannot withstand the flaming of his sky;
And forced to brood upon the higher laws
Men have *through him,* contacted Causing Cause.

He, as Osiris' priest,[47] with others bore
The golden ark in which the precious store
Of sacred books was housed, protected by
The golden hawks which kept a seeing eye
Upon the final truth, its central sun—
"Gods are but names, there is no god save ONE."

A fiercely burning pride was in his heart
As with the Levites he traversed the mart
Of obelisks and monoliths and through
The lotus-pillared porticos to view

The Solar Ark, Osiris' temple, where
The public ark was trusted to his care.
His eyes outshone the fire from Membra's breast[48] —
Burned in his mind and set his soul aflame—
The last great secret, high and holiest,
"He[49] is but One, and I Am is His name."

No pride of place was his, but rather was
His granite soul upthrust by cosmic cause
That like an earthquake lifts the valley floor
To some high peak and with volcanic roar
Proclaims to all the trembling sons of men,
That some great change has come to earth again.
What thought exploded in his seething mind?
What was its meaning to all of humankind?
This! to tell the secret hidden there
For all the earth! to openly declare
That God is ONE and in one mighty blast
Place this truth *first,* which Egypt held as last;
With *this begin* and found a dynasty
Of state and church upon the mystery:
"O Israel hear, the Lord thy God is One
There is no other God, yea, there is none!"[50]

How stern the task! All other seers before
Created faiths for people to adore;
To Moses only was this task assigned—
From slaves and tribes and chaff of humankind
Create a people for a faith![51] and find
A way to lead them to some Promised Land
Through flood and desert, foes on ev'ry hand;
And to this end to use the cosmic force
Which he had learned from priestly intercourse,
The secret knowledge of Egyptian sages,
That mind created matter through the ages—
Not matter, mind.
        And *by his word,* he drew
Upon the cosmic life and overthrew

Magicians, kings and all the soldiery
And forced Rameses to set the people free.

The Farer's Second Vision

The scene was changed, I saw his granite face
On Sinai Mount where desert winds unbrace
The storms. I heard the tempest shriek
And thunder echo back from Serbal's peak
Across the plains of Horeb and Pharan—
Where Israel had encamped her caravan—
This noble soul endowed with wealth and wit
Who for the Law led forth this mob, unfit
For sacrifice like his. I marveled now
To read the pain, deep-chiseled in his brow,
Why had this demigod so willed his soul
To suffer for the sins of those whose whole
Desire was fleshpots back in Egypt's hand—
Who cared no more to seek the Promised Land.

He came to Sinai and the Great I AM
To claim the promise made to Abraham
And to himself, still unfulfilled. No tears
Had dimmed his eyes through all the tortured years,
For most he grieved for stubborn souls and cruel
With whom he waged a never-ending duel.
And even as he pled their cause before
The Elohim-Ieve, rebellious clans
Of Canaanites and Edomites and hosts
Of Arabs, Semites, Beni-Israelites
Revolted, cast their ornaments and rings
Into the melting pot to mold a calf
Of gold to worship Belphagor; and set
The wooden Ashtaroth upon an altar;
Then killed the bullocks and the ram;
And, drinking blood, they danced in nakedness
To tunes of tabors and *nevels*.

But by
His prayer the hand of God was stayed from wrath
And He inscribed in stone the Ten Great Laws;
Yet as his finger wrote, it flamed with fire
Because the Law bore punishment within
Itself, and lightning leaped along the walls
Of Sinai.
              Woe, woe it was that fell on
Israel when Moses came. For in despair,
He broke the tablets, ground the golden calf
To dust and strewed it on the water which he made
The people drink.
              Stern was his soul yet he
Once more went back to Sinai and once
Again received the tablets of the Law.
When he returned again, they were so filled
With awe they could not look upon his face
Because it shone with radiance from I AM.

I cannot tell the wonders that he wrought
Through knowledge of the cosmic force, the *Od*
Telesmic. Nor can I well describe
How he appeared in that great final scene
Upon the Mount of Moab where he viewed
Afar the Promised Land. And first he set
A curse upon the race, "who have betrayed
Their God, and shall be scattered to the winds,"
Yet then he prophesied: "The Lord, thy God
Said this to me, 'I will raise up to them
A prophet like to thee and I will put
My words into his mouth and what he speaks
Shall be required of him who hears, he must
Obey'"[52]
              Did he, perhaps, that moment see
The promised Christ and find reward for all
Those famished years? I know not though I think
He smiled ere angel's hands interred him there
On Moab in the desert wastes.

The Farer's Third Vision

But this
I know, the shifting elemental force
Projected him again upon the screen.
And it was he whom I in vision saw—
This mighty soul, proclaimer of the Law;
Before the Altar of the Ages, he
Stood reverently and bent his knee;
And that high priest who blessed great Abraham
Now blessed the prophet of the Great I AM,
Who stood among the mighty men of old,
Of Jewish priests and prophets manifold,
Saul, David, Solomon and Jeremiah
And Jesus—no people have stood higher
In God's esteem than that which Moses built,
To serve a faith, from Egypt's clay and silt.
He bore great dignity, yet such as shares
Humility which only greatness bears.
The cross of David on his breastplate shone,
Set with twelve jewels, each a precious stone;
But his own eyes were on the ark; he bowed
His head to the Shekinah,[53] mystic cloud
That hid the Presence twixt the Cherubim
Which through the wilderness had guided him.
He spoke:

"The promise is fulfilled and He
Enshrines Himself in all humanity.
In man is temple, ark and sacred shrine:
To every land and people I consign
The tablets of the Law, the scrolls, the rod,
The open secret of the I AM God."

Then priests and Levites joined in chant supreme
That came to me within my cosmic dream:
The Promised Land is reached,
The word fulfilled, the Covenant of God
Is justified. His name is known,

His people safely pass from sea to sea;
The plains exalted, the mountains are laid low,
The river of life flows through
The garden of our God,
Where blooms the fruitful tree.
The flocks are safe, the eagles soar,
The sparrow does not fear the hawk.
The lion and the lamb together lie
In pastures green—
And there is food for all.
The young are suckled at the breast
Of Cosmic Motherhood.
The serpent bears no sting
And life no more must feed upon
Itself, for God is All.

I, The Farer, Heard:
I heard angelic voices coming from
The wilderness and choirs antiphonal
Responding from above. The grandeur of
The theme was like an echo from the deep
Unchallenged spaces of eternity,
To ring upon the walls of time and space
And fade into infinity...
                              O chorus grand!
I have no words to tell the beauty and
The power and majesty of sound that rang
With vibrant life the while the chorus sang:
Holy, holy, holy, Infinite and Mighty,
Holy, holy, holy, Splendor of Life Divine,
Holy, holy, holy, Now and Forevermore,
Holy, holy, holy, Throngs of heaven progressing,
Holy, holy, holy, All that dwells within Thee,
Holy, holy, holy, In earth and sea and sky,
Holy, holy, holy, Sons of men united,
Holy, holy, holy, God and man united,
Holy, holy, holy, Heaven and earth united,
Holy, holy, holy, And all that is to be.

I, The Farer Saw:

The cloud of the Shekinah spreading wide
Enfolded all the singing priests inside
Save Moses, but out beyond the altar
I heard a million voices sing the psalter
And saw the singers: the Shekinah spread,
Illumined them and Moses spoke and said:

Moses

Children of the Most High God,
Followers of the I AM,
Keepers of the Ark of the Covenant,
Bearers of the Eternal Light,
Knowers of the sacred name,
Inheritors of the Promised Land:
What was revealed to me on the heights,
What was revealed to me in the silence,
What was spoken in the burning bush,
Is now proclaimed unto the world,
Is now made known to all men,
Is now the promise fulfilled to all people.

Hear, O Is-ra-el!

The Lord Thy God is One Lord,
The Lord Thy God is the Lord of All;
He who brought you from the land of suffering,
He who brought you from the land of burden,
He who brought you from the land of darkness,
He who overcame your enemies,
He who fed you in the wilderness—
It is He who speaks to you in the heart,
He answers you in the mind,
He is with you in trouble,
He leads you into life,
He delivers you from the dead,
He is your shelter from the storm,
Your rock in the weary land,
Your strength in need,

Your counselor and your keeper.
Holy, Most Holy is He.
He who opened the sea,
He who from the rock brought forth living waters
Has laid his mantle over the world,
Has gathered all nations together,
Has caused His sun to shine on all,
Has caused His rain to fall upon all,
Has brought fruit to the gardens of all,
Has spread the branches of the tree of life over all.

Hear, O Is-ra-el!
Followers of the Self-Existent,
He who gave me the tablets of the Law,
He who gave me the rod of power,
He who gave me the staff of peace,
He who revealed His name to me,
He who lighted the pillar of fire,
He who is in the cloud
Is the Most High, the Most Holy.

Hear, O Is-ra-el!
The Lord Thy God is the One and Only,
His people are one and only,
His altar is one and only,
The whole world is one and only.

Hear, O Is-ra-el!
This is the day of fulfillment,
This is the day of liberation.
The need of fasting is no more,
The day of sackcloth and ashes is spent;
The laughter of the Most High
Is upon the lips of children;
Weep not nor let the tears of sorrow fall;
The fear of night is past,
The Lord Thy God is with thee.

Hear, O Is-ra-el!
> The Lord Thy God is One,
> The Lord Thy God is over all,
> The Lord Thy God is in all,
> The Lord Thy God is through all,
> The altar of the Lord is one altar,
> The promise is fulfilled,
> The law is unbroken,
> The cup uplifted is running over,
> The prophet has passed into his prophecy!
> Time has melted into Eternity.
> The Lord Thy God is One,
> The same yesterday, today and forever.
> O Lord God of Truth,
> Set Thou Thy seal and signet on this day.

I, The Farer
> Then once again I heard the songs supernal
> In praise of God, Almighty and Eternal.
> The luminous Shekinah spread to fill
> The earth and sky. It faded. All was still!

Thus in one age the same great truths broke through

The mind of Orpheus which Moses knew.

Philosopher and poet, mystic, too, and priest,

He brought to Greece the wisdom of the east

Which he in Egypt's templed shrines acquired

By many years of Mysteries inspired.

Orpheus and the mysteries

10

The Farer

Now comes a priest in pure white linen drest,
Bound with a golden girdle, who has prest
A wreath of myrtle on his head, a wand
Or ivory-handled scepter in one hand;
And with his arm across the shoulder laid,
He soothes a child lest he should be afraid;
While all about him notes of music sing
Like birds invisible upon the wing.
Who is this priest, who seems half-man, half-god,
This one who bears a serpent-wreathéd rod?

The Presence

Another age, another place and need,
Another harvest of the age-old seed!
So short the span of faiths! They live, they breathe
And fill the air with incense, and men wreathe
The sacred altar and light the candle flame;
It burns, it dies, leaves nothing but a name.
So long is faith! that faith itself lives on
In fervid hope of newer, clearer dawn.
And, lo, the Cosmic Mind behind the screen
Grows dense with forces longing for the seen
Which seek a vent and like a current pour
Into those souls who leave an open door.
Thus in one age the same great truths broke through
The mind of Orpheus[54] which Moses knew.[55]
Philosopher and poet, mystic, too, and priest,
He brought to Greece the wisdom of the east
Which he in Egypt's templed shrines acquired[56]
By many years of Mysteries inspired.
Mark well my words, ye seekers after Truth,
Nor look with lifted brows upon this youth
Because you found his name in your mythology,
He was a man—yet all but God was he!
His eyes of azure blue, his auburn hair,[57]
His half-sad smile and yet his manly air
Gave rise to this, "He is Apollo's son;

With him on earth, a new faith is begun."
He came not to destroy their faith, but light
The torch of Truth to guide the soul aright
Through those dark groves where priestesses attended
The worship of black Hecate! and ended
The blood and lust of lunar deities
And brought the dark Bacchantes to their knees;
Yet not in wrath; in love he led the way
Through darkened tomb into eternal day.

To Orpheus

For it was you, who brought to Grecian shore
The sacred mysteries and cosmic lore—
One only God, both Bridegroom and the Bride,
The Father-Mother. Sitting by their side
The Manifested Word, celestial Son—
The Triad formed, yet still remaining One.
You called him Dionysos, demiurge
Whose blood and flesh with men so closely merge
That they are one and, though into the pit
They fall in shame, there is escape from it;
Because the Son of God could not be lost,
Though dark the way and bitter be the cost.

The Presence Continues

How oft men curse the saviors of a race
Because they have but little wit to trace
The very sources in the ages gone
Of their own faith when history was born!
Yet fail not, sceptic, in Orpheus to find
A prophet, priest and singer intertwined
Who first[58] portrayed in what you name a myth
The Son of God in conquest over death.
He dramatized within the Delphic grove
The heart of Dionysos who, to prove
The triumph of the soul, to hell descended
And rose again, the power of Pluto ended.
He helped to form the Passion Plays[59] which sway

The hopes of men down to the present day,
Confirmed by Jesus who on them set his seal,
And died and rose again and made them real.

Like Moses, Orpheus from Egypt came
To form one word to signify the Name
Above all names; With Moses, it was IEVÉ [61]
With Orpheus, the great term, EVOHÉ.[62]
"In us, God dies, in us returns to birth,"[63]
He said, "Initiates upon the earth
Become a Hermes[64] to the things above[65]
And weave from patterns dedicate to love.
All-powerful and heavenly-Eros[66] be
In all your loves—Whom I invoke for thee.
Love all, love ev'rything, for ev'rything—
This is the tune to which all souls must sing—
Is moved by love; the gods of time and space,
Or very demons of the deep must trace
Their power to love, the all-embracing force
That holds the worlds sent spinning on their course.
Love light, not darkness, lest your souls returned
Shall bear the hideous stains that they have earned.[67]
Hail all who have been born again and who
Are passing to new birth. Rejoice, all you
Who suffer from your rounds of births and pain,
You shall emerge and be yourselves again—
One body and one soul, tuned to the lyre
Of seven strings that tamed the lakes of fire.[68]
Help thou the weak and comfort suffering,
Once more I say, show love in everything."

. . . . .

"But now mine hour has come by death to show
My sacred mission, the god has willed it so;
I shall to hell descend, from thence shall rise,
Nor shall ye see again with mortal eyes
My human form....This my last word I give,

Through love I found the Truth; in love so live
That pure and strong ye leave the world of night
And live forever with the Son of Light."

The Presence

Yet even as he spoke, his sight pierced through
The hills and groves of Greece, to bring to view
The evil sorceress of Hecate
Who with an army camped maliciously
Upon the Ebro where she might o'erthrow
The solar gods and once again bestow
The rule of Hecate and lunar deities
And force the Sons of Light to bend their knees.

Yet without fear he faced them when he came
Among the soldiers, speaking in the name
Of gods of light and truth, of love and peace,
That health and plenty come when wars shall cease;
Half dazed by speech and beauty luminous,
They cried, "A god is speaking now to us."

Yet moved by jealousy and lust insatiate
The chieftains yielded to the priestess' hate
And pierced him with their swords. He fell and cried,
"I die but Gods live on, forever." Thus he died.

His soul took flight and yet he *left* a soul,
A living spirit, sacred gloriole
To shine around the heads of saints and seers—
Pythagoras and Plato who in the after years
Bore witness to the latent ego and
Enlarged the Mother-Doctrine to expand
His science, arts and logic and release
The Orphic soul to be the soul of Greece.

The Farer

Above his head I heard a sanctus bell;
For love of souls, he dared descend to hell.

It is by knowledge that man rules his fate,
The knowledge of the One: its correlate
That man is mind *and can participate*
In cosmic life. When freed from base desire
His soul is luminous with Living Fire.

Pythagoras the genius

The Presence
>Truth makes no haste; unmeasured by the years,
>It seems to sleep until its time appears;
>But when we wake to it, it opens wide the gate
>Nor need we plead to Providence or Fate.
>Thus seven centuries revolved on earth
>Before Pythagoras was brought to birth;
>Who in the sequence of a lofty mind,
>You now can see, great Orpheus behind.
>For it was he who brought his genius to
>Proclaim in numbers[69] and demonstrate anew
>The ancient Mother-Doctrine thus to prove
>All things are formed by One Creative Love.
>The ONE is Dyad; this atom-unit[70] holds
>The two in one; which from itself unfolds
>Its essence into substance—from which then
>Mother Nature brings forth worlds and men.
>The Spouse of God in "matter" is terrestrial
>But is in "spirit" immortal and celestial.

The Farer
>By what logic did Pythagoras seek
>To solve by numbers—

The Presence
>>Listen, he will speak.

Pythagoras
>The great enigma in which all nature slumbers
>Can be resolved, reducing it to numbers.[71]
>The number "1" assumes a point in space
>Which moves to form a line, the line will trace
>A plane which moves to form a cube: dimension
>Is but the number "one" in full extension;
>The line is "two," the surface "three," while "four"
>Denotes the solid—thus "number" is the core
>Of knowledge;[72] appearances of sense
>Are then reduced to essences, and hence

The mind of you can be aware and know
The "real" from which "substantial forms" must flow.
So from the elemental noumenal
Is built the "solid" world phenomenal.
The "holy tetracty" have I designed
To form a pattern for the human mind
By which the number "four" is clearly shown
To hold all numbers cased within its own.
For "1" plus "2" plus "3" plus "4" are "10,"
The "perfect number" whose numerals again
Will add to "one" in which all things begin.[73]
All science then from numbers is evolved:
Philosophy is thus to "principles" resolved:
Those who interpret numerals with skill
Reduce the universe into the terms of "Will."
The "four" is square, four-square, and so is shown
As Truth or Justice. "One" (1) is aptly known
As Monad, sentient soul who journeys through
A trackless world but when its hour is due
Returns at length to feel the warm embrace
Of Father-arms, eternal dwelling place.
It is by knowledge that man rules his fate,
The knowledge of the One; its correlate
That *man is mind* and can participate
In cosmic life. When freed from base desire
His soul is luminous with Living Fire.
He holds dominion in the world of things,
Who knows that mind moves on itself; and flings
His word out where the cosmic forces swarm
Which give it soul and bring it forth in form.
Man is a spirit who builds himself a soul
Out of the substance of the cosmic whole,
Creation's fluid, a form ethereal
Surviving death—a body spiritual.
Man has the power to make, remake, and evermore
Return to earth or reach the Farther Shore.
The *subtile chariot*[75] will bear the soul
Into the realm of light, if pure and whole,

Or it will fall once more to the embrace
Of matter, forced again to run life's race.
As Moses formed the Tetragrammaton[76]
To seal and yet reveal the three in ONE
So I perceive the universe as three
Immersed in One to form a true Quaternion.
All things resolve to numbers, the first four
Include them all—nor is there less nor more
Than ONE which manifests expressing endlessly
In man and matter and cosmogony.
The universe itself is BEING; soul
On soul are stars and planets[77] (for the whole
Wide solar system is a living thing)[78]
Which unsupported through the ethers swing
Around the sun and as they run they sing.[79]
The spheres are tuned in space to number seven,
The lyre is but a replica of heaven,
Harmonic intervals unfold the plan
By which the *monad* moves up to the man.

Celestial Monad,[80] who from sphere to sphere
Through endless ages reached thy natal year,
Born into time but drawn from timeless space,
Thou hast on earth a moment's dwelling place;
Entombed in matter; yet now aware of soul,
Thou shalt take wing,[81] let heaven be thy goal!

The Farer
What means did he, Pythagoras, provide
For this escape for which *my* soul has cried?

The Presence
With Hermes, Egypt, Orpheus, he taught
That by each self a subtile form is wrought,
A "chariot of the soul," as light as thought,
Etheric double which oft at death is seen
And bears a likeness to the earthly mien.
Sublime and radiant or with the mark

Of beast it takes its journey through the dark
And mystic door of death; and some there be
Who enter life and solve the mystery;
While some will wander in torpor or despair
Nor find relief though searching ev'rywhere,
Until in Horeb, Erebus or in
The deep abyss of Hecate[82] they win
Release from bonds; and from its self-forged chain,
The soul is freed to come to earth again.
None shall be lost though ages roll and roll,
God would be lost were He to lose one soul.

The Farer

Does then the primal psyche enter bliss
When it has purged itself in the abyss?
Will it find peace at last from earthly blight,
And pass to the eternal life and light?

The Presence

Pythagoras taught that expiation will
Through many lives set free the soul until
The upward spiral leads at last to rest
In some far sphere among the spirits blest.

"There comes a time when body, soul, and mind
Alike are pure, the Psyche so refined
That it is bound no longer to this plane
But takes its flight from death to life again."

The Farer

Hark! Hear you music falling from afar?

The Presence

It is perhaps from the vesperian star[83]
Of that far galaxy whereon the spires
Of some fair temple rise; you hear the choirs
Of spirits glorified by love. For by
The thought of souls and by the soul's reply

The notes of music formed become a melody
Which poureth forth in song and poetry.
The highest music is philosophy [84]
And he, Pythagoras, defined the last
And final state of souls when they have passed
Beyond the *antichthone,* a counter-earth of bliss[85]
And left behind the worlds—both that and this.

The Farer

Speak, Presence, speak: what was the seer's reply
Concerning souls? Do we forever die?

The Presence

When all the "repercussions of our lives"[86] have ended
And each has freed the soul and has amended
Each wrong and feels no urge and no desire
Save that which leads to good, he shall retire
To fields of cosmic consciousness, the state
Of spirit pure, the self immaculate.
On that eighth sphere, the number seven passed,
An octave new begun, the Psyche shall outlast
All time, all light of stars, no need of sun
For God is light, eternity is won!

It was the work of Plato to portray
The threefold concept opening the way
To understanding of the mysteries
Though not in terms of monad and the dyad
Which formed the substance of the Sacred Triad,
(Induction in the secret mysteries
Forbids revealing matters such as these.)
Yet he made clear the threefold path to enter...

Plato and the ideal

12

Socrates

The Farer

Around two heads a single halo ran,
Two souls seemed knit in one composite man;
The first, I knew, was Socrates whose wit
Was gentle, though with one blow of it
He cracked the skulls of Sophists, 'til the youth
Turned from half-truths to learn Eternal Truth
From this great soul who proved that power and pelf
Bear little weight with him who knows himself.
His rough and almost satyr face aglow
With earnest kindliness, he sought to show
That Beauty, Truth and Justice are not three
But root in *one* and form a trinity
From which all lesser truths can be evolved
And through which social problems can be solved.
He taught by questions based on moral law
And though he had belief in gods, he saw
That in himself man holds an equity
In all the wisdom of divinity.
"Look thou within thyself and thou shalt find
A law to govern all of humankind,
The Good, the Beautiful, the True; for Good
Is but intelligence when understood,
And virtue, wisdom, so that both are one,
The wise are good, the good are wise and shun
All ugliness in form or thought, and view
Alone the Good, the Beautiful and True."

Nor had the gods left Socrates without
A guide who never kept the sage in doubt,
His daimon[87] knew and spoke and he could hear
The voice of soul that fell upon his ear,
The inner source of all the sages' lore,
And even in that hour when his accusers swore
That he was enemy to state and youth,

He spoke not for acquittal but for Truth;
And he forgave those men whose ev'ry breath
Had sworn the lies that brought the sentence death;
And when the hour drew on, he stood upon the brink
Of the eternal life, he did not shrink
But took the cup of hemlock, smiled and said,
"Be not dismayed nor say that I am dead,
But that the body only lieth here."
He breathed his last faint words, "Be of good cheer."

My eyes were full of tears as though
The death of Socrates had been a blow,
For eyes entranced by astral light can view
All of the past, yet see the present, too,
The life-events and suffering of the sages
Seemed present at the Altar of the Ages.

.   .   .   .   .   .

I had no need to ask the name of him
Who shared the halo; he is half-synonym
For Socrates; none can disengage
The mind of Plato from the Athenian sage
In those great dialogs by which they sought
To utter truth and clarify the thought
Of youthful searchers, helping each to find
The vein of truth that runs through ev'ry mind.
Yet by the same device, we see their query draws
The teeth of falsehood from sophistic jaws
Of scoffers—by logic makes the dissident
Disgorge the truth to their own wonderment!

How can I best portray this noble sage?
Soul-son of Socrates, a mind for ev'ry age,
He will survive in his immortal fame
Known as Plato, though that was not his name,
But nickname given in a playful mood
Because his shoulders were both wide and good

For those athletic sports in which in youth
He had excelled as now he did in Truth.
Here was, save one,[88] the last of those great seers
Who taught the sacred doctrine through the years
And who inscribed on philosophic pages
The triune wisdom of the ancient sages.

Would that my speech held pigments that would draw
A living portrait of him who took the law
Of mind in action from the ancient seers
And proved its truth for the eternal years!
His strong kind face, his eyes so clear and blue
They seemed to pierce straight to the heart of you;
His voice high-pitched, though ever soft and kind,
He was the incarnation of his mind.

What made his genius shine like some great star
At zenith of the universe? What are
His gifts of truth that lift the questing soul
To highest hopes of union with the Whole?
He taught what Krishna and great Hermes knew,
Pythagoras, Orpheus and the Mysteries, too,
But by the use of myth, of logic and of art,
He gave to reason a newly-beating heart.

The Scribe

The Farer paused a moment to reflect
Upon the Mother Doctrine and retrace
The varied forms in which it had been taught
Down to the present hour and to include
Socratic doctrine out of Plato's mouth.

The Farer

Trisect a circle and on the radii
Write out the words depicting Trinity[89]—
Father, mother, son; and once again
Write Bride, and Bridegroom and the Word; and then
Inscribe the numbers, One and Two and Three;

Or body, soul and spirit, a triplicity.
Then write the words, Good, Beautiful and True,
And once again bring Trinity to view.

The Farer (continues)
It was the work of Plato to portray
The threefold concept opening the way
To understanding of the mysteries
Though not in terms of monad and the dyad
Which formed the substance of the Sacred Triad,
(Induction in the secret mysteries[90]
Forbids revealing matters such as these,)
Yet he made clear the threefold path to enter;
All lines are ONE when they have merged at Center.
His metaphysics was a duplicate
Drawn from Pythagoras; and in his great
And all-embracing mind he formed anew
The code of Hermes, that what the eye may view
Is not the *real*, but is an image of
A pattern drawn and held in realms above[91]
Seen through the camera's eye, the center of
A snowflake holds the pattern[92] and the form
Of man-made objects manifold and so
Reveals that man but reads the mind of God
In all he claims that he himself creates.
The things of earth are but derivative
And incomplete, mere copies that will live
Their little day, the shadow of ideas
That are eternal in the higher spheres.
This "doctrine of ideals" makes test of wit
And few there be who grasp the truth of it.

The art lies here—to think in concepts, bring
Together in one total group the "thing"
And *all we think about the "thing"*—the whole
Will then be known—no longer "thing" but soul
Or being. The metaphysical ideal[93]
Is thus perceived as permanent and real.

It can be proved that senses do not see
Nor hear nor touch nor taste *reality*.
An object, let us say, stands on the lawn,
Around its edge twelve numbers have been drawn;
A pin or gnomon set upon its face
Creates a shadow which the eye can trace
And WE tell time, the dial does not tell
Nor know the sanctus from the vesper bell.
To untaught minds the dial is but form;
But to be *used* it must arouse a swarm
Of thoughts—the purpose, plan, the law
Of measurement, of time, anterior
To NOW which must relate the future and
The past—it takes all these to understand
The dial set to capture time. The real
Of any thing is known through the ideal,
The thoughts and concepts which surround "a thing"
Give meaning to it (nor all the arguing
Of atheistic minds has power to prove
A force so great as that which rests in love).
The soul of man springs from the universe
And he is victimized by his own curse,
But he escapes when he has understood
The highest truth, the Idea of the Good.
If he but turn to heaven, he shall find
The perfect pattern in All-Creative Mind.
Let him reflect the pattern and be free
From pains of matter and its mockery.

The Farer

I listened well to Plato for I knew
What modern sciences had brought to view—
A confirmation of the world unseen,
Intangible to sense; for senses screen
Magnetic fields which form the pattern-molds[94]
For cosmic substance; that such substance holds
No other quality than the ideal
Which mind conceives to make the world seem real.

Yet as I read the mind of Plato there
Who stood serene beside the altar stair,
I was disturbed by thoughts that ran like this—
How oft is truth bedaubed by well-meant kiss!
Our very words betray the meaning of the real,
And as we speak, we often seem to steal
From truth if we by *logic* seek to prove
What is unknown save by the grace of love
And by the *feeling* roused in each of us
Through recognition of the marvelous.
Say not "another world," above, beyond,[95]
Nor "separate"; nor does it "correspond";
The subject and the object are the same
In *this one world;* and *opposites* are name
We give to those divisions of our view;
The "I" and "Not-I" are devices to
Clear the thought and form a heliostat
Reflecting truth in symbols—THOU ART THAT.

The Farer (continues)

Again I pierced the Mind of Plato, read
The parable by which he sought to shed
A light upon the meaning of "ideal"
And prove that *concepts* only are the real.
He told of men who in a cave from birth[96]
Are shut away from sight of things on earth,
Save that they see upon the rearward wall
The shadows cast by unseen figures, all
The movements of soldiers or women who
Bear jars upon their heads. And they can view
No other things and they can only hear
The *echoes* of men's voices and suppose
The moving shadows speak—and only those.
To such as these the shadows would be truth
For they had known no other thing, forsooth.
But one of them escapes! He sees the light
That casts the shadows in the cave; the sight
Of everything that comes within his view

Appears illusion; the shadows only, true!
And should some guide point out that objects here
Are source of all the shadows that appear
Within the cave, he is by wonder caught,
His mind confused and he is quite distraught.

Or when the "cave-man" mounts some height
And sees the sun come blazing from the night,
He will be dazzled and not at first aware
Of what is real though he can see it there.
At length he looks into the sun as Cause—
The source, the substance and the laws
Of manifested forms, and knows them all as ONE—
The light, the shadows and the rising sun!
The thing, the thoughts about the thing, the ear
That hears, the hour, the place, the time of year,
Are categories, qualities that embrace
The whole of any thing and give it place
And meaning in the mind; and thus, the only real
Is doctrine of ideas where Plato set his seal.

The Farer (continues)
I heard the Presence speaking thus to me:

The Presence
Judge not by sense, by what you hear or see,
And yet beware lest you befuddle sense
When you deny a real experience;
For pain and poverty and shadows tell
How you can hold the very thought of hell—
Not place, not thing, but failure to proclaim
The Beautiful, the Good, the True—the Name
Of *Him*[97] whom Socrates and Plato knew,
The Just or Good, the Beautiful, and True.

The Farer
Though well conversed with abstract thought because
The Presence taught me to behold the laws,

The qualities, the purpose, the sentiments that cling
Around the visible and make a thought a "thing,"
I still was like a swimmer in the sea
While waves of wonder thundered over me.
I followed Plato into far-flung lands,
To Egypt's temples in the golden sands;
To Croton, where Pythagoras met death,
By fire and sword (where Plato witnesseth
His reverence for the seer from whom he caught
The yearning for the mysteries and sought
Initiation in the Passion Plays
First brought to Greece by Orpheus whose rays
Of light spread over western skies) and in
Eleusis,[98] Plato found the origin
Of his conception of the migrant soul,
Of its descent in "matter" and the whole
Long story of suff'ring and re-ascent—
The drama of Demeter, the Great Mother,
Divine Intelligence and of her daughter,
Persephone, psyche, restored to breath
To prove the soul is never bound by death.

I passed with Plato through the Mystery
And saw the source of his philosophy
Of life, and how Pythagoras and seers
Of ev'ry age had poured the gain of years
Into his mind and heart. I felt his warm
Rich wisdom as he turned the *thought to form*
Or back again to thought, the noumena
Equivalent to all phenomena,
I saw the world as it passed through his mind
How ideas changed to concepts, saw him find
That they exist not as congeries
But metaphysical realities.
And since "ideas alone can be the real,
GOOD is supreme, unchangeable, ideal."

Plato escaped the martyr's death, 'tis said,
Became an exile from his home instead,
But I who read the mind of Plato saw
He never wavered from the mental law
That sits supreme upon its throne,
And kept his faith in Mind, One God alone—
The God of Socrates whose brow One God had kist,
Though he was murdered as an atheist.

The Scribe

Then Plato bowed before the sacred fane;
He touched his brow and bowing once again
He gave Melchizedek a leather roll
That held his sacred doctrine of the soul,
While from the mists that screened the Cosmic throne
Exalted voices praised the Lord, his God alone
And bid attendance of the saints and sages,
The seers and saviors of unnumbered ages.

Song of the Sages

Come join ye your voices in praising the Lord
Who maketh the worlds by the power of His Word;
All hail and all praise to the love and the might
Of God the creator, whose marvelous light
Dispels all the darkness of chaos and night.

We praise and adore Thee, Thou Ruler Divine,
Whose kingdom the world is; Thy love shall entwine
All hearts and all hopes in one union of praise;
To Thee, God of men and of nations, we raise
Our soul's adoration, Thou Ancient of Days.

His soul impassioned by his yearning for
These victims of a sacerdotal law,
He turned his heart and mind and sought to bend
His every word and act to one great end...

Jesus, last of the great masters

13

(I)

His Life and Purpose

Then Jesus came, the last to take his place
In that great line of masters of the race
To shed his radiance upon the saints and sages
Who bowed before the Altar of the Ages.
With quiet dignity he took his place
Beside the altar with men of every race
And color, of humble ranks or great,
The learned, the unlearned or the potentate,
And priests of ev'ry faith, apostles, who
Had died for him, and Judas with them, too;
And most of all the children stood with him,
And faintly seen appeared the Cherubim;
While dressed in robes of white before the altar
They sang in chorus from the cosmic psalter.

I looked into those eyes of mystic blue
That met me at the altar, and I knew
The swift involvement of the soul in bliss
And fell entranced into the great abyss
Of cosmic memory, while all the ages flew
Back to his youth and, in a swift review,
I saw the child of Mary and her spouse
Who lived upon a hillside in a house
Beside the Sea of Galilee. It clung
Against the cliffs, a small white house among
Pomegranate groves, or fig trees or the vine
From which was crushed the sacerdotal wine.
A flock of doves flew lazily around
Above a lad who lay upon the ground,
Half-clad, a cloth about his slender hips,
A smile half-raptured on his tender lips.
His gaze was set upon a further view
Than was enclosed within those walls of blue

For he was thinking of the Father there
Beyond and yet within the vaulted air;
And those strange words that all-unbidden fell
From his own mouth when he had tried to tell
His mother why he, a child of tender years,
Had stopped to argue with the Temple seers
Who had confirmed him in the Hebrew faith,
When he had answered her most courteously,
"Do you not know that it is time to be
About the work the Father gave to me?"
Long years would pass before fate would unseal
The secret of his mission and reveal
The meaning of this strange symbolic scene—
The sky, the sea, the youthful Nazarene,
The dove—the cosmic emblem[99] of the Mother,
Or Holy Spirit—while above, the Father
Keeps loving watch upon the sacred Son
Who shall proclaim the doctrine of the ONE.

How long or short those years to Jesus seemed,
What work he did, what dreams he dreamed
We know in part from fragments, bits of speech
Or habit-ways of life, his mental reach,
For he appeared with doctrine well-defined
In full accord with the Essenes,[100] aligned
With that fraternity, the pure in heart
Who practiced cleanliness and taught the art
Of healing; took no life, no sacrifice
Save from the heart to win to Paradise.
He knew their doctrine of the soul, the same
As that Pythagoras taught. He knew the sign
Of that great cross of stars which had been shrine
To Japhet's sons and Egypt's golden seers
Taught by Essenes to him in tender years,
And that it symbolized the mystery
By which the One is known as Trinity.
With them he saw in it the "sacrifice"
Of God who shows himself in thrice

297

To walk as man, and saw in this trisection
The portent of life, death and resurrection.
He had been taught that Egypt's temple walls,
And shrine and tombs—when death at last befalls—
Had been inscribed with starry cross, a sign
That souls survive in the eternal trine.

Thus early was the Teacher brought to face
The great enigma, and by what means to trace
The doctrine of the soul, the what and why
Of life and how is man to live and how to die.
Yet it took time, for though he had attained
Such powers of mind as seldom have been gained
Or given men, or avatars or seers,
Yet wisdom needs the ripening of years.
But came the day which prophecy foretold
In ev'ry land down from the ages old
When "He" should come, the mightiest and best
Of all the seers by whom the earth was blessed.
Not ushered in by thunder and by might
Like Moses gleaming with celestial Light;
But, dressed in simple robe with sandaled feet,
He made a temple of the village street.
"Take my yoke upon you and learn of me,
For I am meek and lowly. Ye shall be
Like to a child with soul so crystalline,
Ye need but knock, the Father lets you in."

The Farer (continues)
It seemed so simple and so real that I
Could scarce repress my eagerness to cry
How all the wisdom of philosophy
That I had gained had failed to bring to me
Such depth of faith, such sure and deep release
From earthly doubt; nor had it brought such peace
As came to me in these etheric spaces
Where I could hear these words and see these faces.
Akashic vision telescoped the years

And I was back with Jesus in those spheres
Where he brought forth such truths as rocked the ages;
So simply said for children, yet the sages
Have not explored their depth, nor breadth nor height
Save those who read the message in the light
Of that transcendent doctrine of the One-
In-Trinity, the Father, Mother, and the Son,
And see in Jesus Christ the twofold being.
Behold the Son of Man! yet in your seeing
Behold the Son of God!

       O Golden Son of God, the minted mold
       Of Heaven, the coin of life struck off to show
       Two sides; the seal and sign of God enscrolled
       On one; the face of man to see and know
       Upon the other—between them purest gold!
In Him behold the man!—god-man ideal,
The prototype of heaven and the real!
Then deeper look and turn your gaze within
Yourself, the Christ that is or might have been!
And still is there though feeble seems the flame,
Thou art the Son of God and Christ thy name.
Such simple words, Forgive and be forgiven!
Blessed are the pure in heart. In heaven,
The childlike soul shall see the Father's face...
Search not for Heaven in some other place,
But in your heart...You need not beg for bread,
Ask and receive...He who believes is fed.
And all his wants are met...who plants the seed
Shall reap the harvest he has sown...No need
To pray a mournful sacerdotal prayer,
Or search for God on some high altar-stair,
But in your heart and He will meet you there."

Come unto me; whoso believes in me
Shall find eternal springs *within,* and be
Aware of life forevermore.
             Then he

Was silent and I could feel the power
By which he healed the sick. And in that hour
Beside the grave of Lazarus he said,
"Arise, O Lazarus, there are no dead!"

Then Krishna spoke; I listened and I heard
This other Son of God, Incarnate Word,
"Search for the Me, Immortal Me, and find
Within yourself the One Eternal Mind."
And then I heard their voices synchronize,
"I say that ye are gods, nor otherwise;
All that the Father has is in the One—
The Holy Ghost, the Father and the Son.
You are the Son of God and you are blest
Who find within the answer to your quest."

Then Krishna spoke those words of ages past,
"Nay, and of hearts which follow other gods
In simple faith, they rise to me,
O Kunti's Son! Though they pray wrongfully,
I am Receiver, Lord of sacrifice.
Who follow gods, to Me their prayers shall rise.
And whoso loveth Me, cometh to Me.
And none shall be outcast. Search for thc Mc,
The true god is within thyself, and He
Who looks for God shall find Him in the Me."[101]

My vision pierced behind the screen of time,
I saw the past as in a pantomime
And read the thoughts of Jesus from the tape
Of the Akasha and found them taking shape
From ancient Masters and the Mysteries;
Felt his revulsion to the obsequies
Surrounding death, the hopelessness, the vain
Attempts to comfort that followed in its train.
I felt with him the anguish like a spear
That pierced his heart and saw the tear
That fell in sorrow for another—

He who had shared in all of them as brother—
The leper with his rotting flesh who lay
Among the rocky wastes beside the way
And wept in loneliness, devoid of hope;
The blind shut up within an envelope
Of black and never-ending night!
But most of all the children, Baalite
Or Jew sold into slavery for debt—
The scenes of Tyre and Sidon sharpest set,
Those little ones of six upon whose back
Was borne the blood-stained, cruel sack
Of snails dug from the sands to fill the vat
And brew the dyes to clothe some plutocrat
In crimson robes, or purple for the priest—
And Jesus wept because worse than the beast
Was fate of little children falling by
The rotting piles of filth and left to die.
Such were the scenes in which inhuman lust
Enslaved mankind and turned their hopes to dust
And ashes. First of all the Master sought
To change the system and to this end he taught
The better way and by all means to bring
The hearts of men to share the suffering
Of other men. But entrenched evil in
The very Temple held such discipline
Upon the people that the Mosaic Law
Was flouted there and held no more in awe.
Then did the Master turn his back upon
Judaic priests, to bring a surer dawn
To rise upon mankind, assured that men
Could change the world if hope were filled again
With that first light that broke the Vedic dawn—
The light that once so brilliantly had shone
From Moses, that man and God are one and he
Who knows this truth has known Eternity.

His soul impassioned by his yearning for
These victims of a sacerdotal law,

He turned his heart and mind and sought to bend
His every word and act to one great end—
That he should give his life to demonstrate
There is no death, pass through the cruel gate
Of suffering but leave his body here;
Die to the world and then would reappear
But this would be no Passion *Play*—to be
Concealed from sight in sacred mystery
In which the Savior *seems* to die and then
The drama ends when he is seen again.
The world should witness, it should clearly see
There is no death, save to mortality,
And he who builds the temple of the soul,
Will find the future life in his control.

He turned away from gentleness to those
Who damned his Father's house and chose
To name them what they were with such a blast
The temple shook, Jehoshua[102] at last!
This was his plan, though with it he foresaw
How the unholy twisting of the law[103]
Would bring his death about and how that he
When lifted up and hung upon a tree
Would center all the eyes of humankind
Upon his faith, to see in him the Mind
Of God, and, rising from the grave, would prove
The soul unbound by death which soars above
The body lying in the narrow room
To be with God at rest beyond the tomb.

The law of resurrection had been known
To other minds—the purpose was his own—
In the Essenian doctrine of the soul[104]
From subtile ether sprung to play the role
Of life within the body-prison, then
In joyfulness to take its flight again
Enriched by service to the needs of men.
The hour drew near, his feet were firmly set

Upon the path that led to Olivet
Where he could view the hills of far Judea,
In purple-tinted light and he could see a
Bit of the Dead Sea bathed in sulphur mist;
While, just below, the dimming sunset kist
The Temple towers that crowned the sacred wall
Where even now, unmindful of the call
To worship, the politicians[105] laid their plan
To murder him, anointed Son of Man
And Son of God.
          The hour was set and they
In cruel farce convicted him, a play
On justice, won the Law's consent, with grim
Admission that "I find no fault in him."
They nailed him to a cross and hanging there
In agony too great for humankind to bear,
It seemed to him that God had turned away
As though this *were* another Passion Play;
Yet though his thorn-crowned brow with blood was red
He looked upon his murderers and said,
"Father, forgive, they know not what they do,
I trust my spirit, Living God, to You."
It was the end! He died upon the cross—
Yet it to him was gain and not a loss,
For he had planned that all mankind might see
"If lifted up, I draw all men to Me."

Behold! The proof! What all the seers had taught,
And what the Passion Plays sincerely sought
To demonstrate was brought at length to sight,
For Jesus rose and showed himself in light!
Untouched by death he broke at last the spell
That grips the common mind with fear of hell
Or feels the anguished torment of despair
Lest they shall see no more the face so fair
Of their beloved.
          It came upon this wise—
That on the dreadful day of his demise

His followers had run away. Their fears
Of the unknown and the inhuman leers
Of mobs aroused to frenzy by the sight
Of blood drove them in frantic haste at night
To seek concealment and escape their doom
Within the shelter of an upper room.
Not one of them remained courageously
To take the Master's body from the tree.

A certain Joseph of Arimathea
Who loved the Lord, pursuing an idea
Asked Pilate for the privilege to take
Away the body of the master and to make
A sepulcher for it, and binding tight
In linen cloths, bore it away at night.
Then cometh Mary Magdalena to
The tomb of Jesus, she who knew
Him well, but found the stone was rolled away
And Jesus was not there that Sabbath day.
But as she wept a man appeared to stand
Against the morning light; she reached a hand
To touch his garments; "Touch me not," he said,
"But tell your brethren, ascended from the dead,
I go unto the Father," and passing from her sight
He disappeared dissolved in morning light.

Meanwhile his followers, in anguishment
Had hidden from the mobs, their garments rent,
Their faces veiled and in a secret room,
They cowered through those two days of doom.
And then he came! Yea, Jesus came through tight
Closed doors, around his face an auric light
Which glowed within the room and spoke and said,
"Peace be with you." To prove his soul not dead
He showed his form as he appeared at death
And they could feel a stirring like a breath
Of air. "The Holy Spirit be upon
You all," he said and, saying, he was gone.

Shall I say more? I saw it all within
Akashic Mind and felt that I had been
A witness to the soul-form of the Master
That shone like glowing lamps of alabaster
As it had shone two thousand years ago
When he appeared in spirit-form to show
He was not dead.

           Again and yet again
He reappeared to women and to men
Who had been dear to him. In Emmaus
His apparition was just synchronous
With his appearance to the women who
With Mary Magdalene held him in view.
Some seven miles apart they were! And they—
The two who walked with him that day
And had so many times communed with him—
Now knew him not because his form seemed dim;
But when he vanished from their sight
And disappeared in a celestial light,
They knew that it was he.
               It needs no more
Of telling save that he passed the shore
Of earthly life; his words, a last command;
"Bear witness to the truth in ev'ry land
That I have risen from the dead and I
Have given proof that only bodies die,
Fear not, all ye who hear, you will survive,
That which has seemed to die is still alive!"

Thus did the Christ fulfill for all the ages
The promise of the Passion Plays and sages
That one should come to play the final role
And prove to man survival of the soul.

(2)

His Philosophy and Religion

The Scribe

The Farer seemed to sleep, so still he stood,
His eyes still fixed upon the multitude
That stood before the Altar of the Ages,
But unaware of saviors and of sages.
It seemed that all his faculties of sight
Had been withdrawn—no need for outer light
Nor outer sense; as though it now sufficed
To find *within* the image of the Christ;
Nor did he know who spoke, the Presence or
The Christ or self, his soul so filled with awe
Because the Living Spirit seemed to be
His all-in-all; he *was* Eternity...

Then fell these words prophetic and profound,
That seemed to fill all space with soundless sound
As though Infinity Itself awoke in him
Amidst the chanting of the cherubim:

Know that flesh and blood and sinew
Are as waters of a river
Flowing from a hidden source,
Are as form made up of Spirit,
Are as shadows cast forth from It
From a source no man has seen.

This is Alchemy of Spirit
That the food we take in body
Should itself become a body;
This the miracle of life.

Is not this the secret meaning?
Is not this the holy meaning

Of the flesh and blood of Christ?
When of bread we take in body,
When of air we breathe in body,
When of wine we drink in body,
Is not this the eucharist?

He the one who knew its meaning
Is the one who spread the table
Is the one who broke the bread.
This He did to teach the lesson,

This He did to show that substance
Is of Spirit formed and held,
Is by Spirit freely given,
Is by Spirit gladly given,
Is by Spirit always given,
By the universal law.

This the secret of the ages,
This the wisdom of the wise men—
Body has a perfect pattern,
Body has an unseen substance,
Body has a complete likeness
In the life and mind of God.

But this unseen, perfect likeness,
Is not hidden in the heavens,
Is not distant from the planet,
Is not poised in air above us,
Is not buried in the ground.

Where then, is this perfect pattern;
Where then, is this subtle body;
Where then, is this unseen likeness
To the body that we see?—
This the teaching of the ages,
This the secret that they found—
Everything on earth has pattern,

Everything that is, has likeness;
Every form we see has mooring
In the subtle inner substance,
In the life and mind of God.
In this pattern ever given,
Is the likeness of our body,
Is the pattern of each member.

And this body in the ether,
With its head and hands part of us,
With its eyes and feet part of us,
Is the substance of this body,
Is the likeness of this body,
Is the pattern of this body,
Is the life and mind of God.

This the body that the Christ knew,
This the body that he spoke of,
This the body that was in him,
This the body he took with him,
On the mount of his transition,
On the dawn of resurrection,
On the day he left behind him
Nothing that man's eye could see.
For the pattern he brought with him
And his likeness in the unseen
Could not die nor be destroyed.
Only image of his pattern[106]
Hung upon the cross of treason
Or was buried in the tomb.
And because he understood
That the likeness of his pattern
And the image of his pattern
Were not separate in truth,
He could raise the image fleshy
To the likeness of its pattern,
To the form forever given,

To the body so eternal,
It will never pass away.

This the message that He gave us,
This He told His closest followers—
What He did they too could do;
And He told them when He left them
That the Spirit, ever with them,
Would reveal to them the meaning
Of the words He spoke unto them,
When the likeness of His pattern
Sojourned here on earth among them
Till the day of His ascension,
Till the dawn of His transition,
Till the time of His departure
To the unseen realms above.[107]

So the Spirit that was with them
And the life that never left them
Caused them to awake and listen
To the message of creation,
Caused them always to remember
That they, too, had unseen pattern,
That they, too, had inner likeness,
That all mankind, too, has likeness
In the mind and heart of God,
Have identity with God.

The Scribe (continues)
Though he was long accustomed to the range
Of knowledge and the swiftness of the change
From forms of verse to prose and back once more,
As though he held a key to ev'ry door
That opens up to science and philosophy
Or to the star-lit towers of prophecy,
Yet now the Farer heard in wonderment
This recapitulation of the mode
And method of creation. Like an ode

It awakened music in his heart; he heard
A voice that spoke for the Eternal Word.

The Voice

All souls are born of God and are devised
To prove on earth the ever-living Christ.
He who attains awareness of the Me,
Becomes absorbed into the Trinity.
Give heed to him, for in the voice of sages
My word shall be salvation for the ages.
In Christ of Galilee, my greatest Son,
Ye find example; his work will not be done
Until his spirit fills the soul of ev'ry one.
He still remains the last best hope of men,
For when they call he ministers again
To human hearts in grief or pain or death;
And touching him, the soul that slumbereth
Awakes to life; and those who feel the chill
Of dread despair, because they cannot will
To will, shall come once more to grips with sin.
And through incarnate truth, they, too, shall win.

The Farer

I who had seen the astral forms of seers
Who ring the circle of the wheeling spheres
(Those souls that throng the interstellar spaces
And bring new life, new energy and graces
To lift men's hearts to faith and higher hopes
For which the earthbound man so vainly gropes)
Perceived in Jesus Christ the Living Word
Who spoke for God. I listened and I heard,
"It is the Father's pleasure that He give
His kingdom to you—enter in and live!"

It seemed to me that in that moment's sight
I saw a real incarnation of the Light
That brings redemption[108] to the soul, until
Through faith in Christ, man has the will to will.

The shackles broken, the soul is bound
Back[109] to its Source, salvation has been found.

The Voice
Yet Jesus made no claim that he had paid
Man's debt to God, nor must God's wrath be stayed
Nor be appeased by sacrifice of blood.[110]
Look to his life, for Jesus understood
That "I, when lifted up, will draw all men
Back to the Me. I say to you again
It is not I, but rather it is He
Who lives in all who also lives in Me."
It was the sweet simplicity of Christ
That made of bread and wine the eucharist
So that the soul might feed, the heart be satisfied,
That cleansed the mind of doubt; and he decried
Long drawn-out speech and abstract subtility
And said in simple words, "Come unto Me."

If, then, in him the Light of Light shone bright
Until he is to us Eternal Light,
It is because a God-filled mind sufficed
To turn the soul into a living Christ,
And those who follow him shall surely find
Christ Universal waking in the mind.
"He who hath seen the Son, the Father sees,"
And thus the Son doth mediate and frees
The soul from abstract concepts of ideal
And proves the life of God in man is real.

The Farer
How sweet thy words, how true, how sure they sing,
Removing doubt; how great the faith they bring
To human hearts who in the darkness grope
Until in Christ they resurrect their hope!

The Scribe

Deep into night the Farer sat to ponder,
His soul upraised in ecstasy and wonder.
Then back he flung to a divided mind
Because he dragged old shibboleths behind—
The so-called "verities" that once stood sure
As solid rock, forever to endure.
Their power regained, they sank him in the sea
Of ancient doubt and old uncertainty.

The Farer

How can it be that I should lose the ray
That pierced the dark and showed to me the Way
Through doubt and gloom until I thought I saw
How love transmutes and substitutes for law.
With other so-called wise, I thumbed the scroll
Of ancient wisdom; in the inverted bowl
Of inner space I marked the star of hope,
Cast off old anchors and cut away the rope
That bound me to the past of ignorance
To sail the sea of spiritual romance,
Only to find myself as firmly bound
By the dead letter of the intellect
As I had been by ignorance. I checked
The frenzied thoughts that galloped through my brain
And sought once more to bring them under rein.
There must be still another way to waken
Those deep convictions by which I had been taken,
That I might daily know my first consuming bliss
When first I felt upon my lips the cosmic kiss.

I found it! In dual measure it began
With my clear vision of an earth-born man
Whose words and life brought clearly to my view
That men of earth are born of heaven, too!
In Jesus Christ I found a mind so clear
A child could understand, and yet the seer
Has never plumbed the depth so deep or high

Its splendor sweeps beyond the earthly eye,
And in one moment's vision we can see
How man is heir to all Eternity.
I felt it then as I can feel it now
And I shall feel when I have crossed the brow
Of Western hills and down the slopes I go
To follow him into the sunset glow.

What did he say? How was it that he brought
Conviction to my mind? How was my thought
Founded at last upon the Rock of Ages?—
I, who had plumbed the depth of ages,
I, who had claimed to find the mystic key
To occult science and philosophy
And stood upon the pinnacles of ecstasy,
Had slipped so often from the lofty height
Down, down and down in the abyss of night,
Now found in Christ a way that led me on
To light and life and love that filled the dawn
With joy and peace and full serenity!
How was it that conviction came to me?
It was because in his simplicity
I found the answer that a child can find—
Not in the thunder and the raging wind
But in the Truth that Jesus Christ imparts
To those who search with open minds and hearts.
He gave new names to God; I heard him say,
"I am embodiment of Him, I am the Way,
I am the Truth, I am the Light, and he
Shall find the truth who follows after me.
I am the Bread of Life, I am the Vine,
There is no death for him who drinks this wine..."

At last the Living Word! And it sufficed!
A lamp to guide my steps, the Crystal Christ!

The Scribe
The Farer brooded on the mystery,
"I am in the Father, and ye, in Me,"
And then he spoke in partial memory:

The Farer
How shall I tell the story
Of that life in whom the glory
Of the Father was transmuted
Into flesh and blood and brain
Of the Son of Man again?
For the life of Christ is rooted
In the mystery of being,
Source and substance of our seeing,
And in him is brought to birth
God incarnate on the earth—
Symbol that all souls have birth
In the Godhead here on earth.
I found it joy to search for God anew
In imitation of the Christ and through
His eyes to see, his ears to hear, his life
To live the life of God, set free from strife.
Keep ye my word; who conquereth
Himself shall never taste of death.

The Scribe
Thus did the Farer ruminate upon
The simple words of Christ till break of dawn.
While from his lips the broken phrases fell,
Half-quoted, half with interludes to tell
His deeper thoughts upon the simple way
And words of Jesus; I could hear him say:

The Farer
"Blessed are the peacemakers for they shall be
The children of their God." This do I see,
For God is Peace. "Blessed are the meek" for they
Alone survive...Seek solitude and pray

In secret; be brief, direct, with little speaking,
Thy Father knows whatever thou art seeking;
"Fear not, your Father gives..."

But I, O God, have only part accepted,
One half received, the other half rejected;
Half-willing, I, and half-afraid because
I have so often failed obedience to laws.
Why have I robbed myself? How poor am I!
How wrong! The bread of heaven and the wine!
Yet I have failed, O Lord, to make them mine.
O heavenly vintage! I with down-turned cup
Have still complained Thou didst not fill it up.
Yet though it be, as Jesus Christ has said,
To all who ask, the Father giveth bread,
Still He doth give thee freedom of the will
To walk in light or in the darkness still.
I am aware that heaven waits for our
Acceptance of it, though soon or late the hour.

O Perfect Son, Thou best of best, Thou true,
Lead thou my way my earthly journey through,
It was thy word that man must perfect be
As is the Father who is shown in thee.
Nor need we pray for contact with the Whole
For even now he liveth in the soul.

The Presence

"Fear not," he said, "it is the Father's will
To give his kingdom to you and to fill
Your life with love and joy and peace divine—
Ask and receive, all that He hath is thine."
Absorb the consciousness of Christ, make thou
Of him the pattern of thy living now,
And, lo, thine inner life shall suddenly
Become aware that thou thyself art He.

The Scribe

The Farer spoke as one who talks in sleep
And draws old memories from treasures deep
With love and longing; or who desires to keep
The fleeting vision of some beloved face:

The Farer

Stay thou with me, O Christ, and by the grace
Of God, I shall through thee become aware
That heaven waits for him who finds the altar-stair
For there God is and He is everywhere.
And Jesus said that everyone must be
As perfect as the Father and must see
That that perfection lies inherently
In ev'ry soul...It is the Father's will
To give to you the kingdom; he will fill
Your heart with heaven now. Today thy soul
Shall be with me in Paradise. Be thou made whole.
Abide in God and ye abide in Me..."
O Christ of God, let me abide in thee.

The Scribe

The Farer's ecstasy seemed all but spent
But looking up he saw in wonderment
Convulsive shaking of the astral scene
And Jesus stood, as once it might have been
In Galilee with children singing, and
They had clustered round and held his hand.
"Permit the children thus to come to me,
For in the Kingdom they shall ever see
The Father's face."...What sweet simplicity!

And he who saw the face of Jesus knew
That in that face he saw the Father, too.
Who sees the Son, the Heavenly Father sees;
Bow down, O soul, bow down upon thy knees,
Not to one Christ but every Christ within
The mind of man. Behind the face of sin,

A god! My claim to God? Why this I say
That "ye are gods"[111] and ye are gods alway...
If he said this to those who sought to murder him
Doth he not say to you, do not bedim
The inner light, you are not made of sod,
Man is divine, man's other name is God.

The Farer saw or felt himself projected
Into the scene before him, felt connected
With past and present and the future, too,
And stood above himself and seemed to view
The stream of life eternal flowing through
His being and it seemed to him that he
Faced either way into eternity
And found in Jesus prototype of man
Whom God conceived before the ages ran
Into the dark, dead waters of the sea
Of death and fear and of futility.
The Farer felt that Jesus took his hand
And led him on and up to higher land
And showed him all the wonders man can do,
Who worships God, for soul and body, too.
How practical the Master who had said
Ye cannot live alone on daily bread
Yet still ye must have bread! and wine and meat!
And fed the hungry,[112] sitting at his feet.
And when the fishermen were sore beset
He showed the place where they should cast the net
And from the mouth of one great fish[112] he drew
A coin to pay the taxes for them, too.
How practical he was, how simple was his word!
Yet oft in parables—to enemies absurd,
But to his friends encouragement and hope,
A glass through which to view—an astroscope
To bring all heaven in sight to mortal eyes
And show the domes and towers of Paradise.

The Sower and the seed, the talents of pure gold
And how to multiply and make them manifold!

Another mood was on him and he paused
To wonder how the Christ employed the laws
Of Cosmic Consciousness and by his birth
Had brought some part of heav'n down to earth—
More likely still, a greater gift was giv'n—
He stooped and lifted up the earth to heav'n.
And Jesus' speech was tuned to simple things,
The lilies of the field, a bird on wings,
A sparrow's nest, the children in the street
Who played the hours away with dancing feet.
How childlike minds of oft unlettered students
Confound the wise who boast of jurisprudence!

The Farer

Must I who soared in rarest atmospheres
To heights where earth has shrunk till it appears
A swinging pendulum to measure out the years—
Must I, a master of humanities,
Be taught in simple parables like these?

The Presence

Yet, what is life but living day by day
Not in uncommon but in a common way?
A deeper search reveals the subtility
So oft concealed beneath simplicity.
Such occult meanings in the allegory
Of payment to the workers in the story
Of the vineyard where the toiler for a day
Receives no more for labor than the pay
Accorded those who work one hour alone—
Yet here a principle is clearly shown:
When once a man makes contact with a Power,
It works for him, unmeasured by the hour.
The Law is just and equal the reward

For those who once made contact with their Lord.
"Once" is forever to him who contacts Truth.[113]

The Scribe

On Jesus' face the Farer fixed his sight,
Longing for the wisdom of the Nazarite.[114]

The Farer

I do revere thee, so simple and so wise,
And many are the parables that I do symbolize.
But most of all the story of the son,
The Prodigal, the wastrel. I was one
With him. I lost my way. But when at last
I found myself, stripped down to primal Me,
I woke within the Father's house to see
That I am son of God eternally.

The Presence

This is the story of awakened man
A sweeping drama of all evolution,
Who has the eyes to see, the ears to hear
Shall know a world behind this world, and he
Shall sometime enter in thereat, perhaps
With other eyes to see and ears to hear.
The soul possesses such. But man must build
A soul to house his self when he shall take
His way among the stars...See how it grows!
The mustard seed is small but from itself
Evolves, expands and putting forth its limbs
Gives ample shade and shelter for the birds.
The flower giveth not in *parts* but as a *whole*
And from the first it is totality [115]—
My Father *Is* and He and I are one.

The Scribe

The Farer, gazing on the astral scene,
Could not in clarity discern between
The Christ, the Presence and himself; for he

Recalled the words deep hid in memory
But lost awhile through failure to obey.

The Voice

Let your light so shine on men that they
Shall glorify your Father. It is true
That that same light that shone through him shines through
The soul of every man whose lamp is set
Where men can see upon the parapet.
Light thou the lamp of truth! and lift it high!
Give bread of hope to ev'ry passer-by.
To him who gives, a greater shall be given,
The gift of faith and love, of God and Heav'n.
Have trust in Me; whoso believes *in Me*
Shall find the springs of life within and he
Shall never thirst—the waters are supernal
A fountain stream that flows through life eternal.[116]

I am comfort to the sorrowing,
I am shepherd to the sheep,
I am water to the thirsty,
I am rest and peace and sleep;
I am soil and fruit and harvest,
I am wisdom to the wise,
I am seed by faith implanted
Which bears fruit in Paradise.

The Scribe

And then at last he knew beyond the reach
Of earthly consciousness or mortal speech
That Christ and God and self identified
Were truly one. The Christ had never died
And he who finds his life within the Me
Has found his place within the Trinity.
The panorama trembled and the form
Of Jesus seemed half shadow and half light
As clouds appear translucent and opaque
In part, and the soul-body of the Christ

Which he had built with density so deep
It could be seen when he was visible
To his disciples following the death,
Of body, so-called, on the cross, began to move
Away. But as it moved, the multitude
Moved with him—all the followers of Hermes,
All the sacred throngs of Rama,
Krishna, Buddha, Moses, Zoroaster,
Orpheus, Plato and Pythagoras
And seers of far-off China who are named
Laotse, Fu-Ke and Confucius;
And worshippers of Zakatol,[117] led on
By Can and Coh the founder-architects
Of ancient Yucatan; all these and more.
I saw them all in one vast multitude,
Beyond the reach of numbers or of name
Save that each standard bore insignia
For the Triune Deity, the Father,
Mother and the Son.

Hidden in My Very Presence,
Father of all Time and Timeless
Uncreated, the Creator,
Is the Spirit and the Substance,
Is the Pattern of Creation,
Is the Source and Life of All.

Song of the Father

14

The Farer

The Presence took my hand and guided me
Across the bridge and up the heights, and he
And I stood on a pinnacle to face
And gaze into an endless reach of space.
Then near at hand there seemed to rise a mist
That turned to gold with fringe of amethyst.
All, all was silent until at last a breath
Was breathed which sighed as one who whispereth
Before he speaks and fills all space around—
The Voice of the Eternal; and the sound
Was joined by voices singing all about;
And through, above, below, within, without,
They gave response in tonal waves of thunder
That shook my soul with glory, awe and wonder.

The Father

Hidden in My Very Presence,
Father of all Time and Timeless,
Uncreated, the Creator,
Is the Spirit and the Substance,
Is the Pattern of Creation,
Is the Source and Life of All.

The Chorus

Thou, O Blessed One and Holy,
Clothed in splendor, from the Formless
Moldest all the forms of nature
Into beauty ever-changing.
Thou art Power that firmly holds them
In the hollow of Thy hand.

The Father

I AM HE the Word Eternal,
I, the Word Divine and Perfect,
Am the Maker and the Law,
For all things I have created,
For all beings I designed.

I who made them am Creator
Of all songs and of all music.
In my hand I hold life's scepter—
Mine, the image and the pattern,
Mine, the ancient store of wisdom,
Mine, the substance and the meaning,
Mine, the law that governs all.

The Chorus
Blessed He the Sole Creator,
Blessed be the Primal Cause.
From the stillness of the Spirit,
From the deeps of inner silence,
From the Ancient Cause-of-Causes,
From the One and Only Being,
Comes the Word of All Creation
Brought to form upon the earth.

The Father
I am source of word and feeling,
I am form that molds the formless,
I am impulse of creation,
I, Who loves and blesses all.

The Chorus
From the heart of the Eternal,
From the mind of the Creator
Comes the law of all created,
Comes the Word that is command.

The Father
Close then to my very nature,
Close to all that is my being,
Close to all that I have imaged
Are the beings I have made.

The Chorus
They are those He has anointed,

They the ones He has appointed;
Let their vision ever-perfect
View the Father and the Son.

The Father

Emanating from My being,
Sons and daughters of My being
Are sustained by Me alone;
Let them glorify My presence.

The Chorus

All do glorify Thy presence
And Thy name is ever written
In the Soul of Thy created,
In the things that Thou hast done.

The Father

I, the secret of all beings
I, the source of their becoming,
Have in them the symbol hidden,
In the heart and mind of man.
I, the Lord of Lords ordain this,
I, the Power Supreme, command it—
That the heart of all created
Be not separate from Me.
I, my being ever-sharing,
I, Divine, forever giving,
Have imparted of my being
To incarnate in the Son.

The Chorus

Glory to the Source of Being,
Glory to the Heart of Being,
Who gave sons to share His being,
Breathed His breath of life into them,
Poured His love that wrought creation
On the children of his love.

Then as he spoke the Farer's soul was all
But spent and lost in pure beatitude.
The great gray dove spread wide its wings until
They seemed to brood upon the universe
And gather all the children of Her heart
In one embrace of mother-love and She
Began to merge in oneness with the All.

Song of the Mother

The Farer
Above the vapored mountain heights a cloud
No bigger than a hand appeared and grew
And took on shape, a great gray dove[118] with wings
Outspread, and by a slow descent it came
To settle at the Altar of the Ages.
It brooded there.
      My very breath was stilled
With wonderment, the more because within
The symbol of the Cosmic Motherhood
I saw unnumbered forms and faces of
The yet unborn, the embryonic sons
And daughters of the race still in the womb.
And I beheld the cord celestial
That binds the souls of all who live
Or who have ever lived back to the heart
Of Cosmic Motherhood.
      In ecstasy
I knew that it was given me to see
The age-old mystic form of Her Who is
One aspect of the Trinity,
I caught half-vision of Her changing faces
As Nari,[119] spouse of Nara; and Devaki,
The virgin mother clasping Krishna in
Her arms; and Istar holding on her knees
The infant Tammuz; Isis standing on
A crescent moon with Horus at her breast,
And Mary, symbol of the Motherhood[120]
Of God, who brought the Christ to mortal birth.
And it was given me to know by sight
The truth the seers had voiced in ages gone.
The mystery of Trinity was here
Revealed. The glorious Motherhood
That had been vaporous in my thought
Took on reality and She Who is
The essence of all created things was
Evidenced as substance—the Eternal
Feminine which, plastic to the will of

The Eternal Masculine conceives
And brings the holy son[121] to birth.
                                        I saw
Into the essence of all wisdom and
Understood the mystery enfolded
In the Holy Ghost.
                        O Holy Dove, who
Through the ages hath revealed to aching
Hearts the Motherhood of God, I praise and
Worship in Thy name the Holy Trinity!

The Scribe
Then as he spoke the Farer's soul was all
But spent and lost in pure beatitude.
The great gray dove spread wide its wings until
They seemed to brood upon the universe
And gather all the children of Her heart
In one embrace of mother-love and She
Began to merge in oneness with the All.
Then the mother-voice of Nature rose in
Song, and angel voices lent their rapture
To its sweetness.

The Chorus
Hid beneath the veil of Nature,
Screened by never-ending ages,
Are the patterns of creation,
Are the forms of all created;
And these seeds of life were planted
In the womb of Mother Nature.
She, the Mother of all being,
Ageless, birthless, changeless, deathless,
Bore the seeds of life on earth.
As to time, there is the timeless;
As to form, there is the formless;
And the ages, past and present,
Flowing from this unseen river,
Bear the seed of the conception

Which contains the primal thought;
In the seed-time and the harvest,
In the sowing and the reaping
Is fruition of the pattern
Brought to vision and to form.
And to Thee, O Holy Mother,
Be the praise of all creation—
Thou dost bring the form to birth.

The Mother

This the nature of my being,
I, the Mother of Becoming,
I, the stream of evolution,
Am the substance of creation;
I am matrix of all form;
I am chalice for Creator;
I, the Virgin Mother waiting
For the time of my deliverance
Feel the life within me stirring
Of the Holy Spirit's mating;[122]
For my love responding to Him
Finds a holy union with Him
To create the Holy Son.

The Chorus

Yea, thou Mother of Creation,
Yea, thou breast of cosmic being,
In your womb forever holding
All the patterns of creation,
Do conceive, give birth to all;
And forever will replenish
Life within the universe.

The Mother

Oh, the joy of my conception,
Oh, the wondrous child of love—
Ye, the children of my love.

The Chorus

    All the vigor of the Father,
    All the wisdom of Creator,
    All the love of Holy Mother
    Are incarnate in the Son.

The Mother

    All my love is lavished on you,
    In my arms so tender holding,
    Sons and Daughters of the earth;
    Holy children in life's manger,
    Born of wisdom and perfection,
    Fruit of cosmic impartation,
    Ye are born of grace above,
    Ye, my offering of love.
    Ye, my children, born of heaven,
    Are the offspring of the leaven
    Of the All-Creative Being
    And ye glorify my being
    With perfection of your love.
    Drink ye from the river flowing
    From the fountainhead above.
    By its waters, life-sustaining,
    Ye forever shall, remaining,
    Be the children of my love.

The Chorus

    Hail, Mother, full of grace,
    We the children of the race
    Do adore thee...

The Scribe

    The far dim echo of the choralists
    Was heard no more, dissolving in the mists
    That closed around the great gray dove between
    Her and the Farer. As She left the scene
    The clouds assumed an incandescence white
    And like the moon they shed a holy light

331

Upon the altar; for a moment he
Could see Her face in calm serenity.
A halo spread around Her, rimmed with stars,
The holy radiance of celestial bars
That framed the clouds with brilliant rainbow hue
Against a far-flung screen of heavenly blue

The altar of the ages dissolved into the mist
That drew its folds around the visionist.

The Farer
It is not given man too long to fix his eyes
Upon the sainted forms of Paradise,
Lest he, like Lazarus, with deadened sight
Should walk the earth bedazed with heaven's light.
Yet I who face fulfillment of my span
To work and live the normal life of man
Walk in a glory, seeing that my quest
Is all but solved and I am nearing rest.

The ether quivered and slowly fading light

Withdrew the sacred altar from my sight

But just beyond upon the western rim

Of mountain heights I saw the form of him

Who spake as man and God and grouped around

Were his disciples: then I heard the sound

Of angel choirs; they disappeared from me

Across the rim into Eternity.

Song of the Son[123]

I breathed a warm sweet fragrance like to flowers
That bloom unseen before the waking hours;
I felt a Presence, heard a whispered sound,
And in the stars above, in all around
I knew that God was coming into birth,
Incarnate soul of all the things on earth:
"Look thou behind the face of things and see
The Son of God proclaiming, 'Come to Me';
I am in all, through all and thou shalt find
Behind all form the evidence of mind.
Behold thy God incarnate in the Son[123]—
He is the soul of all and all are one."

Then as the caravan moved on in space
I still recalled the finely chiseled face
Of *One* who seemed embodiment of Him
Whom none has seen; and through the spaces dim
I heard a voice, a strong and youthful voice:
Be glad, O man! Again I say rejoice!
I am one with the Eternal,
I am universal Son;
In my life has the Supernal
Shown that God and man are one,
Not the only, not in nature
Is the Christ the only one,
For each soul can have the stature
Which proclaims him as the Son.[123]
I, the Son of God incarnate;
I, the holy child of nature;
I, his sacred word embody;

I, his wondrous name proclaim.
From the deep and hidden matrix
Of the womb forever bearing,
I, the son of God's becoming,
Through the ages past and present,
Come in form to be beholden,
Come in spirit, mind and body,

Come in likeness of the human,
Come to earth as his own Son.
Never parted from his presence,
I am pattern of his being;
I, the likeness of that being,
Am the word of God made flesh.
All the secret longing, yearning
In the heart of the Eternal
Finds its joy in my expression,
Finds its happiness in me.
For the One who is above all,
And the One who is within all
Is the Father of all being,
Is the Cause of all that is.
Not alone in ages ancient,
Not alone in ages present,
Not alone in time prophetic,
Nor in ages yet to be
Is my birth, my incarnation,
Is the time of my appearance,
When the word of God proclaims me
Into manifested form.
For the ethers of the silence
And the fertile womb of nature
Are forever stirring, stirring
With celestial fire from heaven;
And the Mother of creation
And the Father of created
Are forever joined in union
And forevermore conceive.
I the Son forever 'gotten
By the Father and the Mother,
Active always in begetting,
Am eternal with creation.
In the ages long forgotten,
In the dim and vast forever,
In the future, past and present
Is the sacred impartation,

Is the holy impartation,
Is the constant incarnation,
Is the form and life and action
Of the Universal Son.
God the Father of creation
Moving in the womb of nature
Stirring in the holy mother
Evermore begets his Son.
And the joy of this creation
And the joy of the created
Are as heav'nly songs united,
Are supernal in their bliss.
And the light within the Father
And the love within the Mother
Fill the earth and fill the heavens
With the radiance of their beauty.
And the Sons of Love Supernal
Bear the strength of Holy Father,
Bear the beauty of the Mother
And unite the two in one.
This the secret is of sonship,
This the glory is of union,
This the consummate of ages.

For throughout all time and ages,
Through the wise men and the prophets,
Through the humble and the lowly,
God has brought to each his sonship.
God has lighted lamps in heaven,
God has set his signet on us.
Wise or foolish though man be,
I, the son of love proclaim this;
I, the word of God announce it;
I, the spirit, now incarnate,
Do proclaim this truth forever.
This my hymn to the Creator,
This my song to all creation,
This my word to the created:

God and man are joined in one!
Humbly now I kneel in reverence
To receive a benediction
From the wise and Holy Father,
From the Universal One.

Wondrous is the chalice lifted
To the lips of the devoted;
To the heart thus consecrated
By the one he has anointed.
Now the sacrament completed
Joins all life in sweet communion
With all times and with all ages;
Sweet the bread refreshed with wine.

The Farer
The ether quivered and slowly fading light
Withdrew the sacred altar from my sight
But just beyond upon the western rim
Of mountain heights I saw the form of him
Who spake as man and God and grouped around
Were his disciples; then I heard the sound
Of angel choirs; they disappeared from me
Across the rim into Eternity.

With eyes upraised, amazed,
The Farer stood and gazed—
So captured and enraptured as to seem
In some ecstatic vision or a dream—
Toward some horizon far
Where shone the rising star
Of first creation when the worlds were born,
And pure ethereal substances of dawn
Took shape, solidified,
And space was occupied.
While through the vasty deep a shudder ran,
And then a voice proclaimed "Let there be man!"

The awakening 17

The Scribe
> With one last look upon the fading faces,
> One final cadence from the singing spaces,
> The Farer was alone, with eyes upraised
> At first in glory, then with pain bedazed.
> For deep within, he heard a tolling bell
> And knew at once—alas, he knew too well—
> The Presence, too, had faded from his sight;
> Though still he felt a stirring in the astral light.

> Long, long the silent Presence lingered near,
> None but the keenest sense could see or hear
> That he was there; he strangely seemed to merge
> Into the Farer's form and face, his demiurge.
> But now he spoke:

The Presence
>   Be not afraid, my friend,
> I have not left you; this is not the end,
> But it is time for you to find that he
> Is not alone who dwells in unity
> With God, abiding always in the Me;
> Nor think the human self and soul are two
> Or that two voices speak, for both are you!

The Farer
> I do not comprehend this wonder; nor heart
> Nor head consents that you yourself depart.

The Presence
> It is expedient I do not stay
> Lest you should turn from your own self away
> And think causation rises from without
> And not within. Such concept put to rout!
> When *first* the soul becomes of *self* aware
> He thinks *another* self, *another* mind is there—
> He has no scale, no laws, no abacus
> By which to measure out the rapturous;

But when a voice is heard, believes some Power
Above himself, beyond the present hour,
Has come to visit him, some *being* from afar,
Some astral form, some spirit from a star;
So thou, whose vision glimpsed eternal Me,
Ascribed the inner voice to outer deity.
If now that voice seems faint and far and dim,
It is because *thy self* embodies him.
Henceforth his voice encased within thy tone
Shall speak with force, but it shall be thine own.
Forevermore thy wide-eyed soul shall be
Awake, aware that thou thyself art Me.

The Farer

Thou hast lit my death with lamps of life,
Unshackled me from chains of earthly strife;
Eternity has passed through me in Time
And I no more am creature of the slime
But know myself as born again; yet so,
I cannot part from thee and let thee go.

The Presence

You must escape at last from bondage to
The sense of separation. Hold it true
That he is not alone who knows that he
Is ever one with the eternal Me.
The secret of existence is unbarred
And even now the temple bell is heard
Inviting all to worship at the shrine
Of the Eternal Truth—this is the sign
That he will find the Father-Spirit hid
Within himself and do what He has bid.

The Farer

I vow myself to this and I will ever hide
Myself in Him and there will I abide;
Still does my yearning heart desire to know
That you will go with me where'er I go.

The Presence
> One does not stand alone who stands
> With love, for love is God and God is All.
> This truth above all others must remain,
> Which I have taught again and yet again;
> This I repeat and leave with you alway
> Which you must hold against the coming day—
> Despite today's bewildered Parthenon—
> The Lord, thy Holy God, the Lord is One.
> Thy God is One and heaven thy habitat,
> All shall be well with thee for THOU ART THAT.
> The living truth proclaims thy deity,
> He who abides in love abides in Me.

The Scribe
> The Farer's face was luminous;
> It seemed to light the night,
> As when the stars united spread
> A pure unearthly light.

The Presence
> At last you see! The *heart* can understand
> And lead the *mind* into the Holy Land.
> This truth doth hold in life and death the same,
> That he who seeks with an unfailing aim
> Shall reach the goal of wisdom for today,
> And at the hour when he shall put away
> This mortal world, his new-built soul shall be
> So filled with memories of the self that he
> Shall wake Beyond still conscious of the Me.

The Scribe
> The Farer's face was eloquent with deep
> And awe-filled stirrings of the mind as if
> He bore some burden back and forth across
> A bridge uniting two infinities.
> And twice he called out to the Presence; when
> The Presence did not make reply, he cried:

The Farer

>Speak clearly; O my best and only hope,
>Thy voice grows dim, and shadowed is thy form;
>Do not depart. I fear thou leavest me.

The Presence

>I chide thee, O my double, for this word;
>Fear not for anything on earth nor in
>The universe. Unlike the prison door,
>The mind unbarred is free forevermore
>From superstition and belief in Two
>And brings the long-sought goal to view.
>Thyself, thy senses and thy heart today
>Have found their unity; I need not stay;
>Should I remain, you would divided be
>And think that you and I and God are three,
>The time has come to merge them in the Me.
>Retain thy faith in thy true self alone;
>In thee is Father, Mother and the Son,
>In thee the Lord thy God, the Lord is One.
>For this I came, for this I go away
>That you be born again. This is the day
>That your divided selves find unity,
>Embraced within the allness of the Me.

The Scribe

>Upon the Farer's face emotions now
>Played out their parts across his mobile brow,
>While joy with sadness vied in equal part
>To fill the aching void within his heart—
>The hour had struck! He must assume the role
>Of one who knows no master but his soul;
>Admitting now what he had long suspected
>But which before he had in fear rejected,
>The Presence WAS HIMSELF!
>   The truth that lay
>Behind the mystery now saw the light of day,
>While sudden joy put ghostly pain to rout

And freed him from the ancient depths of doubt.
And in this hour supreme he seemed to be
The Voice of Truth and of Philosophy,
For in a single sentence so profound
That future man will listen for the sound,
He summed up all the wisdom of the past—
The riddle solved within his soul at last.

The Farer

The Great Enigma, human life and destiny,
The meaning of the soul, the what and why,
The whence and whither of all life, which once
Outpoured in vials of despair, are now
Resolved into a synthesis which leaves
Me breathless with a glowing faith and joy;
For now I know directly that I draw
My life from Cosmic Life, and I am merged
With God through Love and Knowledge, and I see
They are the same, and that with Beauty they
Do form the highest Trinity.

The Scribe

Then for the last time he addressed his word
Of recognition to the Presence:

The Farer

I know now whom thou art, thou vision blest:
Thou art my soul-self; with thee, celestial guest,
I shall expand throughout the firmament;
I am Thy voice, with this am I content.

The Presence

When self on higher self doth meditate,
The key will turn that opens wide the gate
Through which the unseen guest shall welcomed be,
Reveal himself and make his home with thee.
When he has come, shut tight and lock the door
Against false guests that they may come no more—

All vain regrets, all memories that bind
Thy lofty soul back to the lower mind,
Old fears and superstitions, and the horde
Of thieves and robbers of thy peace.
                                    Restored
To primal self, bring thou thy mind to view,
The good, the beautiful; abiding true
To vows of love and faith and unity
In that first joy when you discovered Me.

The Farer
A flash, one moment of the passing vision
And I am merged with Everlasting Life!
My soul has slipped into the cosmic river
Which shall flow on forever and forever,
A stream that circles through the Cosmic Sea,
I shall be one with God and He with Me.

The Scribe
Then was the Farer's face enraptured
With that soft radiance which clearly glows
Through alabaster lamps on altars set
And he began to sign a hymn of praise
That magnified the Only Causing Cause
In notes of love that swept across his heart
As waves of music sweep across the harp
Of gifted melodists so that the strings
Appear to play themselves, his soul so rapt.

The Farer
How shall I praise Thy name
From Whom creation came,
By Whom the cords, that bind the human heart
In fear, are loosed! Set free,
My soul in praise of Thee
Will echo endlessly, Thou art, Thou art!

Thou art the life of all,
Revealed or mythical,
In things of form or thought, the secret riven;
In love didst Thou descend,
Revealed Thyself as friend,
With such angelic grace, a Prince of Heaven!

The Scribe

He paused, so overcome by love and awe,
It seemed that he for just one moment saw
His visitor celestial clothed in silver white
Fade into glory in a cosmic light.
With Eyes upraised, amazed,
The Farer stood and gazed—
So captured and enraptured as to seem
In some ecstatic vision or a dream—
Toward some horizon far
Where shone the rising star
Of first creation when the worlds were born,
And pure ethereal substances of dawn
Took shape, solidified,
And space was occupied.
While through the vasty deep a shudder ran,
And then a voice proclaimed "Let there be man!"

The Farer

The search is ended, I myself am He
Who was and is. I am Eternity
And shall abide forever in the Me.

And I yearn that we together
May press forward, kneel together
At the Altar of the Ages
To adore the Central Flame.

The Farer's dedication 18

I shall not call you stranger
For I feel we met before,
Though you dressed in other mantles
And you spoke another tongue;
I have seen you ride the waters,
Heard your laughter through the foam.
I have met you in the desert,
Or the valleys of despair;
I have met you—you were there.

You were in the joy of children,
And the mellowness of age;
In man's faith and his illusions,
In his dreams and aspirations,
In the hour of his fulfillment
Or the pain of his regret.
I was there and so we met.

I have met you at the altar
In the rites of the communion;
I have seen you in high places
Where they heaped the gifts of honor.
Yours the hopeful morn of dreaming,
Yours the sweat and toil of noontime,
Yours the sunset glow of even
And the stilly calm of night.

No, I shall not call you stranger;
I remember we embraced;
It was you who bid me welcome.
At the altar of our being,
Each has been both host and guest,
Each was by the other blest.

All we asked was understanding
So that each in the comingling
Would, like water, flowing freely
In another water merging,

Find that each becomes the other
Since they both are now but one;
God designed and it is done.

It is like the sweet aroma
Of the rose that mingles fragrance
With another sister blooming,
Growing on the self-same stem.
Who has language to express it,
This sweet union and communion,
This delight of understanding!
Eager is the searching, yearning,
And the longing for the merging
Of the streams that seek each other,
That the two of them together
May flow back into the Ocean,
By the Mother-Spirit kist,
Whence they sprang in cosmic mist.

In the joy of our communion,
We perceive at length the secret
Of the sweetness that delights us
In the family of God.
In one soil we have been rooted.
Deep within our final being,
At the very heart of being,
Each is heir to all the beauty,
All the joy and inner sweetness
Of the All-Embracing One.
So it is with eager longing
I return to you, my friend,
Seek from you the love I gave you
That we two, by love united
May together spiral backward
From the very outer rim
To the point of our beginning;
From circumstance to the center—

This the faring of the soul
Into oneness with the Whole.

This is why to each comes yearning
For completeness and for union
Each in each and All in All.
This is why we feel compulsion
That we journey on together.
Let us walk the spheres together,
Let us mount the topmost rim,
Guided by the Seraphim.

I have gone into the garden
Where God walks in cool of even
And have seen the petals open
To reveal the hidden secret;
In the full-bloom of my garden,
I have seen the long-lost faces
Where the wayward seeds have blown
Of the friendships I have known.
Here beside my shrine I linger
And to you have lit a candle,
Placed it on this sacred altar,
Dedicated in my heart.
Here I know and feel your presence
Like an essence, sweet, diffused;
Or like wine outpoured in heaven
From the table of our God.
And I lift it up and drink it,
Quaffing from this sacred cup
To the joy of all our living,
Sweet elixir of our friendship,
As together once we drank it
In the banquet room above
'Til our veins were filled with love.

No, I will not call you stranger,
For I feel we met before,

And I know within this garden,
I have met you once again,
Know that God Himself is with us,
Has in us Himself saluted,
Somehow lonely 'til we met,
Joying that at last we met.

.   .   .   .   .

This is then the dedication
And the final consummation
Of my story as a Farer
On the spiral highway mounting
To the mystic throne of God.
All these gleanings of my journey
I do offer you most freely;
Not a tale of rugged struggle,
Not of failure or achievement,
Not of pain and bitter anguish,
But of Truth that was unfolded
By the Angel of the Presence.

And I yearn that we together
May press forward, kneel together
At the Altar of the Ages
To adore the Central Flame.
Pure the soul that from the Father
Fared upon the outbound journey!
Pure again it shall return.
It is that toward which we yearn!

.

"If we have only hoped in Christ for this life, we are of all men most pitiable...but if we believe that Jesus died and rose again then also all them that have fallen asleep in Jesus (the Christ-consciousness) will God bring with him."

Postword

The explanations in the foregoing epic should be clear in and of themselves. Nonetheless, as we are seriously attempting to outline a full philosophy of Mind and the evolution of doctrines originating in many minds and over many centuries, and as the definitions are transferred across the borders of time and of languages, it seems appropriate to add a few explanations which may enable the serious student to revisit the field of investigation he has just traversed and see it with clearer eyes and a better perspective.

The goal of *The Voice Celestial* has been to bridge the centuries that have passed since Jesus, the last of the great masters, gave his message to mankind and to link it into the present age. The return to religion is not to Paul but to Jesus. It is one of the anomalies of history that the theology, rituals and authority of a great religious faith should be founded not on the teachings of its Master but on the concepts of a man who never saw him, who did not even consult with Jesus' personal apostles for several years, and depended upon garbled reports and a psychic experience in setting the pattern of his interpretation. Although it was not Paul but an unknown author who wrote the Letter to the Hebrews and some other works ascribed to Paul, his footprint is burned into the records of the history of the church.

While the church owes much to the Pauline authors and to the beauty of many of his phrases and concepts, nonetheless he must be looked upon as having been a barrier through which the stream of the unfolding revelations of the great prophets could hardly penetrate.

It is both a simple and profound fact that the two major principles in religion which were the heart of the revelations of the seers, including Jesus, must be restored today as far as possible in their primal splendor.

These two are (1) the Law of Cause and Effect and (2) Idealistic Monism, which hold true in both the field of physics and of metaphysics.

The historic church for many centuries made every effort to disavow its ancient historic origins. In order to enforce the concept of a *revealed* religion appearing spontaneously and in its entirety in the first years of our era, it did its best to destroy its own roots, which ran back through immemorial time. The early church was in fact largely Mithraic and drew from other oriental religions, although it afterwards denied its debt to them and to Appollonius of Tiana, the Pythagorean philosopher of the date of Jesus.

These faiths were monotheistic (or trinitarian, Three-in-One) as taught by the masters. The dualism in the theology of the church was drawn from a misconception of the Mithraic teachings of Zoroaster and other alien sources and contradicts the teaching of Jesus regarding monotheism.

Although in physics we know but One Law of light, heat, power, gravitational separation, elastic strain, etc., and although science posits the principle that man controls his world by obeying its laws, religion still insists on dualism, God and the devil, sin and salvation, heaven and hell, i.e., two opposing principles, and many still propound an entity of personal devil.

Corollary with this is the teaching in regard to Law. While in science, as we have said, there is but One Master Law, we are taught by Pauline Christianity that effects can be separated from causes and salvation secured by theological doctrines and practices, the major Pauline concept being *salvation from the consequences of sin.*

If the reader finds in the epic poem *The Voice Celestial* a stream of references to these two major principles, he may be assured that the authors so intended. The riddle of life and the universe cannot be solved without this knowledge. It can be solved with it.

An endless number of secondary principles evolve from these two; in fact, a whole philosophy of life as taught by those whose lives have been recorded in this book. Not only science and religion are affected by this philosophy, but also psychology, industry, business, the healing arts, and social relationships of all kinds. Great masses of people have been affected by the revitalization and reestablishment of these fundamental principles and have experienced redemption from disease and want, fear and sorrow through faith in the all-embracing consciousness of Universal Love. Above all, they have found God.

The new emphasis on the Father-Mother Doctrine of the ages has not diminished the luster of Jesus, but on the contrary, has brought him into focus as the last and greatest of the Masters. He so summed up their revelations that he became the embodiment of their principles and so impressed himself on the succeeding centuries that we who are heirs to his name call him Christ and ourselves Christians.

Jesus Christ

The greatest single gift ever presented to mankind by seer, scientist, or savior was made by Jesus—the demonstration and proof of a soul! Men had believed in a soul, they had taught their belief, they had fashioned "Passion Plays" to illustrate it, but the final and definite proof lay in the teaching and experience of Jesus. There was only one way to prove it—to die and to reappear, not as part of a "play" in which the hero of the pageant dies, descends into nether regions and reappears, as in the Eleusinian Mysteries; but as an actual experience of death and survival.

The resurrection has been so glamorously emphasized that the church has underplayed the real significance—man has a soul!

It is here that the problem of *words* must be met. What is a soul? What is a self? What is it that lives *here* and survives *there*? We use many terms interchangeably. Let us look at them: We speak of "man"; "what is man that thou art mindful of him?" The Sanskrit MN is the source of the Latin word "Mens" or "mind" and means measurer. Man is a measurer or steward of the Universal Intelligence which he differentiates. He is *being* or that-which-is...The word "self" denotes individuality or identity of a being whose inner life is apart from all other lives. The self persists and is the *same* self always...The word "ego" esoterically means an evolving self, while in psychiatry, it is the conscious self or directing faculty...The significance of "self" deepens when denoted by such words as Logos, Atman and Christ. These refer to the Higher Self and indicate the unchanging or eternal essence of *man's being*. In this sense it is a symbol of the individualized Supreme manifesting in speech and reason...The word "ME" has an equal significance...All these denote individualized Spirit or Being...The word *"soul,"* like "self" is often used to indicate man's consciousness of himself apart from all other individual existences; but it also indicates the *formative principle which molds the body* and which can be influenced by thought and feeling and prayer so that man can build a better body here and also create a vehicle for his consciousness which survives the earthly body...

The word "psyche" is to be distinguished from "self" or *spiritual* being and refers to the natural man, that is to mind-emotions. Psychiatry uses the term psychosomatics to indicate the control of the *soma* or body by the *psyche* or mind. In both the Old and the New Testament psyche is used in the significance of soul.

This was the teaching of Pythagoras and of Plato as seen in the biographies of the foregoing epic. Paul makes use of the same principle when he speaks of the *psychical* body (Original Greek of I Cor. 15-44) (See also Ezekiel 13:18 and following) as independent of the physical body and of the body of the *pneuma* (spirit) as well. He assumes that both the pneuma and the psyche have bodies of a quasi-material nature. The recognition of a soul-body which survives the physical is essential to the understanding of the survival of individuality as taught by the masters and exemplified in the resurrection of Jesus. Nor is such survival contrary to the possibilities of modern science. Physics posits and proves the existence of an unseen and intangible world. A field of force which surrounds the ends of a magnet has both form and extension, but we do not see it. Science knows of worlds composed of substances which our sense organs cannot register. But they are there. An understanding of physics necessitates positing an unseen or intangible world from which the tangible or physical emerges. This is the electromagnetic field from which individual molds or patterns are formed and these are the "stuff" or "matter" of the visible world. All natural objects such as tree, beast, or man are formed or held in such mold. Pythagoras and Plato and most of the ancient faiths taught that the *self* forms a mold which they denominated the *soul* and referred to as the "subtile chariot." It is such a *form* that is visible at times in the astral field as an apparition, its opaqueness apparently due to a quasi-material substance which survives body death. (Dr. Duncan McDougall's experiments in the Massachusetts General Hospital proved that the body loses three-fourths of an ounce at death. Such survival is adequate to account for the appearance of "forms," "shapes," and apparitions. The story of the Bible is the story of exceptional men who held conversations with such ghostly visitants. Such visitations were made by Jesus apparently to certify his survival after the crucifixion.)

The necessities of language in the conveyance of ideas across the barriers of languages of many ages have necessitated our use of words which are not exactly synonymous. This is true in regard to the words we have just examined. We have at times used "soul" and "self" and "ego" and "Me" interchangeably as the "spirit in man." But with the ancient seers we may look upon "soul" as a persistent principle of form.

This was understood by the esoteric Spencer who perceived the psychosomatic relationship when he declared that the present visible physical body is a replica of the invisible soul.

> "For of the soul the body form doth take;
> For soul is form and doth the body make."

And this, of course, remains true for all planes on which man has existed or may exist. The soul, then, is real, but its nature depends upon the life, acts, thoughts, and motives of its creator, i.e., its own persistent self. There is no reason to doubt that all souls survive but that they progress or fall back according to the way in which the entity functions on any plane. It was because of this that the ancients and particularly Pythagoras and Plato formulated the principle of the migrations or the return of souls in repeated incarnations. While the present authors do not subscribe to such returns, the principle remains the same that man—*all* men—are building souls for future habitation.

Referring this now to the purpose and acts of Jesus Christ, we again affirm that the significance of the life of Jesus lay particularly in his teaching and manifestation of the *survival of consciousness in soul-form or life beyond death.* He realized that this assurance could not be afforded by a *"passion play"* but must be demonstrated by a personal experience which could be verified as factual by his disciples.

His concept was not spontaneous but a matter of growth. He had at first believed that the rule of love and justice could be established by a return to pure religion as taught by the prophets and in particular by Moses who had derived his concepts of the religious and social order directly from spiritistic communications, in which the God of Monotheism had revealed the slender barrier between life here and life beyond. There is abundance of evidence that Jesus was a member of the party of Essenes, the final survival of the brotherhood of the prophets organized by Samuel. They were physicians who healed by light and other natural means. Their organization and principles were almost identical with those of Pythagoras, including prayer at sunrise, the wearing of linen garments, a primitive form of the Lord's Prayer, and a belief in the preexistence of the soul which "descending from the subtle ether...is attracted into the body in which it remains as in a prison; freed from its bonds, as from a long servitude, it joyfully takes flight."*

Through the Essenes, Jesus had acquired the doctrine of the divine "Word" which had been initiated by Krishna, developed by the priests of Osiris and elaborated by Orpheus and Pythagoras. The "Word" was the Son of Man and the Son of God, the prototypal or perfect Man who would appear as the Hidden One or the Messiah. In the book of Henoch he was represented as the "Son of Woman."

Such doctrines were instilled into the mind of Jesus and he meditated upon and developed them during the period in which he attempted to bring about religious and social changes in Palestine. He accepted the monotheistic doctrine of the masters and elaborated the thought of the Divine Unity as an individual experience. "I and the Father are One," he said, thus making practical for daily life the inner secret of the great faiths—the identity of "man" with God—(Failure to know and act upon this, his highest teaching, has weakened the structure of the modern church.)

Like Moses, Jesus attempted to make the esoteric doctrine known to all people—"the Kingdom of Heaven is already in you!" It was this truth, emphasized by his resurrection, that transformed the lives of hopeless slaves, of the poor and oppressed, into a life of joyful hope. It was Jesus' belief that an inner change would produce objective justice, advance wisdom, and secure good government. Unlike Plato, he did not deal with it as a thesis. He did not attack governments, but the doctrines and institutions which control the masses and majorities of men. Like Philo in Egypt, who was at that very time synthesizing the Oriental Philosophy, Judaism and Hellenism, so Jesus was presenting a unified concept of truth and faith, of life on earth as a reflection of life in heaven; not in an abstract way but as a matter of personal practice.

He considered that man and the world were "lost" because the spark of divine wisdom had been lost from it.

It was only after his efforts at reform in religion and practice had utterly failed that he resorted to extreme measures, such as the ejection of the money-changers from the temple. At first his enemies were hard put to know how to destroy him because he countered attacks with truth and love. Even when they became violent, his strongest reaction was to deal with them from the point of view of seeing them as

*Josephus' A.J. ii 8.

spiritual malefactors, that is, rejectors of truth or "hypocrites."

He was at length convinced that the kingdom of heaven could not be established on earth without first establishing the conviction of the supremacy of the human soul above the plane of organized religion and government. This was the same objective as the passion plays or "mysteries," but to make it universal it was necessary once and for all for a human personality to pass through the experience of death and to verify the survival of the entity by reappearance among those who had known him in the physical body.

It is this experience that is the climax in our historic picture of the masters of the ages in *The Voice Celestial*. His reappearance after the crucifixion was the cornerstone of Christianity—without it there would have been no Christian Religion. Unfortunately for religion and mankind, the physical interpretation of the resurrection has dimmed its luster and identified suffering with the hope of survival. This has been doubly damned by the doctrine of the physical, rather than psychical, survival—the resurrection of the body—of Jesus. If Jesus had reappeared in the earthly vehicle of the soul rather than the psychical it would have offered hope but *not certainty* to the vast multitudes of the human race, because the survival of the body of Jesus does not give assurance of personal survival. Nor does mankind crave body survival but soul survival.

But it *was* the *soul* survival that Jesus demonstrated! This is proven in the Gospel Story in the Bible itself.

The personality of Jesus returned in soul form, in a body sufficiently dense to be seen but not always easily recognized by his disciples! The evidence is overwhelming, and such occurrences have been duplicated in myriads of similar ones throughout Christian history and will no doubt continue for ages yet to come. Even so, the final significance lies not in the appearances of soul forms but in the assurance of continuity of individual existence. It is the future existence of the self to which Paul alludes:

> "If we have only hoped in Christ for this life, we are of all men most pitiable (I Corinthians 15:19), but if we believe that Jesus died and rose again then also all them that have fallen asleep in Jesus (the Christ-consciousness) will God bring with him." I Thessalonians 4:14.

Notes

The object of the following notes is to give a quick reference, with no intention to deal with the subject from a textbook point of view nor to provide a bibliography. The words "thou" and "you" are interchanged not only by poetic license but also purposely to indicate the half-religious nature with which the Farer views the Presence.

Notes to first book

1. "THAT" represents absolute *being*, apart from all *form*. Plato used the term "Eternal Idea"; the Greeks, *to on;* Moses, IEVÉ: (see Note 45 of Second Book); the Vedantists used the phrase, "Tat twam asi," meaning "Thou art That," yourself is one with the All, i.e. the Infinite and Eternal and that all things are of one substance or "That-which-is."
2. ME is the individualized God, or "thou." It represents the *Infinite in Man.*
3. Not "direction" nor "place" but "state."
4. There are four theological views of "Christ as Redeemer," who "delivers the soul from (1) consequence of sin"; or, (2) from sin; or (3) the power of evil spirits; or, (4) imprisonment in matter. See the Postword and also Note 110 of Part II. The word *redemption* is not confined to the act of a savior. It is not to be looked upon as a transfusion of virtue into the veins of another. Its original or root meaning is "buying back" or *repossession.*
5. Men create different theologies from the same texts and the interpretations change from age to age.
6. Suggested by Ella Wheeler Wilcox's "Vision of Sir Launfal."
7. See Postword
8. Here "soul" is used to signify the individualized self.
9. This paragraph follows the thoughts of Plotinus.
10. As illusion is essentially a psychical experience, no attempt has been made to deal with it separately or sequentially in the field of "physical" and then of psychic phenomena. And the Farer is allowed at any point to retrace his steps and repeat his old doubts, as this is true to experience.
11. See Postword.

12. We use the word "ether" to indicate an Akashic medium where Einstein posits a "void."
13. Compare the Rig-Veda and Gospel of John, Chapter 1.
14. See Postword.
15. See Notes on Plato.
16. Quoted from Browning's "Paracelsus."
17. See Pythagoras.
18. i.e., in appearance.
19. Compare Note 4 and also Note 110, Part II.
20. See Postword.
21. So described by Plotinus.
22. Hinton says that the "intuition of space is the most fundamental power of the mind."
23. See John 12:24.
24. i.e., Being in all its attributes.
25. Name given by the Quiches to the Over-All (Supreme) deity (eleven thousand years ago), in Mayan language meaning "That which existed forever," "The eternal truth." The Egyptian Ra ("Sun") seems derived from it. Ancient Chinese philosophy indicated "The Great Unity" by "Y," since it had no body or shape. Later philosophers have used Y in the same way to indicate the Trinity—the stem being the Source from which the two branches emerge as part of it.
26. Not a "nature miracle" but in a symbolic sense.
27. The word "number" is the comparative of numb and pronounced "nummer."
28. This enigmatic statement is understood when interpreted in light of the law in psychology that whatever is established as a belief in the subconscious creative mind will be objectified in physical states—a principle of psychosomatics.
29. The four steps are (1) preparation, (2) incubation, (3) illumination, (4) verification.
30. Like Kipling's "Kim."
31. This experience of the Farer is typical of that described by mystics as the "dark night of the soul," which often transiently follows illumination or the experience of Cosmic Consciousness.
32. Caution must be observed not to interpret this as dualism.
33. i. e., a sense of unity.
34. The point in the heavens toward which the whole solar system, including the earth, is supposed to be traveling. Not the brilliant star in the constellation of Lyra. See dictionary.
35. The Presence here shows that "Logos" can lead to dualism.
36. So defined by Tagore.

37. See note on Buddha.
38. A saying of John Burroughs.
39. Compare Luke 9:58.

Notes to the second book

1. The experience of seeing and hearing the past is not uncommon. While Einstein changed the concept of ether, his principles gave added support to the claim that what is time at one point can be present space at another, overcoming former ontological concepts that the "past" is purely imaginary. The reality of such phenomona as are referred to in the following pages is verified in the book, "An Adventure," by Moberly and Jourdain, published by Coward-McCann, Inc., N.Y. See public libraries.
2. Quoted from Revelations 22:6.
3. Exact description from Hebrews Chap. 7 and from Genesis 14:18-19. This stupendous genius, priest-king, astronomer, temple-builder, who is most ancient of the ancients, was rightfully designated by the Farer before he knew anything of his earthly history.
4. Based on the principle of archetypal design in the universe, in which all measurements are proportionate; for example, the apparent structural proportionment of tbe human foot with planetary measurements. The pyramid inch is derived from dividing the polar diameter of the earth by multiples of 10 and these measurements are used not only in the Great Pyramid of Egypt but appear in the architecture of the temples and palaces of the ancient ruined cities of Yucatan in Central America, erected some 11,500 years ago, according to archeological research.
5. Photographs of snowflakes show that scores of them contain exact outlines of man-made objects, like household utensils.
6. The Laws of Manu declare that "knowledge of the self is the first (primary) of all sciences because immortality is gained through it."
7. (Quotation, not the words of the authors).
8. Knowable or manifest.
9. Not to be confused with "soma" meaning "body" in psychosomatic literature.
10. Rama and the Cythians were Europeans.
11. Quoted from Valmiki, the Hindu poet. "Man contains within himself all numbers, measures, weights, motions and measurements." Encyclopedic Outline of Symbolism. M.P. Hall.
12. We have dealt with Zoroaster (Zarathustra) here rather than under the heading of India because his teachings are in fact an extension of

Mithra. He is also dated by some back to 2500 years B.C. Max Müller presents evidence that he and his disciples lived in India because his sources reflect the Vedas.

13. Compare note on IEVÉ in chapter on Moses.
14. A ceremonial of the Parsees, described by a traveller, Rabbi Benjamin early in the 10th century.
15. This doctrine was later confirmed by Plato.
16. Moussa—name of Moses, 1300 B.C.
17. Even the highest church authorities agree that the Bhagavad-Gita was written at least two centuries B.C. Others hold with the authors that the year was approximately 1300 B.C. It is unnecessary to debate the parallelism with the life of Jesus Christ. One truth cannot contradict another. Rama, Krishna and Jesus are all historic characters encrusted with traditions.
18. Buddhic theory of purpose of reincarnation.
19. An eternal becoming. See also Pythagoras. See "Postword."
20. Establish the light of Nirvana.
21. Mother of Gotama Buddha.
22. An ascetic or travelling teacher.
23. The modern Kohana River. The site of the garden is marked by a pillar put up by Asoka.
24. Quoted from the Pali.
25. Renamed "Bo tree" or "tree of wisdom" because of this experience.
26. Nirvana means "dying out" of the sins of sensuality, ill-will, and stupidity; not a future state of coma nor annihilation but a salvation which only begins in this life and continues in the next.
27. Compare Chapter XI in 1910 edition of James' Psychology, in which he states the same. Compare also the philosophy of the Greek Heraclitus, who lived in Ephesus c. 500 B.C. and was called the "Weeping Philosopher."
28. Three centuries later, 427 to 347 B.C.
29. Literal Translation from Majjhima 1. 129.
30. Buddha and the poets used Pali, not Sanskrit.
31. Such quotations often appear to have come from the Bible. They are in fact the *original* from which the Bible may have quoted.
32. Enthusiasm, from the gk. words *en theos,* in God, denoting spiritual frenzy or god-intoxication.
33. Mentioned in an inscription of the Fourth Dynasty—that is, four thousand years before Christ, which speaks of its great antiquity at that date. The body of a bull, the wings of an eagle, the claws of a lion, the head of a man depict evolution from the four elements.
34. The great Pyramid at Gizeh.

35. So called by the Greeks in later centuries.
36. Compare teachings of Swedenborg and modern psychology.
37. See *Sacred Mysteries among the Mayas and Quiches* by Augustus Le Plongeon. Plato speaks of "the Lands of the West" and that Solon had learned of them from Egyptian priests in the sixth century B.C. At that time the continent of Atlantis had sunk beneath the sea.
38. See chapter on Plato, who adopted the concept but looked upon the "pattern" rather as an ideal or perfect possibility.
39. This fusing of Hindu and Egyptian faiths is important to understanding of later references. See note 44.
40. The rational soul was *Bai*. The divine spirit is *Kou,* which is potential only in this life and develops after death.
41. The Hindu Laws of Manu.
42. Title of God borrowed by the Egyptians from Rama.
43. Egyptian theology posited no hell.
44. The ram's horns worn by Rama, still seen duplicated in the tiara of the pope.
45. I-Evé, often translated as Jehovah or Jahwe, but improperly, as it is more a *meaning* than a *word.* Evé denotes "light" or mother-of-all, but also means "to be" or "being." Moses adds to it the masculine sign of "I" and thus produces the Father-Mother principle, the Being of beings or the I AM.
46. The astral light, the agent or force which sets universal life, represented by the coiled serpent, into motion.
47. Biblical exegesis of modern times denies that Moses wrote Genesis and even questions that he ever lived, or that Abraham was more than the name of the tribe of Ibram in Mesopotamia. But though the Pentateuch is legendary in regard to his life, it is logical to assume that he was a real person by whom the religion of the Jews was founded. His Egyptian name was Osarsiph. On this Philo quotes the Egyptian priest Manethon. The latter affirmed that Moses was a priest of Osiris. Strabo agrees. Clement of Alexandria believed Moses to have been an initiate. ...Whatever Moses' ancestry, we have some evidence that Moses was a man of authority in Egypt or at least an inspector of the Jews of Goshen under Egypt, and that he had priestly training in the lore of the temple.
48. High priest at this time who wore a breast-plate of flashing precious stones.
49. "He" pronounced "hay" is one of the names for divinity in Hebrew, Syriac and Arabic.
50. In general terms India accented the trinity, Zoroastriasm was

dualistic, Egypt and Israel monistic, and Early Greece polytheistic. Although Egypt was a sacerdotal state, the layman did not know the principle of the One. When the New Testament was formulated in the fourth century, most of the material was taken from Mithraic sources and through misconception was grafted onto Christianity. Even to this day evangelists proclaim a personal devil and eternal damnation. Otherwise the motive of love is replacing that of fear. See also chapter on "Postword."

51. In Egypt only the priesthood held the secret of the *One* God, and in case a layman came into possession of it, he was made to take the priesthood so that he would not divulge it. Moses, however, made this primary and created a religion based upon it.

52. Deut. 18:18-19.

53. The cloud of glory hiding the Divine Presence which accompanied the ark and directed Moses. It remained in the first temple but refused to stay in the temple built by Herod. It is believed by many to still exist as an intermediary presence between man and deity.

54. Orpheus or Arpha from the Phoenician word "aour," light, and "rophae," healing—one who heals by light.

55. This was the 13th century B.C. The same was true in the 5th century with Confucius and Laotze in China, and Socrates and Plato in Greece.

56. According to Herodotus, the Orphics were Egyptians.

57. Early paintings of Jesus represent him in the same way.

58. "First," that is, in the West.

59. The Elusinian Mysteries were contemporary but owed development both to Orpheus and Pythagoras seven centuries later.

60. Like Plato, Cicero, and others, Jesus may have been an initiate. There is internal evidence in the Gospel of John.

61. Moses thus formed a word to signify the Eternal Masculine, while Orpheus formed it to signify the Eternal Feminine.

62. Evohé (He, vau, he) pronounced "aye, wau, aye" was the sacred cry of all initiates of Asia Minor, Judaea, Egypt and Greece.

63. This and following lines are drawn direct from ancient historical records.

64. A title bestowed on an initiate.

65. "Above" indicates a state rather than a place.

66. God as Cosmic Love.

67. i.e., return to earth, a belief in reincarnation.

68. In the netherworld, to which he descended in search of his love embodied as Eurydice.

69. 6th Century B.C.

70. Confirmed by modern science, the primary atom being hydrogen with one positive and one negative charge of energy.
71. This passage is drawn from historical records.
72. Modern science resolves knowledge to numbers; philosophy resolves it to principles, as here.
73. Each number is composed of a dot. Arranged in a triangle of four to a side, we have this figure, according to Pythagoras (the central dot being used to represent the whole figure as a unit in itself):

     .   =1)
     . .   =2)
     . . .   =3)   =10=1+0=1
     . . . . =4)

74. Pythagoras and Plato conceived of "soul" as an ethereal "body," built by spirit-mind, a form which survives death, often visible, like the shades, doubles, or *manes* of Egypt.
75. Term used by Pythagoras and repeated by Plato, i.e., the soul or etheric body.
76. As Pythagoras had learned from Egyptian priests.
77. Fechner, 1801-1887, psychophysicist and philosopher held the view that stars are angel-souls.
78. "The physical world...changed in our thinking to a living universe." — Millikan, discoverer of cosmic rays.
79. First to discover the harmonic intervals that produce musical sounds, Pythagoras formulated the principle of "The music of the spheres."
80. i.e., "man."
81. A favorite symbolism in Greek poetry, as of the butterfly emerging from the chrysalis.
82. This was known as the cone of shadow which trails the earth; and Orpheus, Pythagoras, Homer and Virgil likened the souls that seek escape to whirling leaves or swarms of birds, beaten by the tempest. It was a form of purgatory.
83. The evening star, Venus or orb of Love.
84. Pythagoras used the exact words: "Philosophy is the highest music."
85. Plato developed the concept in his Phaedo, a mid-heaven from which man returns to earth.
86. This is the soul as "Karma" to the Brahmins and Buddhists.
87. Not "demon" but familiar spirit. Savonarola, Joan of Arc, and R. L. Stevenson heard such voices.
88. i.e., Jesus.
89. "Trinity" is not confined to persons.
90. Plato was an initiate of the Eleusinian Mysteries.
91. See Note 65.

92. See line drawings in "The Prophecies of Melchizedek" by Browne Landone.
93. Or Prototype.
94. See Postword, par. 17.
95. See Note 3, Part 1.
96. See Plato's"Ethics."
97. i.e., concept of Deity.
98. A Greek colony from Egypt had brought the cult of Isis (see chapter on "Hermes") into Eleusis under the name of Demeter or the Greek Mother as the Divine Intelligence or Mother of Souls. By means of drama, the priests thus taught the esoteric doctrine to which Pythagoras and Plato subscribed. The soul as Psyche or Persephone was shown to descend into matter, suffering and forgetfulness and afterwards to re-ascend to divine life—a Hellenized version of the Fall and the Redemption or expiation.
99. The dove symbolized the Mother or Holy Spirit in all oriental religions. While the Greek word for "spirit" is neuter, indicating "impersonal creative principle," the Aramaic which was spoken by Jesus was *feminine*. In the "Gospel of the Hebrews," Jesus referred to the Holy Ghost as his mother.
100. From the Syrian, "Asaya" meaning physician.
101. Book IX, The Bhagavad-Gita.
102. The real name of Jesus, taken from the great Jewish hero.
103. The Jewish race has unjustly borne the contumely of martyring Jesus. The historian cannot support such a position. It was in fact a political triangle in which two sides were foreign. In the first place the Herodians were not Jews but Idumaeans (See Edelsheim, "Life and Times of Jesus," Vol. I, p. 31) and Herod the Great had derived the crown from the Romans. His son, the tetrach, who beheaded John the Baptist and took part in the destruction of Jesus, made claim to be the Messiah (See Encylopedia Brittanica) and the Herodians supported his claim, siding with the Pharisees. (See Mark 3:6). The High Priests were political appointees of Rome who cooperated with them for political reasons; and it was a Roman who condemned Jesus to death. The third side of the triangle was composed of politico-sacerdotal parties. An interesting sidelight is found in Herod's later history. He was exiled for life to Gaul where he died, the Emperor having tired of his insistence on a crown which he never received.
104. See Josephus, A.J. ii., 8.
105. See Note 103.
106. This is not denial of the body or the reality of the experience, nor his suffering.

107. See Note 65.
108. i.e., regain the primal nature.
109. Religion is from the Latin *re,* meaning "again"; and *lego,* "gather or bind back."
110. There is no authentic original passage in the Gospels in which Jesus claims that his blood will appease God's wrath. Even with Paul, if we accept him as the author of First Corinthians 6:20, the blood of Christ is the "price" of freedom from the *bondage of sin* or ignorance, not an appeasement of God.
111. See John 10:34 and Psalm 85:6 which continue "and every one of you Son of the Most High."
112. This is not designed to show a nature miracle but an attitude.
113. This parable well illustrates the subtility of the parables. On the face of it, it would appear to the rabbis as a violation of law and ethics to make such unequal payments. But a simple principle of truth underlies it. An electrical current discharges its energy in full and instantly whether it takes a second or a year to make the contact. So with the law of mind.
114. The Scribe employs a term properly used of the ascetic and radical sect of the Nazarites to which John the Baptist belonged.
115. This is also the teaching of the Tao, which is worthy of consideration in this Epic, but although Laotse was almost contemporary with Plato, his teaching did not influence the Father-Mother Doctrine.
116. Compare John 4:14.
117. The Creator Trinitarian God among the Quiches and the Mayas embracing *Bitol,* the maker; *Alom,* the engenderer: and *Quaholom,* "he who gives being." The evidence is almost overwhelming that their astronomical knowledge, architecture and religious doctrines antedate those of Egypt and Asia and may have been the source.
118. See Note 99, also Matthew 3:16, and elsewhere in the New Testament.
119. Mother of Viraj (the "Son" or Creative Word).
120. Represented in Art with the same symbol as Isis, crescent moon and crowned with stars.
121. i.e., all being or the Universal Son.
122. Compare Matthew 1:18.
123. See Note 121.

Index

This index is not designed to be exhaustive, but rather to help the reader find half-familiar passages by the use of key words that unlock the door of memory.

About the authors

E rnest and Fenwicke Holmes were brothers. Born in Maine before the turn of the century, they knew the rigorous practicality of rural life, even as their sense of the transcendent was nurtured in a family atmosphere of spiritual openness and curiosity.

Ernest (1887-1960) became known worldwide for developing a philosophy called The Science of Mind. His book of the same name is used internationally in classes and study groups as a basic metaphysical text. He founded the United Church of Religious Science and *Science of Mind* Magazine, which has been in continuous monthly publication since 1927. He authored scores of books, reached millions of people through radio and television, and today his legacy of simple, practical spiritual ideas continues to have wide impact.

Fenwicke (1883-1973) and Ernest worked together closely in the early years, though Fenwicke was later to function independently, writing and lecturing on philosophical subjects. He is best known in Japan, where his books enjoy a continuing popularity.

Ernest had long dreamed of writing an epic poem which contained the essence of his own learning, experience, and insight. He sought Fenwicke's assistance in bringing that ambitious project to fruition, and the result, *The Voice Celestial,* is a collaboration which stands as a monument of modern metaphysical thought.